University of London
Institute of Latin American Studies

10

Latin America and the Second World War
Volume One: 1939–1942

LATIN AMERICA AND
THE SECOND WORLD WAR

Volume One 1939–1942

by

R. A. HUMPHREYS

ATHLONE

Published for the
Institute of Latin American Studies
University of London
1981

First published 1981 by The Athlone Press Ltd.
at 90–91 Great Russell Street, London WC1B 3PY

Distributor in U.S.A. and Canada
Humanities Press Inc
New Jersey

British Library Cataloguing in Publication Data
Humphreys, Robert Arthur
Latin America and the Second World
War.—(Monographs/University of London.
Institute of Latin American Studies,
ISSN 0776-0846; 10). Vol. I 1939–1942.
1. Latin America—History—20th century
2. World War, 1939–1945—Latin America
I. Title
II. University of London, *Institute of Latin American
Studies*
980'.033   F1414

ISBN 0 485 17710 2

Printed in Great Britain by
The Burlington Press, Foxton, Cambridge

PREFACE

This book has been long in my mind. But only retirement has allowed me to write it. With some reluctance I have decided that it should take the form of two volumes, and the Rio de Janeiro Conference seemed to me to be a suitable closure for the first. I shall hope in the second to carry the story to 1945.

I wish to record my gratitude to many of my war-time colleagues, in particular Miss Katharine Duff, the late Professor W. L. Burn and the late Professor A. G. B. Fisher, and, in the years when I was Director of the Institute of Latin American Studies, to the research assistants to whose work in the Public Record Office I am so greatly indebted.

My greatest obligation is to my wife.

June 1980   R.A.H.

University of London
Institute of Latin American Studies Monographs

CONTENTS

I

LATIN AMERICA ON THE EVE OF THE SECOND WORLD WAR

I

In 1939 Latin America was the richest raw material producing area in the world free from the control of any Great Power. From the Rio Grande, the border between the United States and Mexico, to Cape Horn—roughly the distance from Stockholm to Cape Town—the twenty republics of the region, differing in size, wealth, race and population and in political, social and economic development, occupied nearly a fifth of the inhabited surface of the globe. Three, Cuba, the Dominican Republic and Haiti, were set in the Caribbean sea. Two, Bolivia and Paraguay, were landlocked, though Paraguay did indeed have access to the sea, nearly a thousand miles away, by the rivers Paraguay and Paraná. And one, Portuguese-speaking Brazil, was larger than the continental United States.

The whole population of this immense area, whether of Indian, European, African, Asian or mixed stock, was probably not more than 125,000,000, rapidly increasing, and increasingly young in composition, but unevenly distributed both within and between the several states. Brazil contained nearly half the inhabitants of South America. Yet her population was smaller than that of the British Isles. And while Buenos Aires, São Paulo, Rio de Janeiro and Mexico City each had over a million people, Santiago de Chile, Montevideo, Rosario and Havana more than five hundred thousand, and many other cities over a hundred thousand, vast areas of the Latin American mainland were empty of men. With few zones of concentrated rural settlement,[1] the population clusters, urban and rural, were separated, more often than not, by great distances and sparsely peopled territories. Except in a few favoured regions, as in south-eastern South America, trade and travel overland between the republics and, not infrequently, within their own boundaries were a matter of high adventure, impeded, sometimes even prohibited, by formidable mountain barriers, dense tropical forests, arid deserts and uninhabited wildernesses.

No road joined the northern to the southern continent. Of the great Pan American, Highway, together with its feeder roads, intended to link New York to Buenos Aires long stretches remained untouched or incomplete. Argentina, Brazil and Mexico each had their railway networks, radiating from Buenos Aires, São Paulo, Rio de Janeiro and Mexico City, and Chile its famous longitudinal line. In Perú and other of the Andean countries the railways were miracles of engineering skill. But no lines linked together the capital cities, with the exception of Guatemala City and San Salvador in Middle America, and, in South America, Buenos Aires, Asunción in Paraguay, Santiago de Chile, and, the highest seat of government in the world, La Paz in Bolivia. And, south of Panamá, there was only one direct transcontinental line, the spectacular route across the Andes from Argentina to Chile.[2]

The rapid development of air transport in the 'twenties and 'thirties had done much to overcome, at least in part, the obstacles which nature had imposed and to open up communications. It had brought Bogotá, for example, within a few hours of its Caribbean port of Barranquilla, a journey which, by road, rail and river, could take a week or even a month. Perú's port of Iquitos on the Amazon was within easy reach of Lima, though so difficult had been the land route across the Andes that goods from Lima had sometimes been sent through the Panamá Canal, across the Atlantic and then back again up the Amazon. Bahia and Rio de Janeiro were linked as never before. South America became criss-crossed by air-lines, many of them, as in Bolivia, Brazil, Colombia, Ecuador and Perú, under German control, and the expansion of the domestic air-lines[3] was accompanied by the establishment of trans-Atlantic routes and the great trunk lines from the United States operated by Pan American Airways and Pan American Grace.[4] But though cargo-carrying by plane had been made relatively cheap and profitable in Central America,[5] air travel and air freight were in general expensive. For all that a revolution was taking place with the advent of the air age, large parts not only of South America but of Middle America as well remained dependent on the cart-track, the mule-trail, the raft and the canoe; and while air transport was changing the pattern of travel between the republics—the number of passenger miles flown had rapidly increased—it had done little to affect the pattern of intra-Latin American trade. No more than a tenth of Latin American exports were bought by other Latin American countries.

It was primarily to Europe and to the United States that the Latin American states looked for their trade and prosperity. Each was first and foremost a producer of foodstuffs and raw materials—coffee, cotton, sugar, tobacco, cacao and bananas in the tropical and sub-tropical regions; wheat, maize and linseed in the temperate zones; beef, hides, skins and wool, especially in south-eastern South America; nitrates and cop-per in Chile; tin in Bolivia; petroleum, more particularly in Venezuela, Perú, Colombia and Mexico; and among a variety of other minerals, such as iron, lead, zinc, manganese and tungsten mined in Latin America, the gold and silver which had once made the Indies the envy of Europe still ranked among the leading exports of Mexico. Despite the rapid growth of the cities, mostly due to migration from the country-side, as well as, in some instances, to immigration from abroad, agricultural and pastoral activities occupied more than two-thirds of the total population.[6] But the importance of the extractive industries in such countries as Bolivia, Chile, Colombia, Mexico, Perú and Venezuela was out of all propor-tion to the number of people engaged in them.

With these vast, though unevenly distributed, natural re-sources, almost every country specialised in a single product or group of products for export, and all, in greater or lesser degree, were dependent upon the import of manufactured goods and certain raw materials. Export economies, they had attracted huge investments of foreign capital. Britain had been the pre-eminent source in the nineteenth century, and the amount of British capital invested in Latin America on the eve of the first World War had been of the order of £1,000 million, representing a fifth to a quarter of all British overseas investments.[7] The largest holdings were in railways and government securities. But British investments were spread over a great range of enterprises, in public utilities, in mining, and in agriculture. The greatest accumulations were in Argentina, and, after Argentina, though at a respectful distance, in Brazil and Mexico.[8] So the proportions remained. United States investments, starting late, were much less substantial, as also were French and German. But though British investments increased on a reduced scale in the decade of the nineteen-twenties,[9] the United States had by then become the principal source of the supply of capital. This was the era of the 'dance of the millions', the foreign investment mania, when American investors were as eager to lend as Latin American states to borrow. United States investments quadrupled. By 1930 they had reached a rough equality with British, amounting to more than $5 billion, or about a third of United States investments abroad, and the 'dance of the millions' had extended not only to the northern countries of South America, but to the southern states as well.[10]

Foreign capital had provided the Latin American countries with the 'permanent outfit' which was the economic foundation of their nationhood. It had financed the building of ports, docks, railways and other public utility services, operated banks, insurance companies and shipping lines — the mercantile marines of the Latin American countries had always been small — and it had developed oil-fields, mines, ranches and plantations. But, in the context of domestic social, economic and political conditions, it had enhanced, not reduced, Latin American dependence on the export of a few primary products and the import of manufactured goods. The disadvantages of so great a dependence on overseas demand and sources of supply were first clearly revealed by the impact of the first World War. The Great Depression of the 'thirties drove home the lesson. The prices of many of the principal Latin American exports fell, by 1933, to little more than a third of their 1929 value.[11] Imports declined. The inflow of capital ceased, while rising tariff barriers and autarkic policies in the world at large faced the Latin American countries with a growing stringency of foreign exchange. Governments defaulted in whole or in part on their debts.[12] Tariffs were raised, exchange controls and import quotas introduced. Economic nationalism became orthodox south of the Rio Grande, and while resentment at the proportions of the proceeds taken abroad by foreign-controlled enterprises and the desire to subordinate foreign to domestic interests grew, official policy was increasingly directed to the development of home industries, the diversification of agriculture, and the achievement of a greater measure of self-sufficiency. More and more the Latin American countries, of which Argentina, Brazil, Chile and Mexico were industrially the most advanced, sought to provide themselves with a large part of the articles of common consumption. The growth of the textile industry, old established in Mexico and Brazil, and the processing of foodstuffs were outstanding examples. But the desire to develop heavy industry, which Mexico had begun to do in the early years of the century, while a beginning had been made in Argentina, Brazil and Chile, was also strong. And though these policies had made little difference to the character of the export trade of Latin America, its import trade had already begun to undergo important modifications.

II

Who were the major traders? Japan, less, but not much less, important than France and Italy, can hardly be counted as such. But, starting late, Japanese trade had made marked, though chequered, advances in the nineteen-thirties. In 1938 Japan was supplying 2.7 per cent of Latin American imports[13] —cotton textiles, rayon yarns and textiles, silk tissues, electrical goods and toys—chiefly to the west-coast and southeastern republics of South America but also to the Caribbean area, and was buying raw cotton from Brazil, her most important source of supply in Latin America, and agricultural or mineral products from Argentina, Uruguay, Chile, Perú, Ecuador and Mexico.

This was a new and remarkable development, just as substantial Japanese emigration to Brazil and Perú was a new and remarkable development.[14] Much more striking, however, had been the revival of German economic penetration. Already in 1921 the great German shipping lines had resumed their services and within the next ten years Germany had made marked progress towards the recovery of her pre-1914 trading position. In Argentina, the British Ambassador, Sir Malcolm Robertson, had complained in the late nineteen-twenties of British firms whose principals, instead of visiting Latin America to study the markets, preferred 'to stay at home and wait for business to come to them, in the intervals of their golfing week-ends', and his caustic comments on the 'white beards of commerce' and on 'far too many old men' who were directors of 'far too many companies' had given great offence.[15] No such strictures could have been made about German firms and German sales techniques, which combined efficiency, enterprise and knowledge. And German trade was given a yet more aggressive turn in the 'thirties by the negotiation of barter deals and the application of the Aski, or compensation, mark system. Under this Germany bought with Aski marks the foodstuffs and raw materials which she needed, reserving the marks for the purchase in Germany of those commodities—machinery, metal goods, coal, chemicals and the like—which she was willing to sell at what amounted to subsidised prices.

The rewards for Germany were considerable. By 1938 she was providing some 16 per cent of Latin American imports (slightly less than in 1913) and taking ten or eleven per cent of Latin American exports. In general she had become a more important supplier than Great Britain. In some countries —Brazil, Chile, Perú and Guatemala were examples— the expansion of German trade had been still more spectacular.[16] But bilateral trading of this kind, limiting, as it did, the freedom of the Latin American countries to decide for themselves the sources from which to purchase their imports, had its disadvantages as well as its attractions; and one incidental result was that the accumulated balances held in Germany in 1939 to the credit of the Latin American countries were estimated to be of the order of $250 million.[17]

While German trade had advanced and Germany had built up a network of air-lines in Latin America, British trade had declined. Britain had turned to the cultivation of intra-imperial trade, to imperial preference and the like. But restrictive measures at home and in Latin America alike affected her export trade, and while her textile exports had been particularly hard hit by the growth of domestic textile industries in

Latin America, as also by Japanese competition, in other export lines German gains had been British losses. Nevertheless in 1938 the United States and the United Kingdom accounted for nearly half the trade of Latin America. The United States, whose Trade Agreements Act of 1934 (after the excesses of the Hawley-Smoot Tariff of 1930) opened a new phase in her trading relations with Latin America,[18] was the largest single source of supply and the largest market. She provided more than a third of Latin American imports and received rather less than a third of its exports—proportions almost exactly paralleled by continental Europe. Britain, for her part, bought a good deal more than she sold, taking some 17 per cent of Latin American exports in 1938 and supplying about 12 per cent of its imports.[19] This over-all view of Latin American trade conceals, however, as much as it reveals. South America alone was responsible for more than three quarters of the trade by value of Latin America, and in South America Argentina was both the leading importing and the leading exporting country.[20] It was with Argentina that British trade was largest, and, with certain local exceptions, the main Latin American trading interests of Britain and the United States lay in different areas.

III

Proximity and trade, policy and strategy, alike linked the countries of the Caribbean area closely to the United States. These were the guardian outposts of the Panamá Canal Zone, that immaculately groomed region where the canal, with its satellite railway,[21] was not only one of the crossroads of the world but the key to the two-ocean naval strategy of the United States. It could indeed be argued, and was argued, that the defences of the canal, under contemporary conditions of warfare, extended from Cuba and Puerto Rico in the east to Ecuador and the Galápagos Islands in the west (far beyond the Caribbean area) as well as, of course, to Mexico, the small states of Central America, Colombia, Venezuela, and, still further south, to the great 'bulge' of Brazil, projecting far into the Atlantic.

In Cuba, which the United States had helped to liberate

from Spain and which, together with Puerto Rico and the island originally known as Hispaniola, commanded the eastern approaches to the Caribbean and the Canal Zone, the United States maintained a naval base at Guantánamo. But she had surrendered in 1934 the right she had obtained when the island was given self-government to intervene in order to safeguard Cuban independence and to ensure stable and orderly government.[22] Cuba, meanwhile, had undergone a major upheaval in 1933 when its extraordinarily heterogeneous population had witnessed the overthrow (assisted by the United States in the person of the American Ambassador, Sumner Welles) of an increasingly detestable and detested dictator, a succession of transient governments, including the 127 days of the nationalistic and radically-minded Dr. Ramón Grau San Martín, at first the idol of the university students (but not of Sumner Welles),[23] and the rise to power of a thirty-two year old sergeant of humble origin but great political acumen and assimilative powers, Fulgencio Batista, who was soon to become the 'arbiter' of the country's destinies,[24] though not till October, 1940, its President. The revolution of 1933, with its strikes and disorders, in part communist-inspired, the political activities of the students and the so-called sergeants' revolt, together with economic distress and the reforms promulgated by Grau San Martín, was the forerunner of a more profound social and political upheaval twenty-six years later. But Cuba, in 1939, preserved the outward forms of constitutional government, and, with her enormous investments of United States capital, more substantial in Cuba than anywhere else in Latin America, still remained, if not a protectorate, at least a satellite of the United States.

Haiti and the Dominican Republic, the one a heavily populated, predominantly negro country where an urban mulatto minority held a monopoly of power, the other, larger, less populous and more mixed in race but with small white and negro minorities, lacked the importance of Cuba, despite American holdings in Dominican sugar plantations. While they uneasily shared their small island in peace, at least in 1939 (two years earlier the Dominicans had massacred several thousand Haitian immigrant labourers), their relations with the United States had moved on parallel lines. Both had experienced United States occupation (not without a measure of provocation), Haiti from 1915 to 1934, the Dominican Republic from 1916 to 1924, though not till 1941 did she regain her fiscal as well as her political independence.[25] The country, since 1930, had been under the domination of Generalissimo Rafael Leonidas Trujillo (who had served with the occupying United States marine corps), though he allowed two puppet presidents to occupy the presidential throne between 1938 and 1942. Ruthless, unscrupulous and insufferably vain, he rejoiced, in the fullness of time, in the titles of Benefactor of the Fatherland and Restorer of the Financial Independence of the Republic, and Santo Domingo, the oldest city in the New World, was outrageously renamed Ciudad Trujillo. His régime brought some material advantages to the Dominican Republic, at a high cost in civil liberties, but the main beneficiaries were the dictator, his entourage, the armed forces and the sugar companies. For all his vanity and egotism, however, Trujillo possessed ability and shrewdness, and he was well aware of the value of good relations with the United States.

Sténio Vincent of Haiti had also come to power in 1930. Well-educated and well-read (in contrast to Trujillo), he disliked the name of dictator, but nevertheless ruled as a more or less benevolent autocrat with the support of the *Garde d'Haiti* and a generally complaisant Congress, making some attempt to improve the standard of living of his illiterate and volatile rural peasantry. Important opponents of the régime, however, were apt to find themselves faced with imprisonment or exile.

Like the three island republics, the five states of Central America, together smaller than Texas and among the poorest of Latin American countries, were also virtual, though reluctant, satellites of the United States, the United Fruit Company enjoying a reputation as the sixth Central American state. All but Costa Rica were dictatorships pure and simple. Their doyen was General Jorge Ubico of Guatemala, the most populous and powerful of the isthmian family, who had become President in 1931 and described himself as a 'Liberal Progressive', though his liberal qualities were not easily to be discerned. His rivals in length of office were General Maximiliano Hernández Martínez of El Salvador,[26] a spiritualist but none the less ruthless for that, who had also ruled since 1931, and General Tiburcio Carías Andino, who had been dictator of Honduras, the most backward of the Central American countries, since 1933. The fourth of these mettlesome generals was Anastasio Somoza of Nicaragua, notable both for his acquisitive instincts and for founding a dynasty which survived for forty-three years. President Somoza was apt to describe the United States, where he had received part of his education, as his second country; and whatever their personal predelictions it was still a golden rule among Central American dictators to keep on good terms with Washington.[27] All of them, also, presided over countries whose peoples were predominantly illiterate and composed mainly of pure-blooded Indians as in Guatemala but of mixed race elsewhere, with a small white or near-white dominant upper class. Though Nicaragua produced gold and Honduras silver as well, each country's prosperity was bound up with the export of coffee or bananas or both.

Costa Rica's fortunes were also tied to these products. But to move from the world of the mini-dictators into Costa Rica was to breathe a different air. The press was free, the army diminutive and the level of literacy high. There were, it was said, more school-teachers than soldiers. The population, overwhelmingly European in extraction, included a large number of farmers owning their own land; and though personalities mattered more than parties, and policy and administration were the preserve of a small élite, the country's peaceful evolution had been seriously interrupted only once since the early years of the century.[28] Presidents succeeded Presidents at four yearly intervals, the incumbent in 1939 being León Cortés Castro, who, it was rumoured, had a tendency to favour German interests. Cortés Castro, however, gave way, after peaceful presidential elections in February 1940, to a middle-aged physician, Dr. Rafael Calderón Guardia, who had not.[29]

Finally, there was Panamá herself, once a part of Colombia, but brought into existence (with the timely support of President Theodore Roosevelt) in 1903, and cut into two by the ten-mile wide canal zone which dominated her life. Not, for historical reasons, usually reckoned among the Central American states, she shared many of the social, ethnic and economic characteristics of her more northerly neighbours. Government tended to rotate among a few leading families, and in the interests of stability and order the United States had on several occasions supervised the holding of presidential elections. But, as in Cuba in 1934, so in Panamá in 1936, the United States had renounced by treaty the right of intervention she had acquired when Panamá was born, the two countries agreeing to take joint action whenever needed for the protection of the canal. The treaty, which thus implicitly recognized Panamanian independence, contained, and was coupled with, a number of provisions designed to assuage Panamanian resentments. Ratified by the United States Senate in 1939 (though, by an exchange of notes, the United States reserved the right to take instant action for the defence of the canal in the event of an emergency which precluded immediate consultation with Panamá) it enhanced, at least temporarily, American popularity,[30] and also that of President Juan Demóstenes Arosemena. Arosemena, however, died at the end of 1939 and was temporarily succeeded by the 'First Presidential Designate', Dr. Augusto Boyd, the Panamanian Ambassador in Washington.

American capital played a dominant role in the economies of all of these states. American direct investments in them in 1940 were estimated to be of the order of $800 million, Cuba alone accounting for $560 million, concentrated in the great staple industries and their supporting enterprises—the coffee and banana plantations of Central America, and the sugar industry which dominated Cuba and the Dominican Republic. Trade and direct investments tending to move together and most tropical products—sugar and tobacco were exceptions—not competing with those of the United States,[31] the United States had become by 1939 not only the principal source of supply for the Central American and island republics, but, with the exception of the small Dominican Republic, their principal market. Great Britain was the chief purchaser of Dominican sugar as France had been, till 1936, of Haitian coffee, and both countries retained close British and European connections. As for Central America, where Britain was still an important though declining customer for Costa Rican coffee, German economic penetration had made marked advances not only in Guatemala, where the German 'colony' was largest and many coffee plantations were in German hands, but in Costa Rica, which possessed the second largest 'colony', Nicaragua, Honduras and El Salvador.[32] Much as the island and isthmian republics lay within the sphere of influence of the United States, the Caribbean, with its outer ring of islands from Puerto Rico to Trinidad, most of them in European hands, was not an American lake.

Two South American countries, Venezuela and Colombia, which commanded the eastern approaches to the Panamá Canal, and Mexico, the immediate neighbour of the United States, completed the Caribbean circuit. Venezuela had grown rich on oil, exploited under generous concessions to foreign companies and most of it exported to the Standard Oil and Royal Dutch Shell refineries on the Dutch islands of Aruba and Curaçao and then re-exported to the United States, the United Kingdom and Europe. The spectacular rise of the oil industry in the nineteen-twenties had enabled the country's dictator, Juan Vicente Gómez, to redeem Venezuela's entire foreign and internal debt. But he had done little to improve the lot of his people.[33] When his long, odious, and corrupt despotism (with the army as his praetorian guard) ended with his death in December, 1935, Venezuela could neither feed herself nor provide many of life's necessities. Gómez had provided peace and stability—no mean achievement perhaps—but at the price of 'civic stagnation'; and while the masses lived in misery, the greed and rapacity of the dictator and his entourage had known no bounds.[34] His death opened a new chapter in Venezuelan history. In Caracas the mob sacked the houses of his family and their associates, and serious rioting broke out in Maracaibo. But there was no popular revolution—there was, indeed, no one to lead it. Neither, however, did 'one gang of robbers' succeed another. General Eleazer López Contreras, the Minister of War, popular with the army and said to be the sole member of the government who had not enriched himself in office,[35] was hastily made Acting President and then duly elected President in 1936 by the Gomecista Congress. But though López Contreras had been brought up in the Gomecista tradition and took strong measures to repress political and labour agitation, even expelling a number of communists and alleged communists, the tradition itself was broken. Ruling with a cautious moderation and introducing a broad programme of social and economic reconstruction, he was to retire with an unusual respect, in Venezuela, for law in 1941, having initiated a transitional period in which the country began to move from absolute tyranny to relative freedom.[36]

By contrast with Venezuela, whose political advance was still halting, Colombia appeared to have achieved a high degree of maturity. An educated élite, mostly of pure Spanish descent—Bogotá, with its poets and a men of letters, was known as the Athens of South America—governed a substantially mestizo population,[37] mainly rural but becoming increasingly politically articulate among the workers in the textile factories, on the railways and in the banana plantations.[38] Politics revolved round two major parties, the Conservatives and the Liberals, each of which tended to split into rival factions. A rift among the Conservatives, who had long been the governing party and were staunch supporters of the power of the landowners and the Catholic Church, enabled the Liberals, who believed in constitutional decentralisation, religious freedom and a broadening suffrage, to attain power in 1930, at a time of economic depression. Having obtained power, they retained it, first under Dr. Enrique Olaya Herrera, whose aim was economic recovery, then under the more radical social reformer, Dr. Alfonso López Pumarejo, who, revising the Constitution, disestablished the Church and emphasised the protection of labour and the social duties of property, and, finally, with the election of 1938, under Dr. Eduardo Santos.

Dr. Santos, who owned one of Latin America's most influential newspapers, *El Tiempo* (edited, till 1941, with a certain amount of fraternal independence, by his brother), had represented Colombia at the League of Nations, moderated without abandoning Dr. López's programme, and was a warm protagonist of Pan American co-operation. His sincerity was never in doubt. Neither was the desire of the United States to eradicate the ill-feelings and suspicions which past events, such as the secession of Panamá, had engendered.

Colombia's strategic position brought her into prominence in United States defence plans[39]—she accepted American naval and aviation missions in 1939—and economic and financial relations between the two countries were close. The commercial exploitation of petroleum had begun in 1917 and American capital dominated both the oil and the fruit industries.[40] Almost all Colombian coffee, mainly grown on small holdings,[41] but, in terms of value, Colombia's major export, was shipped to the United States; and the United States not only took rather more than a half of Colombia's exports but supplied rather more than a half of her imports. Germany occupied second place, though a long way behind. As in Venezuela, there were a number of Germans established in the chief cities, and Germans had a minority, but no longer a controlling, interest, in Scadta, the oldest of Latin American airlines.

Mexico, the third in size and the second in population of the Latin American states, was, ethnically speaking, essentially an Indian and mestizo country in which more than thirty Indian languages were spoken.[42] Rich in minerals, her principal exports were gold and silver, lead, zinc, and, as in Colombia and Venezuela, petroleum. In 1921, indeed, Mexico had produced more than 193 million barrels. Those great days were over by 1926, but Mexico was still producing 47 million barrels in 1937 and nearly 43 million in 1939. Despite her mineral wealth and her rising industries—the textile industry, for example, and the steel industry at Monterrey—Mexico was, nevertheless, essentially rural in character. The greater part of the population made their living by agriculture, and nearly a half was illiterate.

The strategic and economic importance of Mexico and the United States to one another was obvious. The United States was Mexico's best customer and source of supply. But Mexico, in the nineteenth century, had lost a half of her territory to the United States. She was the only Latin American country with which the United States had ever been at war, and twice in the twentieth century, in 1915 and 1917, the United States had intervened in Mexico by force of arms. Mexican nationalist sensitivities were acute, and they were enhanced by the great revolution which the country had undergone, and was still undergoing, a revolution properly to be described as the first genuine social revolution in the New World. From its modest beginnings in 1910, it had developed, after years of chaos and violence, of advance and retreat, into a 'social, economic and political movement of extraordinary magnitude and depth';[43] and under General Lázaro Cárdenas, who had been elected President for a six-year term in 1934, it had entered upon its most advanced phase.

Cárdenas was both a skilful politician and an idealist. He ruled virtually as a dictator, with the support of the industrial workers (the Confederation of Mexican Workers, or C.T.M., with Vicente Lombardo Toledano as its secretary, had been organized in 1936),[44] the peasants, and the military, who, together with the so-called 'popular' sector (including the civil servants and the teachers), formed the four constituent parts of the Party of the Mexican Revolution, or P.R.M., so named in 1937.[45] But Cárdenas was a dictator with a difference. He may have been felt to be mistaken and even dangerous. But few doubted his honesty of conduct and integrity of purpose. His aims may be defined as an attempt to raise the economic, educational and social level of the working masses and to give Mexicans, as opposed to foreigners an increasing share of the country's wealth. These aims found expression in three major policies: the gradual extension of state control in the management of national life; the widespread expropriation and redistribution of agricultural land; and an advancing programme of labour legislation. The peasant was to play a more significant part in the nation's agriculture, the worker in the nation's industry; and the strengthening of national sovereignty by the control of natural resources was illustrated most spectacularly by the expropriation in 1938 of almost all the foreign oil companies — the climax of a long labour dispute and an act which came to be regarded as a test case of national sovereignty and independence.

Such a programme caused immense difficulties. Labour and agricultural problems were acute. And the means employed by Cárdenas to implement his programme roused violent hostility outside Mexico and bitter criticism within. Not only mineral but agricultural properties, many of them in foreign hands, were expropriated, and these actions were naturally resented. So far as the oil companies were concerned, British interests were greatly in excess of American both in actual investment and in proved resources, and the reaction of the Foreign Office to what it regarded as an arbitrary and confiscatory measure was so acidulated that Mexico, in May, severed relations with Great Britain. Earlier, the 'Tennessee temper' of Cordell Hull at the State Department might have precipitated a similar break with the United States had it not been for the moderating, and insubordinate, influence of the American Ambassador, Josephus Daniels.[46] As it was, relations were strained but not broken. A movement to withhold silver purchases, which might have been ruinous to Mexico, was only partially sustained, Henry Morgenthau at the Treasury objecting.[47] And though the oil companies, supported by the British Government and, to a lesser degree, by the State Department,[48] did their best to prevent the sale of Mexican oil, Germany, Italy and Japan were eager to buy and Mexico was constrained to sell where she could.[49] Above all, the newly organised *Petróleos Mexicanos*, despite a period of great disruption, continued to operate the fields, and exports of oil, after a precipitate decline, again began to climb in the later nineteen-forties.

IV

Venezuela and Colombia were not only Caribbean states; they were Andean countries, traversed and divided by that majestic mountain chain which marches from Tierra del Fuego to the northern shores of South America; and while the pre-eminence of the United States among the Central American and island republics was unchallenged, her influence in South America, great as it was, tended to diminish along the Andean chain from north to south.

Three of these Andean republics, Ecuador, Perú and Bolivia, were Indian as well as Andean, though in each the ruling minority was predominantly European by descent. Ecuador, the smallest and least populous of the three, lay, with her dependent Galápagos Islands, within the defensive area of the Panamá Canal. Cacao and coffee were her chief agricultural exports, with cacao still in the lead, though its boom days

were over; gold and petroleum (from the Santa Elena penin-
sula) the chief mineral. Of cacao exports three-fifths were
shipped to Germany, and Germany, which also controlled the
Sedta air-line,[50] established in 1937, supplied a quarter of
Ecuadorean imports. Though the United States was responsible for more than a third of Ecuador's trade, the larger share
lay with Europe, with Japan, however, replacing Britain as a
supplier of cotton piece goods.

Here, as elsewhere in Latin America, the world economic
depression had led to unemployment, misery and desperate
poverty.[51] Recovery was slow and political life, exacerbated
by the rivalry between the chief sea port, Guayaquil, and the
mountain capital, Quito, fevered in the extreme. The accession to the Presidency in 1934 of a former university professor,
the young Dr. José María Velasco Ibarra (who was to be five
times President of Ecuador), had roused happier but delusive
hopes. Dr. Velasco's volatile temperament and impetuous
actions led to his removal by the army not quite a year after he
had taken office and the day after he had assumed dictatorial
powers.[52] Having notably failed to cleanse the Augean stables
of Ecuadorean politics, he retreated to Colombia, leaving his
country to a bewildering succession of rulers and abortive
revolutions[53] until the election in January 1940 of a wealthy
lawyer from Guayaquil, Dr. Carlos Arroyo del Río. Dr. Velasco, who had returned from exile to contest the election, was
decisively defeated, whether fraudulently or not, attempted
a *coup d'état*, was arrested, and again beat a by no means
silent retreat first to Colombia and then to Argentina and
Chile.

Ecuador was one of the smallest and poorest of South
American countries. Her neighbour to the south, Perú, with
whom she had a long-standing border dispute, which was to
culminate in open war in 1941, was more than four times her
size, had double her population,[54] and was beginning to be
counted as one of the major republics.[55] Like Ecuador she had
suffered acutely from the effects of the world economic depression, which brought to an end, by revolution in 1930, the
long, autocratic rule of President Augusto Leguía. A country
which had borrowed heavily, encouraging huge foreign investments in its mining enterprises of copper, silver and petro-

leum—the Cerro de Pasco Copper Corporation and the International Petroleum Company, for example—was plunged into economic distress and social and political turmoil, compounded by a recrudescence of regional rivalries. Recovery had to wait for the advent to power of ex-President General Oscar Benavides, nominated to the Presidency by the Peruvian Congress in May 1933 after his predecessor, Colonel Luis Sánchez Cerro, had been assassinated. He remained in power till December 1939. Presidential elections in 1936, in which Benavides did not stand but which resulted in the victory of an anti-administration candidate, were annulled, and thereafter Benavides ruled as a more or less benevolent dictator, with a 'sincere admiration', it was suspected, for the strong arm methods of Mussolini.[56] He was also credited with having raised Perú 'from the depths to the heights'.[57]

As in Ecuador, so in Perú, the United States was the major single source of supply. But whereas Ecuador sent a third of all her exports to the United States, the Peruvian proportion was smaller. Much of her sugar and cotton, cultivated in the irrigated coastal valleys, went, the former to Britain and the latter to Britain and Germany, and Europe also took Peruvian minerals, including petroleum. As in Ecuador there had grown up a by no means negligible trade, in cotton textiles, with Japan. The Japanese 'colony' officially numbered 17,600. Probably far larger, its members were engaged in retail trade and in small crafts and industries, but some of them were successful farmers and cotton planters. There were alarmist reports in the 'thirties that Japan was determined to obtain a firm footing on the Pacific coast by means of this community, was concentrating on Perú as a field for expansion, and might, at some future date, plan to seize the country.[58] A government decree in 1936, limiting immigration, was particularly aimed at Japan, and the military authorities in 1939 were reported to be thoroughly alarmed at the 'Japanese menace'.[59] German interests were dispersed in the larger cities such as Lima and Arequipa and, above all, in the sugar industry,[60] and *Lufthansa Perú*, organized in 1938, was, of course, in German hands. Italian influence had been both older and stronger. The *Banco Italiano*, though technically possessing Peruvian nationality, was especially influential, and while Ecuador had accepted an

Italian military mission, Benavides had welcomed both an Italian Air Force and an Italian Police Mission.

Benavides was sustained in power by the renewal of economic prosperity. As the British Minister remarked, 'men do not make revolutions on full bellies'.[61] The Peruvian upper ranks of society, living, for the most part, between the mountains and the sea, the commercial interests, the 'moderates', and the army all supported him. But the vast majority of Peruvians were Indians and mestizos, or *cholos*. And had 'popular' opinion prevailed (though sustained 'popular' political interest, when some three-quarters of the population was illiterate and only eight per cent was entitled to vote, was difficult to assess or maintain), Perú might at one time have fallen under the control of the *Alianza Popular Revolucionaria Americana*, or Apra,[62] of which Dr. Victor Raúl Haya de la Torre was the leader. Not an orthodox communist party, Apra was nevertheless anti-capitalist, anti-imperialist, and hostile to the United States. It called for mass education, the emancipation of the Indian, the nationalisation of land and industry, the internationalisation of the Panamá Canal and the economic, followed by the political unity of the Latin American peoples; and in support of this programme it sought to enlist the incipient middle class and the urban workers. For the oligarchy it was a standing threat to the whole social and economic order. Its members resorting to violence and murder, many were imprisoned or exiled and the party itself was outlawed on the ground that it had an 'international character'.[63] For this alleged reason it was unable to put forward a candidate in the subsequently annulled presidential elections of 1936, when it threw its support, instead, behind the anti-administration candidate. It was again banned in the elections of October, 1939, which resulted in the return, by an enormous majority, of the aristocratic Dr. Manuel Prado y Ugarteche, a banker, the son of a former President, and the first civilian to hold the Presidency since 1930. Pledging himself to avoid extremes either of the right or the left, Prado professed his adherence to Pan Americanism and world peace.[64]

The third of the Indian and Andean states, next in size (after Colombia) to Perú, but with a population[65] barely

larger than that of Ecuador, was Bolivia. The greater part of
her people lived on that immense plateau, at an average
height of two miles above the sea, where the cordillera of the
west walled it off from the Pacific (Bolivia had been deprived
of her Pacific coast-line by Chile) or in the inter-mont valleys
of the cordillera of the east, which towered over the tropical
lowlands stretching to the frontiers of Brazil and Paraguay. A
small urban oligarchy of the middle and upper ranks of
society, together with an élite of landed proprietors, monopol-
ised politics. The masses, living in conditions of hardship and
poverty, worked under appalling conditions in the tin and
silver mines, or, the majority of them, scarcely less miserably,
in the fields. A landlocked state, with rich agricultural poten-
tialities, Bolivia was forced to import much of her foodstuffs as
well, of course, as her machinery and textiles. The United
States, Germany, Argentina and Perú were her major sup-
pliers. The air-line, *Lloyd-Aéreo Boliviano*, founded in 1925, was
German-controlled; the army had been German trained; and
there were a number of old-established and wealthy German
firms as well as later immigrants in La Paz, the *de facto* capital,
in Oruro, the hub of the railway system and of the tin-mining
area, and in Cochabamba, an agricultural centre, where an
Italian military mission functioned, as well as in other towns
such as Sucre, the legal capital. Germany, however, took only
a small portion of Bolivian exports, of which by far the most
important element was tin. Most of the tin mines were in the
hands of the Patiño, Hochschild and Aramayo interests, above
all Patiño, and the greater part of the tin-ore was exported to
Britain for smelting. Belgium was Bolivia's second best customer.

The Great Depression had borne hardly on Bolivia. The
price of tin collapsed. Financial dislocation and labour unrest
—the labour movement had made its appearance in the first
quarter of the nineteenth century with the growth of an urban
proletariat and among the railway workers, though unionism
was not permitted in the mines—were accompanied by revolutionary upheaval.[66] Then, in 1932, came the major catas-
trophe of the long and costly Chaco War. Bolivia, seeking an
outlet to the Atlantic by means of the Rió de la Platan system,
claimed the desolate region (mistakenly thought to contain

oil) known as the Chaco Boreal, and a port on the Paraguay
River. Paraguay disputed the claim, and the result was disas-
ter. Bolivia lost 60,000 of her young men and reaped in defeat
a harvest of humiliation, bitterness, and despair, made mani-
fest in a violent reaction of soldiers against civilians and a
rising tide of xenophobia. An armistice was signed with Paraguay, who had captured no fewer than 15,000 Bolivians, in
June, 1935. In May of the following year, when the prisoners
began to return, a general strike threatened to paralyse the
country, and the army struck. Two colonels, David Toro and
Germán Busch (the son of a German immigrant and a Bolivian mother) devised a *coup d'état*, Toro assuming the Presidency to inaugurate a brief experiment in state socialism or
what came to be called 'functional democracy'.[67] His programme seems to have been strongly influenced by Italian
fascism and the idea of the corporate state and was made
notable by the creation of a Ministry of Labour and the
seizure in March, 1937, of the holdings of the Standard Oil
Company of New Jersey, whose concessions had been granted
in 1922 and which was accused of tax evasion and the illegal
exportation of oil.[68]

A few months later Toro was displaced by Busch, who had
at least a good war record,[69] which Toro had not. But there
was no reversal of Toro's nationalistic and socialistic policies
as at first had been anticipated. In 1938 a national convention
was summoned which re-wrote the Constitution, with a new
emphasis on social welfare, and formally elected Busch to the
Presidency. Busch, in the following year, frankly assumed
dictatorial powers, proclaimed the need for a 'stern régime of
moral and administrative discipline', issued a major labour
code, and insisted that his government was 'national' in
character and sought the subordination of the individual to
the general good.[70] National and essentially Bolivian it was.
The British Minister, in December 1938, reported, somewhat
optimistically, that there was little sympathy in Bolivia either
for Nazism or Fascism,[71] and again, in March, 1939, that
Busch himself had no obvious leanings to Germany. 'Funda-
mentally', he wrote, 'Bolivians do not like Germany or German methods'.[72] Nor did he consider that the Busch régime
demonstrated any pressure from, or particular love for, the

totalitarian systems of Germany and Italy. Nevertheless, in April, 1939, Busch had privately asked the German Minister, Ernst Wendler, to secure German assistance in establishing 'order and authority in the state through a complete change in the system and the transition to a totalitarian form'—a request which took the German Foreign Office aback.[73] In August, however, Busch died in what are known as 'mysterious circumstances'—he was generally believed to have shot himself under the influence of drink, over-work and nervous excitement[74]—and was at once succeeded by the Chief of Staff of the Army, General Carlos Quintanilla, who, in due course, pledged himself to restore constitutional rule and to hold elections in 1940. The 'post-war era of military socialism' had ended.[75] In December General Enrique Peñaranda del Castillo, a Chaco war veteran, affectionately known as the Bolivian Cincinnatus, was put forward as a candidate by the parties of the right, centre and moderate left, and in March, 1940, was elected.

V

Chile also was dominated by the Andes. But instead of dividing the country against itself, the Andes confined it to a narrow coastal strip, stretching in as long a line as from London to the North Pole. Her population[76] was markedly homogeneous, upper and lower classes, masters and men, often boasting a similar admixture of Araucanian Indian and Spanish blood, though the masses more prominently reflected the Indian strain and the classes were more nearly, and sometimes wholly, European in extraction. The great majority lived in the lovely central valley, the agricultural zone, sandwiched between the heavily forested south and the desert north, the source of Chile's mineral wealth in nitrates and copper. The great copper mines, such as those of Chuquicamata and Potrerillos were dominated by United States capital —$383 millions were invested in mining and smelting alone.[77] Nitrates had suffered severely from the invention of the synthetic-nitrogen process. But between 1930 and 1939 copper and nitrates accounted for 72 per cent of the value of Chilean exports.[78] The United States, closely followed by Germany, was the most important single source of supply, the United Kingdom and Europe the principal customers.

Over the years Chile's social structure had been changing. An industrial proletariat had grown up in the nitrate fields, the copper and the coal mines, and, together with a lower middle class, in the ports and the capital. Labour militancy had appeared and working class movements; and in 1920 Arturo Alessandri, a fiery politician and company lawyer, popularly known as the 'Lion of Tarapacá', for which province he had been a Senator, was elected to the Presidency, not indeed by 'popular' vote—that was scarcely possible—but nevertheless appealing by his silver-tongued oratory both to the educated middle classes and to the working masses. Alessandri favoured a moderate programme of social reform, immoderately opposed by a conservative Senate. Resigning in 1924, he was brought back by a military *coup d'état* in 1925, to supervise the reform of Chile's ancient Constitution, restoring the traditional pre-eminence of the President, which Congress had eroded, separating the Church from the State, and incorporating a number of fashionable twentieth-century social provisions.[79]

Where Alessandri had sown, Colonel Carlos Ibáñez, himself a representative of the middle classes, sought to reap the increase. Ibáñez came to the presidency, after an interval of growing power, in 1927. He, too, appealed to the forgotten man, improved the educational system, and 'constantly advocated, and occasionally actually worked for, amelioration of the social system'.[80] But the 'Chilean Mussolini', as he enjoyed being called, not only ruled in a highly authoritarian manner, he involved the country in obligations far beyond its capacity to meet, and in 1931 was overwhelmed by the world depression. This, though delayed in its impact, affected Chile almost more drastically than any other Latin American country. Mineral exports dramatically fell. The Government was forced to declare a moratorium on the foreign debt, and, in July, after a week of student demonstrations, strikes and bloodshed, Ibáñez, to the relief of the conservative classes, resigned.[81]

But the whirlwind was yet to come. The economic and financial situation continued to deteriorate, unemployment to rise, wages to fall. The Communist Party, founded in 1921, took on a new lease of life; a Socialist Party appeared; the *Confederación de Trabajadores de Chile*, or C.T.Ch., was created on Marxist lines; the navy, hitherto the pride of the nation, was disorganized, the army discontented, and the country demoralised.[82] Finally, on 4 June, 1932, Colonel Marmaduque Grove, a stormy petrel of Chilean politics,[83] organized a *coup d'état* and established a junta of three which proclaimed the 'Socialist Republic' of Chile. It lasted twelve days. The army then intervened. Grove was deported to Easter Island, and Dr. Carlos Dávila, a former Ambassador to the United States, who, as the most moderate member of the junta, had resigned, was reinstated with a new junta which he soon superseded as provisional President.[84] But between the 4th June and early November Chile experienced three *coups d'état* and seven changes in the presidency, as well as serious social unrest.[85] If events in Cuba in 1933 foreshadowed the revolution there of 1959, those in Chile in 1931–2, the expression of deep-seated changes, anticipated the crises of the nineteen-seventies.

At last, after fifteen months of near anarchy,[86] peaceful elections were again held, and Alessandri, in October 1932, was once more returned to the Presidency. Formerly regarded as a dangerous demagogue, he now appeared as the essence of respectability, determined that constitutional government must prevail and revolutionaries be suppressed. He even condoned the establishment of a short-lived 'White Guard' or Republican Militia, dedicated to the preservation of 'democratic republican government'.[87] The nitrate industry was re-organised, unemployment reduced, the external debt partially redeemed, local industries were encouraged, exports trebled and imports doubled. But nothing was done to promote agrarian reform and little to redress the grave problems of Chile's social order. The condition of the rural and urban worker, made worse by an inflationary system of finance, remained unbelievably hard.

So, in 1936, the parties of the centre and left (no country in Latin America was more prolific of parties than Chile), the Radicals (essentially a middle class party), the Democráticos (a small group), the Socialists, the Radical Socialists (both founded between 1931 and 1933), the Communists and the C.T.Ch., composed their numerous differences and established a Popular Front. They chose as their candidate for the election of October 1938 Pedro Aguirre Cerda, a moderate Radical, a well-to-do landowner, though born in comparative poverty, a professor and an educational reformer. Opposed by Alessandri's former distinguished but arrogant Minister of Finance, Gustavo Ross, who was the choice of the parties of the right, the Conservatives and Liberals, Aguirre Cerda won by a narrow majority. His greatest strength lay in the big cities, the nitrate fields and the copper mines. But he was supported also by the followers of Ibáñez, who had attempted to stand as the candidate of the *Nacista* Party, the *Partido Nacional Socialista*,[88] but who was disqualified on account of alleged complicity in all ill-starred rising in September. His programme was comparatively mild. It called for educational, social and agrarian reform, public health legislation, the suppression of monopolies, revision of the tax structure and defence of the democratic régime. But, as President, Aguirre Cerda faced unprecedented difficulties, caused by a severe earthquake, which laid waste six of the richest agricultural provinces early in 1939, and by the coming of the war in Europe, from which Chile was bound to suffer, in the autumn.

As the European skies had darkened, even before the advent of the Popular Front Government, there had been some anxiety in Chile over the presence of German immigrants, the efficiency of German propaganda, and the teaching in German schools.[89] The Germans in Chile were old-established. Many, small farmers, artisans and peasants, had come in the eighteen-forties and fifties to find new homes in south-central Chile. Others, in the eighteen-eighties, had settled in the 'frontier' region north of Valdivia and south of the Bío-Bío river. These German-Chileans had deserved well of the country of their adoption. Many were Catholics; some were Austrians or Swiss; and a few late comers were Jewish refugees. The Germanic element in the population cannot have exceeded thirty to thirty-five thousand;[90] and the Chilean-Germans in general were by no means supporters of the Nazis, though Nazi organisers were active.

VI

On the frontier between Chile and Argentina the Andes reach their greatest heights, and between their eastern foothills and the Atlantic stretches one of the world's great plains regions, the flat, treeless, grassy Argentine pampas. Across the Río de la Plata they merge into the rolling plains of Uruguay, and far up-stream from Buenos Aires border on sub-tropical Paraguay, her irrigated pastures and forested hills to the east of the Paraguay river, the brackish wastes of the Chaco to the west. These plains were cattle country, and, with the invention of barbed wire, they became agricultural country too. They turned Argentina into one of the world's great granaries as well as one of its foremost producers of meat. But the great plains of south-eastern South America were paralleled by the great plains of the United States, and their products were competitive. Not the United States but Britain and continental Europe were Argentina's best customers, buying 40 per cent of her wheat in 1938, 91 per cent of her maize, 74 per cent of her wool, and 93 per cent of her meat,[91] and while Britain led in the trade of Argentina and Uruguay, Germany, after Argentina, had gained the lead in inland Paraguay.

Paraguay was the only country in which an Indian language newspaper was published (in Guaraní), and the majority of her people were either Guaraní or of mixed Guaraní and Spanish blood. There had been little immigration, apart from the German-Canadian and German-Russian Mennonite colonies in the Paraguayan Chaco. But Germans and some Brazilian-Germans had helped to colonise the Upper Paraná and there were small German communities in Asunción and Concepción. The population, drastically reduced by the great war of the eighteen-sixties with Argentina, Brazil and Uruguay, was still under a million, and, though victorious in her war with Bolivia over the Chaco Boreal, Paraguay had lost nearly 40,000 of her young men. Her economy was rudimentary—her exports consisted almost entirely of agricultural, forest and pastoral products, including fine-grade cotton—and the Chaco war had left her exhausted and faced with grave problems of national reconstruction, aggravated by military discontent, labour disturbances and political instability. A war veteran, Colonel Rafael Franco, organized a *coup d'état* in 1936, to inaugurate an experiment in totalitarian socialism. But the experiment was brief. A further *coup d'état* destroyed him in 1937 and he retired to Montevideo to make soap. Finally, the real hero of the war, General José Félix Estigarribia, was elected to the Presidency in August 1939, reluctantly, it would seem, found himself compelled to proclaim a dictatorship early in 1940, promulgated a new Constitution, which was ratified by a plebiscite, but was killed in an air accident early in September. He was succeeded by his Minister of War, General Higinio Morínigo, the absolute ruler of Paraguay, or nearly so, till 1948.

Uruguay, with an almost wholly white population, including a sizeable German and Italian element, was the smallest of the South American states but surpassed by none in her social progress. Under the influence of José Batlle y Ordóñez, the founder of the newspaper, *El Día*, twice President, and the principal political figure till his death in 1929, one of the most turbulent Latin American states had been transformed into one of the most orderly and progressive. As the State entered into business and industry and embarked on a programme of advanced labour legislation, Uruguay might plausibly claim to have become the first 'welfare state' in the Americas.

To avoid the dangers of dictatorship Batlle had also provided the country with a curious dual executive, under which power was shared between the President and an Administrative Council of nine. So long as the President and the Council saw eye to eye, the system worked fairly well. But it broke down in the 'thirties, when, under the impact of the world depression, the livestock industry was prostrated, exports declined steeply, and the national finances were seriously affected. Insisting that energetic action, which the double executive failed to provide, was essential, President Gabriel Terra carried out a *coup d'état* in 1933, dissolved Congress, arrested the principal members of the Administrative Council, convoked a constitutent assembly and secured a new Constitution which suppressed the dual executive. But the 1934 Constitution itself contained a remarkable provision whereby the President had to select three of the members of his cabinet from the largest minority party, which was also to hold half the seats in the Senate. And since the President's action had split both of Uruguay's traditional parties, the *Colorados* (or liberals) and the *Blancos* (or conservatives), political life came to exhibit a scene of extreme confusion. The President himself, illegally extending his term of office, continued to govern by decree till he was succeeded in 1938 by his brother-in-law, General Alfredo Baldomir. But not only was the Vice-President, Dr César Charlone, like Baldomir a Colorado, though of different complexion, on doubtful terms with the President, but a principal section of the Blancos, led by Senator Luis Alberto de Herrera, the so-called Herrerista Nationalists or Herreristas, were entrenched in the cabinet and the Senate, and these, too, were the President's critics. Not surprisingly the question of constitutional reform was much to the fore in Uruguay.

The contrast between Montevideo, on one bank of the Río de la Plata, and Buenos Aires, a hundred miles distant, on the other, was striking. Montevideo retained something of the atmosphere of a Spanish colonial city. Buenos Aires was one of the great capitals of the world. It published two of the world's most distinguished newspapers, *La Prensa* and *La-Nación*, and it was the hub of the richest, most industrialised, and, ethnically and culturally, most European in outlook of all the Latin American states. Argentina, as the capital clearly revealed, had been one of the major immigration areas of South America—the other was Brazil—and, except for a minor fraction, her population was European by descent or birth.[92] The greatest influx of immigrants had been Spanish and Italian. The Italians, indeed, had been closely connected with the whole agricultural development of Argentina, and there was scarcely any trade or profession to which they had not contributed. But there was also a German-speaking population, varied in origin and divided among itself, of perhaps a quarter of a million,[93] and even a 'colony' of Welsh. Such was Argentina's reputation abroad that a contemporary historian could observe in 1929 that a revolution in Argentina was as improbable as in England.[94]

It was, therefore, a shock when the Government of Hipólito Yrigoyen, twice President of Argentina and leader of the now essentially middle-class Radical Party, was overthrown in the following year. Yrigoyen's ageing incompetence and autocratic habits, the increasing paralysis and mismanagement of the bureaucratic machine which depended on him, and a total failure to grapple with the economic consequences of the world depression, all contributed to this result. An almost legendary figure, he had not only lost the support of those upper middle-class groups, the professional and well-to-do business men, some of whom were allied to the landed gentry, but also of the lower middle-class and of the voting section of the urban workers—of all those, in short, who had been responsible for his re-election in 1928.[95] Even the students demonstrated against him[96] and the revolution, almost bloodless, proved to be astonishingly popular. It was engineered, among dissident sections of the army and the conservative landed élite (who detested Yrigoyen), by two generals, José Félix Uriburu and Agustín P. Justo.[97] As the Argentine workers were to discover, it meant the end of the so-called 'era of liberal democracy' (a very corrupt and raw democracy), which had begun with the law of the secret and obligatory ballot in 1912, the great Radical victory at the polls in 1916 and Yrigoyen's first Presidency. It meant also the restoration of the dominance of the traditional ruling groups, the conservative oligarchy, supported by the army. The political clock had been turned back.

For a year the country remained under the provisional presidency of the aristocratic Uriburu, who imposed a state of siege, suspending, that is, a number of constitutional guarantees, persecuted and exiled Radical leaders, and debarred them from presenting a candidate when presidential elections were held in November, 1931. The election of Justo, who belonged to the group known as the anti-Yrigoyen or anti-personalist Radicals, now allied with the conservatives in the ill-named National Democratic Party, was a foregone conclusion. Uriburu's repressive measures were somewhat relaxed. Where Uriburu had supported the organization on military lines of a *Legión Cívica Argentina*, subject to severe discipline and pledged to the support of the provisional government, Justo's attitude was one of tolerance mingled with distrust, and the *Legión* did in fact begin to disintegrate.[98] But he also authorised or condoned fraudulence, intimidation and shameless malpractices to maintain the conservative domination, and, as his own election had been a foregone conclusion, so in turn was that of his Minister of Finance, Dr. Roberto M. Ortiz, the son of a Basque immigrant and himself a student both of medicine and law, in September, 1937. Ortiz, too, was an anti-personalist Radical, but, as President, he struck a different note from Justo. He aimed, indeed, at the purification of politics and the restoration of democratic practices.[99] Was it possible that Argentina was about to witness a liberal, or, at any rate, a constitutional revival? The answer would not be long in coming.

The landed gentry and the British market were closely allied in Argentina. Britain was the principal customer for Argentine products, taking three times as much as any other country, more than 99 per cent, for example, of her chilled beef and heavy proportions of her frozen meat, wheat, maize, butter, wool and linseed.[100] British investments were estimated by the Bank of England in 1936 at £422 million— about a third of all British investments in Latin America.[101] British imports from Argentina in the nineteen-thirties accounted for more than a half of her total imports from Latin America.[102] A former Minister of Overseas Trade had jestingly — and offensively—stated in 1933 that Argentina ought to become 'a fully fledged member of the British Empire'.[103] But Argentina sold more to Britain than she bought. On the other hand she bought more from the United States than she sold, paying for imports under a multilateral system of trade whereby sterling could be converted into dollars. She bought more, partly because the United States had been investing in Argentine public utilities and establishing branch firms which were major consumers of imported goods, partly because, with the growth of Argentine industry, British exports remained too traditional.[104] She sold less, partly because of the competitive nature of the Argentine and United States economies and partly because an embargo had been placed, under United States sanitary regulations, on the importation of Argentine meat, while the equally-resented Hawley-Smoot Tariff of 1930 had raised the duties on many Argentine (and other foreign) imports to prohibitive heights.

To protect herself against the effects of the world economic depression Argentina had introduced exchange control in 1931. Britain, in 1932, adopted a protectionist stance and by the Ottawa Agreements imposed restrictions on Argentine imports of food and those of other foreign countries in the interests of imperial preference. The conjunction of these policies, American, Argentine and British, together with Argentine fears of further possible restrictions, resulted in the Roca-Runciman Agreement of 1933 (in effect re-negotiated in 1936) which seemed to provide benefits and a measure of security both to Argentina and Britain. Broadly speaking, Britain undertook not to curtail her imports of Argentine meat below certain levels. Argentina promised to use the sterling acquired from sales to Britain (after the deduction of a reasonable sum for the service of her public debt liabilities to other countries) for current remittances to Britain, including both interest payments to British investors and payments for British exports; and this preferential treatment was accompanied by the relaxation of some tariff restrictions and a promise of 'benevolent treatment' of the British-owned public utilities, such as the railways and the tramways, which had been the subject of contention.[105]

These arrangements roused acrimonious debate. In the United States they were regarded as highly injurious to United States interests and inconsistent with the principles of triangular, non-discriminatory trade which Britain herself professed to uphold (other than in the Ottawa Agreements) and to which the Secretary of State, Cordell Hull, was deeply attached and had succeeded in embodying in the Trade Agreement Act of 1934.[106] They led, therefore, to a serious clash of interests between Britain and the United States and reinforced criticisms, already heard, that Britain not only sought, and obtained, trading advantages at the expense of the United States but also was anxious to restrain the growth of American influence in Argentina, encouraging her, for example, in her aloof and somewhat hostile attitude to the United States and the ideas of Pan Americanism.[107]

In Argentina the cattlemen and the conservative oligarchy approved the agreements.[108] *The Unión Industrial Argentina*, on the other hand, accused the Government of sacrificing the industrial interests of the country to its pastoral and

agricultural.[109] Britain was charged with trying to turn
Argentina into an 'economic colony',[110] and the promise of
'benevolent treatment' to the British-owned public utilities
stimulated Argentine nationalism, both political and economic. Nationalism, as a political force, was, of course, a general
phenomenon in Latin America, and obtaining an increasing
hold. Argentina was not alone in spawning so-called
'nationalist' groups, which combined national sentiment with
fascist ideas, such as the *Legión Cívica* at the beginning of the
decade of the thirties and the *Alianza de la Juventud Nacionalista* towards the end.[111] And anti-imperialism in Argentina
was directed as much against Britain as against the United
States.

But though a number of right-wing extremist groups had
been making their appearance in Argentina, drawing support
from army or ex-army officers, old-fashioned conservatives,
current ideological doctrines, and idealistic or disillusioned
youth, and glorifying the spirit of hierarchy and discipline,
such groups were comparatively small. Argentines in general
were alive to their dangers, and to the dangers also of the
penetration of non-nationalist ideologies, whether Communist, Fascist or Nazi. Communist activities were made illegal, at
least in Buenos Aires Province, in 1936.[112] German Nazi
activities—and Germans of all kinds found themselves subject to the usual Nazi pressures, a branch of the Gestapo
functioning as a *Hafendienst* or port service—[113] roused much
indignation, particularly the use of the Nazi salute and Nazi
teaching in German schools and the organization of a plebiscite among the German and Austrian communities on the
Anschluss in 1938.[114] The Government refused to be stampeded
into hasty action.[115] But an enquiry was instituted into the
state of affairs in German schools and steps were taken to
supervise the teaching in all foreign establishments.[116] A sensational (and false) report of a German plot in 1939 to seize
Patagonia led not only to a judicial enquiry but to an investigation of local Nazi parties throughout the country and the
introduction of measures to control foreign organizations. By
an executive decree of 15 May the Nazi Party was banned,
only to be replaced by the Federation of German Welfare and
Cultural Societies.[117] But Argentina moved with caution. Ger-

many was her second best customer, and she was quite prepared to conclude a barter deal with her in 1939.

VII

Brazil, like Argentina, aspired to pre-eminence in South
America. Her resources were as immense as her territory was
vast. But her population was not much more than forty-one
millions. To the north and east it occupied little more than a
broken coastal fringe, but penetrated more deeply inland in
the southern and south-eastern regions which accounted for
the greater part of Brazilian agricultural and industrial production. Racially, the country presented a magnificent example of tolerant miscegenation between Indians, Negroes and
Europeans, principally Portuguese. At least a half of the
population could be classified as white. But a high proportion
was mulatto, with a sprinkling of zambos and mestizos and a
strong element of pure negro. The size of the Indian tribes of
the interior remains a matter of speculation. The European
element had been reinforced in the late nineteenth and early
twentieth centuries by immigration, mainly from Italy and
Portugal. But there had also been a much longer and fairly
continuous, though smaller, stream of German migrants, giving rise to a population of German or part-German stock of
close on a million; and of these perhaps 100,000 or more were
Reichsdeutsche.[118] Japan, too, had contributed her quota, carefully controlled by the mother country, the Japanese community in 1939 numbering little fewer than 200,000.

The majority of the Germans and Italians had settled in the
three southern states of Rio Grande do Sul, Santa Catarina
and Paraná and in São Paulo, though there were smaller
communities elsewhere.[119] In south Brazil German agricultural settlements were of long standing, and the Germans themselves had been regarded as hard-working, model colonists.
Their numbers had grown by natural increase rather than by
any very large additions from Europe, and because of the
historical conditions under which their original settlements
had taken place, and their relative isolation, their linguistic
and racial assimilation had been much slower than that of the
Italians. Many of the older agricultural settlers, however, as

distinct from the newer immigrants in the cities, had become Brazilianized and others upheld the traditions of an older, more liberal Germany. The Italians, arriving in large numbers before 1914, had been attracted by the demand for labour on the coffee estates of São Paulo, and, like the Germans, by the possibilities of acquiring land in the southern states. But Italians, and Brazilians of Italian stock, had also played an important part in Brazil's financial, commercial and artistic life. The Japanese, very much less assimilable, had mostly settled in the state of São Paulo[120] as agricultural workers and were conspicuously successful in the cultivation of coffee, cotton, sugar, rice, tea, and in market gardening.[121]

Brazil was still primarily an agricultural country, with some two-thirds of her economically active population engaged in rural occupations. Coffee and cotton remained the chief export crops. The major part of the coffee exports was shipped to the United States, Brazil's most important single customer, and, after the United States, to Germany. The cotton mostly went to Germany and Japan. Thanks to bilateral exchanges under the Aski mark system[122] (despite a Reciprocal Trade Agreement with the United States), so intensive had been the Nazi trade drive in the later nineteen-thirties that Germany had become the largest single exporter to Brazil, selling armaments and munitions as well as coal, chemicals, iron and steel products, and the like. German firms were established in the larger cities. *Deutsche Lufthansa* operated a transatlantic service and *Sindicato* Condor (founded in 1924) not only covered the whole of the Brazilian coast but linked Brazil to Uruguay, Argentina and Chile until *Lufthansa* itself took over the Buenos Aires-Santiago route. German trade had grown at the expense both of Britain and the United States, but more particularly of Britain, and though British investments in Brazil exceeded those of the United States and were far greater than German, Brazil, which had set out on the course of industrialisation and national self-sufficiency, had no great liking for foreign-controlled enterprises.[123] Industry, at the time of the world depression, had still been in its 'adolescent stage'.[124] But the shock then administered, when coffee prices fell by 1931 to a third of those which had previously prevailed, was severe and lasting. From now onwards industrial growth proceeded apace, particularly in the old textile industry, in food-processing, in the manufacture of cement, and in pharmaceutical and metallurgical enterprises. By 1938 the value of industrial production had outstripped that of agricultural production, and plans were being laid for a large-scale steel industry—a project dear to the heart of President Getúlio Vargas, for whom Brazil's industrial growth was not only a matter of national pride and economic security but a means of expanding Brazilian trade with her neighbours.[125]

Dr. Vargas, who had been the Governor of Rio Grande do Sul, had risen to power in 1930 as the result of a revolution which began the destruction of the old political order, brought new men into politics, and marked the advent of new social forces. It was achieved through an uneasy alliance between revolutionary army officers, the so-called *tenentes* or lieutenants, disgruntled machine politicians in several states and genuine liberal reformers, supported finally by the high command in Rio de Janeiro. Its immediate purpose was the prevention of one politician from São Paulo, the richest and most powerful state in the Union, from succeeding another in the Presidency.[126]

Dr. Vargas installed, all representative assemblies, federal, state and municipal, dissolved, federal interventors replacing state governors, and the President ruling by decree, the victorious conspirators found themselves at odds. Vargas, while creating two new Ministries, of Labour and of Education, was forced to tread delicately between those who wished for an early return to constitutionalism[127] and those who feared the replacement of one clique of politicians by another.[128] The states themselves seemed to be locked in incessant rivalries within and between themselves, and one, São Paulo, bitterly resentful of federal intervention, rose in revolt in July, 1932. A full-scale civil war followed, but, failing to win the support she expected, São Paulo was forced to surrender at the end of 83 days. Vargas treated her with magnanimity.[129] What was more, he summoned a constituent assembly in 1933 which promulgated a new Constitution in July of the following year. This, a mixture of conservatism and liberalism, preserved the classic constitutional forms. But the powers of the federal government were enhanced, particularly in social and economic affairs, and an element of functional representation was introduced, together with a number of social welfare provisions designed to appeal to the middle and working classes. Vargas himself was confirmed in the Presidency for a further four years.

But the return to constitutionalism did little to tranquillize politics. On the left the Communists organized the short-lived *Aliança Nacional Libertadora*, a kind of Popular Front, but brought themselves and it into disrepute by the part they played in barrack-room risings in 1935 in Rio Grande do Norte and Pernambuco and even in Rio de Janeiro itself. These were easily suppressed. Severe measures were taken against their instigators and thousands of suspects arrested and imprisoned. On the right the *Integralista* movement, founded in 1932 by Plínio Salgado, a journalist, novelist and politician, made rapid headway. With its green shirts, its symbols, slogans, salutes and parades, it unblushingly borrowed the outward trappings of European fascism, and some of its doctrines as well. It stood for hierarchy, discipline and order, the destruction of regionalism, ultra-nationalism, and the creation of an 'integral nation' supported by an 'integral society'.[130]

For much of the time between November, 1935, and July, 1937, Vargas had governed under emergency powers granted to him by Congress. In 1937 itself, as presidential elections, due to take place in January, 1938, approached, he gave the impression of 'flirting with the integralists',[131] as indeed he was, meanwhile consolidating his position with the military high command, who looked upon the approaching elections, and the victory of any of the candidates who had appeared, with horror. Vargas could not constitutionally stand. But, under the pretext of the discovery of a Communist plot[132] to subvert the state, he again asked for and was given emergency powers. Then, on 10 November, troops surrounded the Congress building and Congress was dissolved. A new, authoritarian and highly nationalistic Constitution, intended, as its preamble declared, to preserve the nation from party dissension, demagogic propaganda and ideological conflict, was promulgated out of hand[133] (to be ratified by a plebiscite which was never held). This was the famous *Estado Novo*, as it came to be called. By a so-called transitory article (No. 187), the nation was declared to be in a state of emergency. Federal, state and municipal bodies were again dissolved; the majority of State Governors were replaced by Federal Interventors; and in December all political parties were banned. The Integralists, who had expected to be welcomed with open arms, now found themselves relegated to the status of a cultural society. In May, 1938, some of them attempted an ill-organised *coup d'état*, attacking the Presidential Palace, where Vargas and his daughter held them at bay until help arrived. The movement was then in effect proscribed. This was the last serious threat to the President. From 1938 to 1945, with no *Estado Novo* party, but with the support of the military and with the states under federal puppets, Vargas governed in complete if relatively benevolent despotism.

These developments led, naturally enough, to fears that Vargas was sympathetically inclined to the totalitarian states in Europe. Sumner Welles, at the State Department, pooh-poohed this. The régime, he thought, was 'essentially Latin American in character'.[134] More accurately, perhaps, it was authoritarianism *sui generis*. Vargas believed—and in this he agreed with the Integralists—in 'Brazil for the Brazilians' and in her increasing cultural, poltical and economic unity. Whatever his relations with the third Reich, he was not prepared to tolerate German control over Germans living in Brazil. There were to be no divided loyalties in the *Estado Novo* and no threats to security within its own borders if Vargas was to have his way.

How far the Germans in Brazil of the fourth, third and even second generations were becoming Brazilianized is not an easy question to answer. Some, undoubtedly, had made their choice between Germany and Brazil during the first World War. Some were refugees, and others, besides the refugees, had little sympathy with the Nazis. But there could be no question at all of the extent of Nazi propaganda and of the attempts of the *Auslandsorganisation*[135] and its satellites to regiment both the *Reichsdeutsche* and the *Volksdeutsche*. Vargas took counter-measures. It was not only the Integralists as well as the Communists who were repressed. Brazilian political organisations with foreign connections were banned—a measure, as the British Ambassador reported, mainly directed against bodies such as the *Casa Alemã*, the headquarters of the Nazi Party, the Front of the German Women Abroad, and the Hitler Youth Club.[136] German schools, of which there were a great many, were closed or restrictions imposed on their teaching. By an anti-Nazi decree of 18 April, foreigners were forbidden to engage in any type of political activity or to maintain clubs or societies of a political nature.[137] After the Integralist putsch in May, 1938, some Germans suspected of being implicated were arrested, anti-Nazi measures were intensified, and in September the disagreeable German Ambassador, Karl Ritter, was declared *persona non grata*. Germany retorted by asking for the recall of the Brazilian Ambassador. Meanwhile thousands of Germans left Brazil in disgust. Further signs of Brazilian caution were the establishment of the headquarters of a new infantry regiment at Blumenau in Santa Catarina, the centre of one of the most completely German districts in Brazil, and a decree in August that all conscripts must only speak Portuguese during their military training.[138] But German interference in the internal affairs of Brazil was one thing, German trade and German military supplies were quite another. Ambassadorial relations were soon restored, and, to the satisfaction of the Brazilian military, always obsessed by fear of Argentina, additional military contracts were signed with Krupps and other German firms.[139]

VIII

Britain and the United States had shared a common concern over the German trade drive in Brazil. They shared also in the disquiet felt in Brazil and elsewhere in Latin America at the activities of the *Auslandsorganisation*.[140] To some extent, indeed, Washington and London exchanged information which their representatives had gathered about these, and on such matters as German espionage in, for example, the Caribbean,[141] and, as the shadows had deepened over Europe, so also had Washington's anxiety to win the Latin American countries to a common stance and to forge a common front in defence of the hemisphere. 'To me the danger of the Western Hemisphere', wrote Cordell Hull in retrospect, 'was real and imminent',[142] and who could doubt but that much depended on Brazil, not only because of her obvious strategic significance but by reason of her seeming vulnerability?[143]

But there had been much lee-way to make up in United States-Latin American relations and a legacy to be overcome of resentment and distrust engendered by past United States policies. Indeed, it had been in part the absence of the United States from Geneva that had encouraged the Latin American states to join the League of Nations, as all ultimately did. Though the degree of enthusiasm varied, some, at least, saw in the League a counter-balance to the power and influence of the United States.[144] Membership soothed their national pride where the United States had most bruised it; it stimulated their self-reliance and appealed to their idealism. But as the authority of the League declined, so did Latin American interest in it. By 1939 half the states had either withdrawn or had announced their intention of doing so. Membership was becoming more a liability than an asset, and, by contrast, the attraction of the Pan American regional system, as embodied in the International Conferences of American States and the Pan American Union, now half a century old but hitherto distrustfully regarded, especially by Argentina, became more marked.

One great step forward had been the proclamation of the 'Good Neighbour Policy' by President Franklin Roosevelt at his inauguration in March, 1933, though the 'Good Neighbour Policy' was in fact built on foundations already laid; and this was followed in December by the acceptance by the United States at the Seventh International Conference of American States at Montevideo of a declaration that no state had the right to intervene in the internal or external affairs of another.[145] A further step was the liquidation by the United States of its previous interventionist policy in the Caribbean. But progress was slow. At Montevideo Cordell Hull whom Roosevelt had appointed Secretary of State, and who certainly looked the part, though his language sometimes resembled that of a Tennessee hillbilly, had gone out of his way to win the confidence of the Argentine Foreign Minister, the extremely vain but able Carlos Saavedra Lamas. But when, at the instance of the United States, a special Inter-American

Conference for the Maintenance of Peace was held at Buenos
Aires in 1936 and opened by Roosevelt in person, Hull found
that the eyes of Saavedra Lamas, who had recently served as
President of the League Assembly and had been awarded the
Nobel Peace Prize, were 'more on the dying League than the
living Pan American idea'. He also felt that his treatment by
Saavedra Lamas was personally insulting.[146] Nevertheless,
the Conference strengthened the doctrine of non-intervention
laid down at Montevideo and it agreed that, in the event of an
international war outside the Americas which might menace
the peace of the republics, they would consult together to
determine the proper time and manner in which they might
eventually co-operate, though Argentina insisted on the quali-
fying clause 'if they so desire'. But no machinery for consultation, such as the United States had wanted, was devised; nor,
to the relief of the Foreign Office, did the United States
succeed in persuading the Conference to adopt her own rigid
and isolationist neutrality policy, because, as Hull remarks,
the League permitted 'the export of arms to a nation that was
being attacked.'[147]

Finally, at the Eighth Inter-American Conference at Lima
in 1938, not only did the new Argentine Foreign Minister,
José María Cantilo, who had been the Argentine Ambassador
to Italy, arrive on a battleship, but, having emphasised
Argentina's strong ties with Europe, he then retired for a
vacation among the Chilean lakes, leaving a surbordinate in
charge of the Argentine delegation. Hull (who knew no Spanish) recalled the next ten days he spent at Lima as 'among the
most difficult' of his career.[148] Argentina, with her European
outlook and her self-appointed rôle of the 'Queen of South
America',[149] prevented the United States from achieving all
that Hull had wished. But she was less intransigent than has
often been supposed, and, on the whole, Hull had reason to be
satisfied, and so had the Foreign Office.[150] The Conference
oonce again renewed the pledges made at Montevideo and
Buenos Aires, and the Declaration of Lima marked a great
advance in its affirmation of the solidarity of the American
states 'against all foreign intervention or activity' that might
threaten them. This time, also, teeth were provided, which, as
it was soon to be seen, were not entirely false teeth. The

Foreign Ministers of the republics were to meet when consultation seemed desirable and at the initiative of any one of them. And the delegates not only condemned racial bigotry and intolerance everywhere but the collective political activity of aliens throughout the continent.

There could be no doubt about the countries to whom these condemnations were addressed,[151] and, given the result, it was of little moment that, in order to achieve it, Hull had appealed directly to President Ortiz of Argentina over the heads of the Argentine delegation and of Dr. Cantilo in his Chilean retreat.[152] Still more important, throughout the Conference the United States had enjoyed the warm support of Brazil,[153] and when Dr. Oswaldo Aranha, the Brazilian Foreign Minister, visited the United States early in 1939, he told the British Ambassador after his return that he had conveyed to Roosevelt a message from Vargas that if a war broke out, Brazil would be in opposition to the totalitarian powers, though, with more friendliness than discretion, he also referred to the pro-German sympathies of some of the army officers and to the influence which the army had on Vargas.[154] Aranha added, early in July, that while he himself did not conceal his sympathies for the democracies, he had so far failed to persuade Vargas to take up a definite attitude, but, a few days later, that at a Cabinet meeting held on the 4th July all present had shown themselves to be whole-heartedly in favour of Great Britain.[155]

II

THE ERA OF NEUTRALITY

I

President Vargas's good faith, or his realism, and Aranha's protestations were soon to be tested. At dawn on 1st September, 1939, Germany invaded Poland. On the 3rd Britain and France, soon followed by the British Dominions (except Eire), declared war on Germany, and on this same September day the S. S. *Athenia*, with many American passengers on board, was sunk by a German submarine off the north-west coast of Ireland. On the 10th a British Expeditionary Force sailed to France and on the 17th Soviet troops invaded eastern Poland. By the end of the month that unhappy country, its capital in ruins, had been partitioned between Germany and Russia. A British aircraft carrier, H.M.S. *Courageous*, had been sunk and a Polish Government in exile formed in Paris.

To millions of the inhabitants of Latin America these events were of unknown significance. But among the educated classes opinion was deeply stirred. Despite the attractions of Franco's Spain or Mussolini's Italy for conservative groups fearful of Communism, or, as in Argentina and Brazil, of Hitler's Germany for army officers in part German-trained, mesmerized by German military might or wanting German military equipment, sympathy for the democracies, enhanced by the fate of Catholic Poland, was widespread. The great Argentine dailies, *La Prensa* and *La Nación* from the first placed responsibility for the war on the shoulders of Hitler. *O Estado de São Paulo*, which had the largest circulation of any paper in Brazil, spoke of the 'democracies fighting against barbarism',[1] and even the right-wing *El Siglo*, the organ of the Colombian Conservative Party, whose horror of Communism had led it in the past to support Franco, Mussolini, and even Hitler, denounced him in November as the 'scourge of humanity'.[2] In Chile the Foreign Minister declared that he himself and four-fifths of the Chilean population sympathised with the Allies.[3] Dr. Aranha in Brazil was at pains to assert not only his support for Britain but that of his colleagues and of the President.[4] President Benavides of Perú was equally outspoken,[5] and in Uruguay the Chamber of Deputies, with the exception of one man, rose to its feet in a demonstration of support.[6]

This was a unique display. But though it illustrated that the Chamber was not neutral in thought, there was no suggestion in Uruguay or elsewhere that the American republics should be other than neutral in fact. Anxious, moreover, as were many countries to preserve their European economic ties, there was a clear understanding that war in Europe presented the Americas not only with common legal and political problems but also with common economic problems, in that sources of supply, export markets, shipping services, credit facilities, all alike were threatened. On 1st September President Santos of Colombia, of whose democratic sympathies there could be no doubt, telegraphed to his fellow Presidents expressing his country's determination 'to act in close agreement with the Governments of America on the principles of solidarity proclaimed in the Pan American Conferences'.[7] José María Cantilo, the Argentine Foreign Minister, who was strongly European in outlook, called a meeting of American representatives in Buenos Aires to announce Argentina's determination to follow her traditional policy of neutrality, in conformity with the rules of the Hague Convention of 1907 on the rights and duties of neutrals, and to propose a common American front.[8] And on the 5th September, at the initiative of the United States and after urgent consultation between the several American Governments, Panamá, at the joint request of Argentina, Brazil, Chile, Colombia, Cuba, the United States, Mexico and Perú, issued invitations for a conference of American Foreign Ministers to be held at Panamá City in accordance with the consultative procedure laid down in the Declaration of Lima.

Meanwhile, most of the republics took emergency measures to control the prices of imported goods and prevent speculation and declarations of neutrality came thick and fast,[9] though a number of states, of which Bolivia was the only

example in South America, preferred to await the delibera-
tions of the Panamá Conference. These declarations were
accompanied or followed by regulations similar to those
adopted at the outbreak of the first World War and designed
to uphold neutral rights and obligations by governing the
conduct of belligerent warships and merchant vessels in neutral ports, preventing the abuse of neutral flags, controlling
radio transmissions, and the like. The Foreign Minister of
Uruguay, Dr. Alberto Guani, actually consulted the British
Minister and his naval attaché before drawing up the final
draft of the Uruguayan neutrality regulations,[10] and, to British satisfaction, Brazil and Venezuela both prohibited belligerent submarines from entering their territorial waters.[11]

The Panamá Conference opened, under the sign of neutrality, on the 23rd September and closed on 3rd October. Not all
the Foreign Ministers could afford to be absent from their
capitals. Cordell Hull was represented by the United States
Under-Secretary of State, Sumner Welles, the Argentine Foreign Minister by Dr. Leopoldo Melo, a former Minister of the
Interior, who was careful to let it be known on leaving Buenos
Aires that no military or political agreements were
contemplated.[12] But it was not only the Foreign Ministers, or
their representatives, who descended on Panamá City. So also
did the German Minister in Central America,[13] representatives of the *Deutsche Nachrichten Bureau* (the official German
news agency) and of Transocean (its overseas news-service),
and a supporting caste of attachés and agents, some of whom
attempted, in vain, to obtain admission to the Conference as
observers.

There were three main subjects for discussion—neutrality,
the protection of the peace of the western hemisphere, and
economic co-operation. In a 'General Declaration of Neutrality' the republics affirmed 'their unanimous intention not to
become involved in the European conflict' and laid down
'standards of conduct' which they would observe as neutrals
and expected the belligerents to respect. Almost all were put
forward by the United States and conformed in the main to
generally accepted norms. But, by implication, each state was
left to enforce them at its discretion—sovereignty was as
delicate a subject as neutrality—and the efforts of Sumner

Welles to secure an agreement banning the entry of submarines into American ports or waters were defeated by the
opposition of Argentina.[14] An Inter-American Neutrality
Committee, composed of seven experts in international law,
was to formulate further neutrality recommendations 'in the
light of experience and changing circumstances', and, by an
additional resolution on neutral trading rights, the Conference, at the insistence of Argentina, Uruguay and Chile,
recorded its opposition to the inclusion of foodstuffs and cloth-
ing intended for civilians in belligerent contraband lists and
its belief that the granting of credits for the acquisition of such
goods was not unneutral.

But neutrality and neutrality regulations were not enough.
Further to safeguard the peace of the western hemisphere the
Declaration of Panamá purported to establish a security zone,
some three hundred miles wide, round the American continents which should be 'free from the commission of any hostile
act by any non-American belligerent nation'. The territorial
waters of Canada and of the 'undisputed colonies and possessions of European countries' (all of them Dutch, French or
British) were excluded from this 'chastity belt'—an exclusion
which led Argentina to reserve her long-standing claim
against Britain to the Falkland Islands and, by implication, to
the South Orkneys, and Guatemala hers against British
Honduras.[15] Joint representations were to be made to the
belligerents to secure their compliance, and the republics
might undertake either individually or collectively a patrol of
the waters adjacent to their coasts within the defined area.

This was the most sensational act of the Panamá Conference. It harked back to proposals made, and shelved, during
the first World War. But the idea was Roosevelt's own, warmly
supported by Sumner Welles (though Cuba also claimed
paternity), and derived in part from a suggestion privately put
forward by the President in the summer, and agreed to by
Britain, for an American (not a Pan American) patrol of the
Atlantic.[16] Cordell Hull did not believe in it, and he was not
alone in this scepticism.[17] Three days before it was approved
the British ship, *Clement*, was sunk off Pernambuco by the
German pocket-battleship, the *Graf Spee*, but it hardly needed
the report of this action to underline, what the Declaration

admitted, that the security of the zone depended on the willingness of the belligerents to respect it and the establishment of an effective naval patrol to safeguard it. It was one thing for such countries as could do so to establish a patrol of their territorial waters, and, at Roosevelt's express orders, the United States Navy had organized early in September a patrol to report and track any belligerent air, surface or underwater forces approaching the coasts of the United States and the West Indies.[18] But this was not a question of territorial waters or the like. There was only one navy, that of the United States, most of whose ships were in the Pacific, which could provide anything like the kind of patrol required, and Sumner Welles promised its assistance, though the Navy Department was 'appalled' at the idea of patrolling so vast an area.[19]

Less dramatic but more important was the decision (for which the initiative again came from the United States) to establish an Inter-American Financial and Economic Advisory Committee, consisting of twenty-one economic experts, one from each of the republics, who would meet at Washington not later than the middle of November. It was to consider and make recommendations on all aspects of economic cooperation between the several states in order to protect their financial and economic structures, expand their industries, intensify their agriculture and develop their trade on those liberal principles so dear to the heart of Cordell Hull. Of all the economic projects submitted to the Conference, this alone, in the opinion of Dr. Herbert Feiss, the economic adviser to the State Department, was of real value.[20] For the rest, the Conference exhorted the belligerents to conduct their operations on humane principles and the American republics to prevent the spread of foreign ideologies antipathetic to the 'common Inter-American democratic ideal'—a somewhat ironical phrase. It resolved that if any region of America 'subject to the jurisdiction of any non-American State should be obliged to change its sovereignty' to the danger of hemispheric security, a further consultative meeting should be held 'with the urgency that the case may require', and it agreed that it would be desirable for the Foreign Ministers to meet again at Havana, Cuba, on 1 October, 1940, or earlier if necessary.

II

For six weeks after the fall of Poland the armies in Europe remained inactive, though the Soviet Union took the opportunity to invade Finland—to the universal execration of Latin America, Argentina and Uruguay taking the lead in demanding the expulsion of the U.S.S.R. from the League of Nations. But the war at sea remained alive, and not only at sea but in the waters of the 'safety zone'. So far as this was concerned, Sumner Welles professed to be anxious to work out the details of the proposed neutrality patrol and other points also with Britain and France,[21] and Winston Churchill, as first Lord of the Admiralty, told Roosevelt, with cabinet approval, that Britain quite understood the desire of the United States to keep belligerents out of her waters and liked the idea of a wide limit within which no belligerent submarines should act. There would be a difficulty about surface ships, because if a raider operated from or took refuge in the zone, Britain would have to be protected, or protect herself. 'We should have great difficulty', he added, 'in accepting a zone which was only policed by some weak neutral. But of course if the American navy takes care of it, that is all right'.[22]

To some extent the shield of the United States was indeed extended over the Caribbean sea. Rumours abounded in the first three months of the war that German submarines were refuelling from bases in Mexico, Central America, Haiti, and the Dominican Republic. All apparently were unfounded.[23] But vigilance was increased. El Salvador, for example, dismissed the German Director of her Military School and gave 'leave of absence' to the head of the State Mortgage Bank, who was also the German consul and the local Nazi leader.[24] Guatemala was reportedd to be making provision for the patrol of her Atlantic coast[25] and Cuba to have improved her coastal supervision.[26] The Dominican Republic offered the United States all possible air and naval facilities.[27] In Colombia a close watch was instituted on the air ports and on the Scadta airline and its German pilots, and Shell, in Venezuela, agreed to make a substantial contribution to coastal defence.[28] By the end of the year the United States had succeeded in establishing a reasonably effective air and sea patrol over the

Caribbean area generally, Britain making available a limited use of base facilities in Bermuda, St. Lucia and Trinidad for United States naval vessels and aircraft assigned to the neutrality patrol.[29]

For the rest, except in the western part of the North Atlantic, where the Germans were careful to observe it until early in 1942, the zone remained a paper zone. The *Graf Spee*, a 'Nazi corsair', as *El Día* of Uruguay called her,[30] roamed the South Atlantic intercepting and sinking British shipping until, on 13 December, she was caught off the estuary of the Rió de la Plata by three British cruisers, *Ajax*, *Achilles* and *Exeter*, with much inferior gunpower, was severely damaged and took refuge in Montevideo. She was given 72 hours to make repairs, and then, on 17 December, while the cruisers waited for her, scuttled herself some five or seven miles out from the port. President Roosevelt expressed great satisfaction to Lord Lothian in Washington,[31] and the Argentine Foreign Minister telephoned his congratulations to the British Ambassador in Buenos Aires. He also remarked, more than once, 'The only thing that really matters is that you should win the war'.[32] The sailors from the *Graf Spee* were taken off by a German merchantman, the *Tacoma*, which had followed her out from Montevideo, transferred to lighters sent by a German firm from Buenos Aires, and interned in Argentina, though a number were allowed to take jobs and some to escape. Her brokenhearted commander, Captain Hans Langsdorff, in true naval tradition, shot himself.[33]

By now few Latin American Governments felt any great enthusiasm for the zone. The Panamá Declaration, wrote *La Nación* of Argentina, had only been accepted with misgiving by some of the republics and as an act of deference to Washington. *El Día* of Uruguay called it 'absurd'.[34] The Uruguayan press supported with one voice the action of the Government in expelling the *Graf Spee* and ungrudgingly praised the gallantry and courage of the British sailors fighting for the freedom of the seas, and the reactions elsewhere in Latin America, in Brazil, Colombia and Perú, for example, were very similar. But, without loss of face, so spectacular a disregard of the Declaration could hardly be passed over without comment, combined, as it was, with the capture, also in December, of the *Dusseldorf* by H.M.S. *Despatch* nine miles off the coast of Chile, and following repeated German violations of the zone. A common front was called for, and, the United States taking the lead, a joint note of protest against violations of the zone and hinting at sanctions against belligerent ships committing war-like acts was sent to the belligerents on 23 December, though the Chilean Foreign Minister remarked a few days later that Chile, like Argentina, had never favoured the zone, nor indeed had she introduced it, and Uruguay only agreed to the note with reserve[35]. Churchill, in a friendly message to Roosevelt, pointed out that Britain had cleared the South Atlantic of German raiders, to the benefit of the American republics[36], and the formal British reply of the 14th January, 1940, was sympathetic but firm. It pointed out that the only effective method of preventing belligerent acts within the zone would be to ensure, first, that the German Government should send no more warships into it, and, secondly, that since so much German shipping had taken refuge in American waters, if the Allies were to forego the opportunity of capturing these vessels, it would also seem that they should be laid up under Pan American control for the duration of the war. Anxious as the Allies were for the fulfilment of American hopes, they must reserve their rights in order 'to fight the menace presented by German action and policy and to defend that conception of law and that way of life' which they believed to be 'as dear to the peoples and Governments of America as they are to the peoples and Governments of the British Commonwealth of Nations.'[37]

This reply coincided with the first meeting on 15th January, 1940, of the Inter-American Neutrality Committee at Rio de Janeiro, inaugurated with a resounding declaration by President Vargas that the Americans had as much right to proclaim a peace zone as the belligerents to declare a war zone — a view echoed both by Dr. Aranha and by Dr. Cantilo.[38] But the Committee did little more than discuss the various ways in which neutrality regulations could be strengthened before adjourning on 3rd February. By the time it again met in April further 'incidents' had occurred—the scuttling of the German freighter *Wakama* about fifteen miles off the coast of Brazil after being hailed by a British warship, of the *Heidelberg* and *Troja* off the coast of Venezuela, and of the *Hannover* off the Dominican Republic. Further protests were on the way, and the Committee drew up a number of recommendations for transmission to the American Governments, including the denial 'by collective action' of admission to their ports of warships or airships guilty of violating the 'safety zone'.[39]

By now, however, the question of sanctions had become little more than academic. The 'twilight war' was ending. On 9th April, Germany, without warning invaded Denmark and Norway. On 10th May, she invaded Holland, Belgium and Luxemburg. The American republics, at the initiative of Uruguay, protested. But protests were vain. Hitler's massive war machine moved on. Dunkirk was evacuated, France fell, while Italy, in that brilliant June summer, stabbed her in the back. By the end of the month Britain, in Europe, stood alone. As for the 'safety zone' round the American continents, never well thought out, it was, in Cordell Hull's words, 'tacitly abandoned'.[40] It is true that when in December, 1940, Britain enquired how the United States would regard the construction of a British base in Trinidad, Summer Welles declared that that would be 'a clear and flagrant violation of the letter as well as of the spirit of the Declaration of Panamá';[41] nor would the United States agree to allow British warships in 1940 and 1941 to intercept shipping in the Caribbean in order to prevent blockade running to Japan; and as late as February 1941 the United States joined in yet another protest, this time over the seizure by Britain of the French ship, *Mendoza*, within the zone off the Brazilian coast. But the 'safety zone' in fact was replaced by what Hull described as a 'flexible' zone, not defined by any 'watery boundary' but by the distance to which, for her self-protection, the United States wished to extend her own neutrality patrol.[42] The Neutrality Committee was indeed asked at the Havana Conference in July, 1940, to prepare a draft convention on the juridical effects of the 'safety zone' and the measures which the republics were prepared to take to secure respect for it, and another on all neutrality principles and rules generally recognized in international law, especially those contained in the Panamá Resolutions and in the recommendations of the Committee itself. But, its practical value diminishing, the Committee was finally reconstituted in 1942 as the Inter-American Juridical Committee.

III

The Declaration of Panamá was intended to prevent the war from spreading to the western hemisphere. The Inter-American Financial and Economic Advisory Committee, which first met under the chairmanship of Sumner Welles on 15 November 1939, was concerned with the economic defence of the hemisphere, with measures, that is, to minimise the adverse economic effects of the war and the dislocation of international trade.

At the beginning of the war Britain had established a blockade of Germany by a line drawn across the Straits of Dover and another from Scotland to Norway. She had issued a declaration of contraband, had established contraband control bases in the English channel and the Orkneys and at Gibraltar and Haifa, and had placed some German and neutral firms trading with the enemy on a Statutory or Black List and still others on a suspect list. The Statutory List did not apply to the United States, and until the United States in 1941 issued its own Proclaimed or Black List the effects of the War Trade Lists policy in Latin America were doubtful. Listed firms found difficulty in obtaining navicerts, or commercial passports, from the British missions in Argentina, Uruguay and Brazil (where the system was applied in December, 1939, and extended by July, 1940, to Bolivia, Chile, Perú and other Latin American States)[43] certifying that cargoes destined for Europe were not intended for Germany. But they continued to trade internally and with the United States and Japan,[44] and the system caused a good deal of ill-feeling. The Chilean press and government, for example, were at one in criticising the Black List. In Argentina *La Prensa* declined to publish listed names and Dr. Cantilo deplored the Allied attitude to neutral shipping and maritime control.[45] The Uruguayan Foreign Ministry held that Black Lists were contrary to the freedom of international trade, and President Baldomir described them as an example of disregard for neutral rights.[46]And if listing caused annoyance, so also did the blockade and the British declaration of contraband.

A Reprisals Order in Council of 27 November 1939 ordered the interception of merchant vessels having on board goods of enemy origin. In certain circumstances, however, German exports were given free passage if they had been paid for prior to the Order and were on board a vessel which cleared from her last neutral port of departure before 1 January, 1940. This enabled Brazil, for example, to receive a substantial amount of war material from Germany, and occasional concessions were made to other countries. Otherwise the system was rigorously enforced, not without causing delicate problems—the dispute over the *Siqueira Campos*, loaded with arms at Lisbon but detained at Gibraltar in November, 1940, en route for Brazil was a notable example[47]—and since Germany had been an important Latin American market and a still more important source of supply, the effects were severe. It was not, however, till the summer of 1940, when Italy entered the war and Germany came to control the coast of Europe from the south of France to North Cape, that the full impact of the blockade, which was now extended, was felt. It now meant the loss not only of the German but of most of the European market, which had absorbed some thirty per cent of Latin American exports, and from some countries a still higher quantity, and had provided a rather larger proportion of imports.

British purchases continued. But they were more and more confined to essential supplies—Dominican sugar, but not Cuban tobacco, Venezuelan oil, which provided some forty per cent of British oil imports,[48] but not Chilean copper, which was replaced by imperial supplies, Bolivian tin, all of which was smelted in England, though the Bolivian Government was anxious for a smelter to be built in the United States,[49] small *ex gratia* purchases of cotton from Perú, and, above all, large quantities of foodstuffs and raw materials from Brazil and the south-eastern states of Latin America—meat from Brazil, meat and wool from Uruguay, meat, hides, wheat and other commodities from Argentina. As a result the value of British imports from Latin America actually increased in 1939 and 1940. But, in order to conserve Britain's gold and hard currency reserves, these imports had to be paid for, so far as possible, in special account sterling which could only be used to finance exports from Britain or the empire and for payments to British creditors.[50] By the end of the war Argentine sterling balances had risen to £100 million and Brazilian to £40 million.[51]

Britain, of course, was anxious to maintain South American good-will and her trading connections, and a mission, headed by Lord Willingdon, an ex-Viceroy of India and former Governor-General of Canada, was sent to South America in October, 1940. It was to explain Britain's economic, financial and blockade policies and her wish to damage the South American economies as little as possible. It was also intended to promote British exports. These had been fairly well-sustained during the first year of the war, and export trade generally had been vigorously promoted in order to secure the exchange necessary for foreign purchases, more particularly under the 'cash and carry' regulations of the United States. But by the time the mission sailed the cabinet had already decided that for financial and shipping reasons it would be necessary to limit the amounts which the Ministries of Food and Supply could buy from foreign as distinct from Commonwealth and imperial sources, and, with the concentration on the necessities of the war effort, what Britain had to offer for export was becoming less and less. Some of the representatives of the export groups attached to the mission appear to have sailed with a misplaced optimism, rapidly dissipated on their return, and, as Willingdon himself somewhat bitterly remarked, with whatever good-will the mission was received, the trade side 'went to the Devil when Government had practically to shut down any exports to South America' and to class nearly every country as among those 'which had no exports to send us which were of real interest'. British exports to Latin America in fact fell off in 1941 and continued to fall. The mere presence of the mission in South America in 1940 and 1941, while Britain was fighting for her life, made a considerable impression.[52] But there was now no question of exporting to increase British trade. Export trade was 'ruthlessly abandoned',[53] except in so far as the Government continued to need to secure currency resources for essential purchases. 'We threw good house-keeping to the winds', said Lord

Keynes. 'But we saved ourselves and helped to save the world'.[54]

Whatever the propaganda value of the Willingdon mission, it could do nothing, either, to reduce freight rates and rising import prices, nor, despite hopes which may originally have been entertained, could it help to solve what had become the major economic problem in Latin America in 1940—the accumulation of huge export surpluses—surpluses of agricultural products, wheat, maize, linseed, coffee, cacao, sugar and bananas, whose prices inevitably fell, and surpluses also of hides, wool, cotton, nitrates and metals, for which, however, the war was creating an increasing demand. The countries most seriously affected were those whose trading connections with continental Europe had been stronger than, or as strong as, their connections with the United States. Thus Brazil, where the fall in coffee exports had at first been counterbalanced by British meat purchases, had lost a third of her former markets, and her coffee, cotton, fruit, hides and nuts were all in world surplus.[55] The blockade had cut off some forty per cent of Argentina's normal export trade,[56] and there the maize crop, which had been particularly good, hung round the Government's neck like a millstone. Chile was faced with a prospect of surpluses of agricultural products, wool and timber as well as nitrates. Paraguay had lost her chief market for hides, and by June Perú had sold only one-third of her cotton crop.[57]

Not surprisingly one non-European country, Japan, made every effort to take advantage of the European blockade to ensure her own safe supplies of essential raw materials. Japanese trade and good-will missions toured Central and South America in 1940, penetrating both to Bolivia and Paraguay. Three new ships, the *Loyalty*, the *Patriotism* and the *Promotion of National Power*, were added to the *Osaka Syosen Kaisya's* service through the Panamá Canal to ports on the Atlantic coast of South America.[58]A barter deal was completed with Argentina in May, a trade pact ratified with Uruguay, an oil agreement signed with Mexico, and purchases of Chilean minerals and Peruvian and Brazilian cotton were increased. But there were considerable difficulties in the way of the Japanese trade drive. For one thing, Japan was unable to supply the kind of goods which Latin American countries wanted and which Europe had formerly furnished. For another, her economic activities had long caused anxiety, particularly on the Pacific coast. There were anti-Japanese riots in Perú in May and in Ecuador in June, and the signing of the Tripartite Pact in September, with its recognition of Japan's 'New Order' in Greater East Asia, transformed vague apprehensions of Japanese imperialism into definite fears. The Pact was seen in Chile as a threat to Latin American independence itself.[59] The continent, remarked *El Día* of Uruguay, could now be attacked on both sides.[60] Nevertheless, the trade drive continued in 1941, Japan seeking strategic minerals, such as Mexican mercury and Peruvian molybdenum, as well as other raw materials, doubling, for example, her 1940 purchases of Peruvian cotton. But it was increasingly hampered by agreements between the United States and various Latin American countries for the acquisition of their strategic and critical materials and by other pre-emptive purchases, by the closing in July of the Panamá Canal to Japanese shipping ostensibly 'for the purpose of effecting repairs' but in reality because of fears of sabotage,[61] and by the freezing of Japanese funds in the United States in the same month, and it came to an end with the attack on Pearl Harbour.

Pearl Harbour was far distant in the summer of 1940. But Washington was well aware of the dangers to Pan American solidarity inherent in Latin American economic difficulties. The Inter-American Financial and Economic Advisory Committee had indeed decided to create an Inter-American Development Commission intended to stimulate the increase of non-competitive imports from Latin America to the United States, the trade of the Latin American republics between themselves, and the development of industry, particularly the production of consumer goods. It had also drafted the charter of an Inter-American Bank to assist in the stabilisation of currencies, the promotion of economic development and the increase of trade. But the Development Commission was not organized till early in June, and the idea of the Bank, in which each Government was to take shares, met with a mixed reception both in Latin America and the United States: it continued to be discussed but never came into existence.[62]

In the belief that immediate and drastic measures were necessary, President Roosevelt put forward on 21 June a proposal for 'an effective system of joint marketing of the important staple exports of the American republics', the creation, in effect, of a gigantic cartel to control the trade of the western hemisphere.[63] This was plainly inspired by fears of an autarkic Europe controlled by the Axis. But it met with more criticism than approval in Latin America, where fears of United States economic imperialism were still strong, was not well received in the United States and died at birth.[64] The President then reverted to more conventional methods. A Rubber Reserve Company and a Metals Reserve Company were set up on 28 June to acquire reserve supplies of strategic and critical materials, not solely in Latin America, but, so far as the latter company was concerned, with Latin American countries very much in mind. And on the eve of the second meeting of American Foreign Ministers, at Havana, which had been brought forward from October to July because of the gravity of the international situation, the President announced plans for increasing the lending power of the (Second) Export-Import Bank and removing some of the restrictions on its operations. A relatively new institution, the Bank had been primarily concerned with making loans or credits which would promote the trade of the United States, and, since the beginning of the war, it had approved modest grants for operations in various Latin American countries.[65] With Congressional approval a further $500 million was now to be added to its capital and its sphere of activities enlarged to assist the 'Good Neighbours' in the development of their resources, the stabilisation of their economies, and the orderly marketing of their products. It became a major instrument of United States policy.

The Havana Conference itself ignored the cartel scheme and did little more in the economic field than lay fresh burdens on the Inter-American Financial and Economic Advisory Committee. The Committee was to take steps, *inter alia*, to try to increase trade between the various republics, 'to create instruments for the temporary storing, financing and handling' of surplus commodities and 'for their orderly and systematic marketing' and to develop commodity arrangements.

As a result, it drafted an Inter-American Coffee Convention in November, and this, put into effect early in April, 1941, came to the partial rescue of the coffee-producing countries by allocating basic export quotas. It also summoned an Inter-American Maritime Conference, which met in Washington late in November, to consider the problems and maintenance of inter-American shipping services.

As Sumner Welles rightly observed, clearly 'the main brunt of the hemisphere effort to maintain the inter-American economic and commercial structure' fell, of necessity, upon the United States.[66] As yet, however, the brunt was not very heavy nor did the effort extend very far. An Office for the Co-ordination of Commercial and Cultural Relations between the American Republics, with Nelson Rockefeller at its head, was established on 31 July.[67] Congressional approval for the enlargement of the resources and activities of the Export-Import Bank was given late in September, when an agreement was also concluded with Brazil for a credit of $20 million towards the construction of a steel plant at Volta Redonda, which the German firm of Krupps had been offering to assist.[68] The Metals Reserve Company contracted in November to buy for five years almost the entire output of Bolivian tin other than that of the Patiño mining companies (much the largest producers) which was sold to Britain.[69] The United States also bought Chilean copper and nitrates on a considerable scale, thus relieving Chile of what Sumner Welles, somewhat prone to exaggeration about Latin American affairs, called a 'desperately serious' economic situation.[70] The Export-Import Bank allocated a credit of $60 million to the *Banco Central* of Argentina for agricultural and industrial purposes and the United States Treasury a stabilisation loan of $50 million, though neither of these loans was ever taken up.

Meanwhile trade between the United States and the Latin American countries, including those of the southern bloc, increased by leaps and bounds. As compared with 1938, exports from the United States to Latin America rose by 45 per cent in 1940 and imports from Latin America by 37 per cent,[71] and the expansion was to continue, though by the end of 1941 Latin America's unfavourable balance of trade was reversed. Negotiations for a Reciprocal Trade Agreement with Argen-

tina had broken down in January, the concessions on imports
into the United States failing to satisfy Argentina, and the
agreement itself being strongly opposed by United States
agricultural interests, though there was a disposition in the
United States to lay the blame for the failure on Argentina's
inability to convert sterling into dollars and to accuse Britain
of obtaining a stranglehold on Argentine trade.[72] But despite
this alleged 'stranglehold', United States exports to, and imports from, Argentina alike showed a spectacular increase in
late 1940 and in 1941. There was one other significant trend—
the more limited increase in intra-Latin American trade and
efforts to enhance it still further. Argentina, for example,
signed agreements with Brazil, Bolivia, Colombia and Cuba
and ratified a pact with Chile, and plans were laid for a
conference of the River Plate countries to be held in Montevideo in January, 1941.

IV

The blockade and the submarine warfare, quite apart from so
spectacular an event as the 'Battle of the River Plate', had
early brought the war home to the Latin American Governments in an inescapable manner. But while it had begun to
touch the pockets and disrupt the trade of their peoples, it had
not touched their persons. They had been spectators of events,
horrified by the fate of Poland and the invasion of Finland,
applauding the end of the *Graf Spee,* and in general strongly
disposed in favour of the Allies. But neither in the United
States nor anywhere else was there an inclination actively to
intervene on their behalf. 'Neutromania' prevailed.

The ending of the 'twilight' war with the sudden invasion of
Denmark and Norway on 9 April was a fresh shock to Latin
American opinion, which had tended to be critical of the
Allied failure effectually to aid Finland. From the Soviet
Union almost anything might be expected. Was she not engaged
in swallowing the Baltic States? But this new act of aggression
came not from the U.S.S.R. but from Germany, and virtually
the whole of the Latin American press denounced it in bitter
terms. The shadow of the swastika, now more clearly than
ever, overhung the hammer and sickle.

The most remarkable reaction came from Argentina. There President Ortiz had shown, what the nation had doubted, the reality of his determination to restore institutional normality and to curb the scandalous abuses and corruption of politics.[73] For a while he had proceeded cautiously enough. But, outraged, in 1939 and 1940, by the gross electoral frauds perpetrated in the gubernatorial elections in the province of Catamarca and the much more important province of Buenos Aires, he decreed federal intervention in both, amid popular approval but to the indignation of certain members of his cabinet, and, in particular, of his Vice-President, Dr. Ramón Castillo, himself a native of Catamarca. *La Nación*, as early as 20 December, 1939, talked of a new era having dawned, and the Radical Party, so violently discriminated against since the revolution of 1930, took new heart, participated in the Congressional elections of March, 1940, and succeeded in winning control of the Chamber of Deputies.

Not content with these efforts to restore some semblance of purity to politics, the President, in February, insisted that the time had come to strengthen Argentine defences by the creation of adequate air and naval forces and a proper surveillance of the 3,000 miles of coast line[74]—there had been constant but unverified rumours of the use of Patagonian anchorages by German ships and submarines. What was more, he proposed in April that the American republics should abandon their status of neutrality in favour of non-belligerency. This proposal was put by the Foreign Minister, Dr. Cantilo, to the United States Ambassador, Norman Armour, on 19 April. The Pan American neutrality zone, said Cantilo, was in practice a dead letter; the United States, despite its official neutrality, was in reality aiding the Allies; neutrality had become a fiction and should be abandoned. Instead, the American republics (with the example of Italy before them, but with opposite motives) should proclaim themselves non-belligerents. This, as *La Prensa* later said,[75] was not intended 'even indirectly' to bring the Americas nearer to war. But it would relieve them of the rules of neutrality and give them liberty of action. Undoubtedly this new status would favour the Allies, but Germany, in view of the conduct of Italy, could hardly protest. Should the United States agree, Dr. Cantilo concluded, he would take up the matter with Dr. Aranha of Brazil, and, if Brazil also agreed, the United States could issue a call for a Pan American Conference.

Taken by surprise, Armour immediately reported the Ortiz-Cantilo proposal to the State Department both by telegram and by letter, recommending an appreciative reply, while Cantilo instructed the Argentine Ambassador in Washington, Felipe Espil, to lay a summary of it before the Under-Secretary, Sumner Welles. Much disturbed, Welles stated on the 23rd that the adoption of the proposal would be regarded as clear evidence in the United States that the Americas were moving towards war, that it would entail a complete abandonment of the Panamá agreements, that differences of opinion would doubtless arise among the American governments which would destroy unanimity, and even that it would violate the principles of international law; and Cordell Hull, on the 24th, rejected it, repeating some of Welles's arguments and adding, for good measure, a lecture on international law. Curiously enough, in view of later accusations against Argentina, the Argentine initiative passes unnoticed in Hull's *Memoirs* and Welles's writings.[76]

Ortiz and Cantilo had meanwhile seen the Brazilian Ambassador and the proposal was put to Dr. Aranha. It was also re-stated, in modified form, to Washington. But Aranha's attitude was that the established safeguards of neutrality were preferable to a plunge into the unknown,[77] and Washington maintained its stance. Finally Cantilo revealed the proposal to the press. It received some support, particularly in Uruguay[78] (though not in the Foreign Affairs Committee of the Argentine Senate). But on the whole Aranha's view, which was also Washington's, prevailed, and by 14 May, when Germany had compounded her aggressions by invading the Low Countries and the Dutch army was on the eve of capitulation, Ortiz and Cantilo knew that the idea was dead.[79] Ortiz had to content himself in his Annual Message to Congress on 14th May with the declaration 'we are neutral. But Argentine neutrality does not and cannot signify an attitude of absolute indifference or insensibility',[80] and with joining in a collective protest initiated by Uruguay against Germany's 'ruthless violation' of the neutrality of Belgium, Holland and Luxemburg.[81]

It is not for the historian to speculate what might have happened had an inter-American conference been called in May to consider the Argentine proposal. By the middle of June, when France was falling and dangers from within and without seemed to menace the western hemisphere, the United States was anxious enough that the republics should meet. And it is a curious coincidence that at the moment when Ortiz and Cantilo were resigning themselves to failure—the text of their proposal was printed in *La Prensa* on 13 May— Churchill himself, in his first message as Prime Minister to Roosevelt on 15 May, asked him to proclaim the non-belligerency of the United States—a step which would have cleared the way for all-out aid to the sorely pressed democracies—telling him that the voice and force of the United States might count for nothing if delayed too long, and asking for forty or fifty old-age destroyers and much else.[82] He also told the defeatist and isolationist American Ambassador, Joseph P. Kennedy,[83] that England would never give in and that, if necessary, the Government would move to Canada, take the fleet, and fight on.[84] No lecture on international law was delivered to Churchill.

In Argentina—and the Americas—there was a sad sequel. Ortiz had been trying to build up the armed forces; and the news in June of the fall of France, to whose culture Latin America acknowledged so great a debt and whose collapse came as a devastating shock, actually strengthened the President's position. With strong public support, despite German sympathies in some army circles, he was able to secure in mid-June the termination of the German military mission[85] and the passage of an internal security law. But there was a contrary current. An Argentine freighter, the *Uruguay*, had been sunk, to public outrage, off the coast of Spain at the end of May. Germany refused to make any compensation. Yet not only was the attitude of the Argentine Ambassador in Germany extraordinarily conciliatory—he emphasised, on 10 June, the opportunities 'of an economic and political nature' in Argentina which would present themselves to a victorious Germany[86]—but Cantilo, a few days later, on 18 June, took occasion to state that while Argentina would remain firmly attached to the principle of Pan Americanism, her watchword was 'continental solidarity, liberty of action', and that she was bound to consider the effects on her economy of a Europe organised by a totalitarian Germany.[87] Further, the Secretary-General of the Foreign Ministry, informing the German Ambassador, Edmund von Thermann, of the forthcoming meeting of the American republics at Havana, underlined the excellent state of Argentine-German relations, declared that Argentina would adhere to a policy of complete freedom of action, and hinted that a friendly note from Germany might be advantageous to the Argentine Government at the Havana conversations.[88]

Did this reflect a new caution in the policy of Ortiz, or the influence of his Vice-President, Dr. Castillo? It is tempting, perhaps too tempting, to believe that, though the hand was the hand of Esau, the voice was the voice of Jacob. Ortiz had recently lost his wife; he was suffering from diabetes and failing sight; and, a very ill man, he was losing his grasp on affairs of state. On 3 July he delegated his executive powers, temporarily at least, to Castillo, a staunch conservative, nationalist and neutralist, totally out of sympathy with the President's aims. As for Cantilo, for all his pro-Allied leanings he was a legalist and a pessimist. He had been much mortified, and in view of the deteriorating situation in Europe, he may well have thought that prudence was the better part of policy. Ortiz himself, in the aftermath of an army land scandal—in which his War Minister and warm supporter, General Carlos Márquez, was implicated, though the personal honour neither of the minister nor of the President was involved—submitted his resignation to Congress on 22 August, to have it rejected by 170 votes to one. This was a personal triumph. But nothing could hide the fact that the President was an invalid and that Argentine politics in the hands of Castillo would change for the worse. A light was failing.[89]

But what of Brazil? Unsparing in his eulogies of President Vargas, Sumner Welles saw him as the man who had transformed what might have been 'a disintegrating federation into a closely knit, unified nation.'[90] The aim of the *Estado Novo* was indeed to establish Brazilian unity, both politically and economically, by curbing the powers of the several states, destroying regionalism, exploiting the country's great natural resources, developing industry, diversifying agriculture, improving communications and strengthening defences. It was infused by an intense spirit of nationalism,[91] while a signal example of Vargas's social programme and of his aim to keep in touch with the masses—unlike his predecessors the President never forgot the common man—was the enactment of a minimum wage law on 1 May, 1940. The nationalisation programme found expression, *inter alia*, in the emphasis which the President laid on the rôle which the army could play in the education of the foreign-born,[92] in the reinforcement of the much disliked Department of Press and Propaganda, in the arrest of alleged communists in December, 1939, and April, 1940, the closing in March and April of a large number of German and Japanese schools in Santa Catarina and São Paulo, in the President's insistence that the Germans in Brazil must be Brazilians first and Germans afterwards, and in the strengthening of the garrisons in the German-populated districts.

But Vargas was nothing if not shrewd. In his Foreign Minister, Oswaldo Aranha, he had a devoted friend as well as a warm supporter of Pan Americanism. But his Chief of Staff, General Pedro Góes Monteiro, and his Minister of War, General Eurico Dutra, both accepted German decorations and were both impressed by Germany's military strength. In November, 1939, Vargas had congratulated Hitler on his escape from an assassination attempt, and, with a careful eye on the political scene, both domestic and international, he had been at pains to point out in March that Brazil was neither pro-British nor pro-German.[93] On 11 June he startled the continent with a speech in which he declared that the 'era of improvident liberalism, sterile demagoguery', and 'useless individualism' had passed and that mankind was witnessing the 'tumultous and fruitful beginning of a new age'[94]—a speech which both he and Dr. Aranha were at some pains to explain away. Meanwhile, on 6 June, a United States liaison officer had arrived in Rio, where he was to remain as head of the American Military Mission, to be assured that Brazil would co-operate with the United States and the other American Governments in the event of aggression from any quarter.[95] But Vargas, in June, was no less prudent than some of his

Argentine contemporaries. Germany had been promising to buy large quantities of Brazilian products once the war had ended, provided 'no substantial change' was made in Brazil's neutrality[96], and, at much the same time that the Secretary-General of the Argentine Foreign Ministry interviewed Ambassador von Thermann, Vargas, without the knowledge of Aranha, held an interview with Ambassador Kurt Prüfer. Vargas, so the Ambassador reported, said that he 'very much regretted the deterioration in economic relations with Germany, which had been caused by the war, and in whose continuation he saw Brazil's salvation', proposed to examine 'even at this time' whether Brazil and Germany could not reach a definite agreement for commercial exchanges, emphasised his determination to maintain neutrality, and expressed, both his 'personal sympathy for the authoritarian states' and his 'aversion to England and the democratic system'.[97]

The Ambassador was naturally delighted, and so was the German Foreign Office, which saw a 'broad and lasting field for co-operation', and the Presidential-Ambassadorial conversations were continued on 28 June, when Vargas appeared to be 'visibly pleased' with the German response and declared that he would supervise the negotiations himself, while the Ambassador was again lavish in his promises of increasing German imports and exports.[98] What, it may be asked, would Sumner Welles have made of all this, had he known it? What he did know was that Vargas was still in touch with Krupps over the Volta Redonda steel project, and this knowledge did much to hasten an agreement with the United States instead.[99] In April and May, therefore, Vargas was in no mood to accede to the non-belligerency proposals of Ortiz and Cantilo. He still kept his options open. It was the failure of Germany to move swiftly against Britain after the fall of France, as well as his hopes of aid from the United States, that finally solved his dilemma. And while German promises proved specious and the United States gave practical assistance, the deeds of the Royal Air Force during the Battle of Britain, which began on 10 July, were soon to capture Brazilian, and Latin American, imagination.

As in Brazil, so in Chile the Argentine proposal for non-belligerency fell on stony ground.[100] Chile was the last of the

American Republics to join in the collective protest against the German invasion of the Low Countries, the German Ambassador telling the Foreign Minister that this would be regarded as an 'unfriendly act'.[101] This intervention did not count for much. Chilean sympathies, except to some extent in the army, which, until recent years, had been German-trained, some of the younger naval officers, members of Jorge Gonzáles von Marée's *Vanguardia Popular Socialista*, and some of the Communists, who, as a result of the Soviet-German pact, had been making common cause with pro-German and anti-United States elements, were mostly engaged on the side of the Allies. The entry of Italy into the war was greeted by a spontaneous boycott of Italian shops. But the Government could not afford to ignore the substantial Germanic element in the south, subjected, as it was, to Nazi propaganda and penetration, nor, still less, the attitude of the Communists, who were themselves part of the ruling Popular Front. Above all, it was precoccupied with tensions within the Front itself, where Radicals quarrelled with Socialists, Socialists with Communists, the Confederation of Chilean Workers with both, and all of them—a habit of Chilean parties—among themselves. The administration of Pedro Aguirre Cerda was faced with repeated cabinet crises, while his social and economic programme roused violent opposition among the parties of the right, that is, the Conservatives and Liberals,[102] both of whom represented the landed aristocracy. The history of the Popular Front became that of a 'war on two fronts'—against the parties within it and the parties outside it.[103] Spain, on 16 July, added the insult of breaking off relations with what she described as an 'anarchical régime. Popular Front governments were decidedly unpopular in General Franco's Spain, and Spain's action was decidedly unpopular in Latin America. Preoccupied with her internal affairs, and distracted both by politics and economics, Chile, not surprisingly, remained determinedly neutral, though she welcomed all signs of inter-American co-operation. No other policy was possible for an Administration which represented so great a variety of opinion and which was fighting for its life. There was a serious crisis in July when the Government announced the discovery of a subversive plot by right wing elements with the support of the *Vanguardia*.[104] But, remarkably enough, the Popular Front continued to survive, not finally to disintegrate till January, 1941.

It remains to consider one other country—the small state of Uruguay. With an ultra-democratic press, no country in Latin America had shown itself more strongly in favour of the Allied cause, though the followers of Senator Alberto Herrera,[105] who had paid a long visit to Germany before the war and was a thorn in President Baldomir's side, were covertly hostile to Britain and openly critical of the United States, and the Vice-President, Dr. Charlone, was also believed to entertain totalitarian sympathies.[106] The President, on the other hand, and his Foreign Minister, Dr. Alberto Guani, who had presided both over the Assembly of the League of Nations and over its Council, were decided partisans of the democracies. As for the people of Montevideo they broke the windows of the Italian Bank when Italy entered the war. But Nazi agents were believed to be active in Uruguay—the Germans had been, and still were, employed on the great Río Negro hydroelectric scheme—and no South American country was more strategically placed, commanding, as it did, the entry to the Río de la Plata, forming a natural stage on the northward route from the Falkland Islands, and providing also a link between Argentina and Brazil. With a small army and a diminutive navy, none, moreover, was less adequately defended.

Early in October, 1939, a Socialist Deputy had drawn attention to Nazi activities in Uruguay and a young Professor of Philosophy in the University of Montevideo, Hugo Fernández Artucio, had been tireless in denouncing them. In March, 1940, he placed a detailed indictment before the Minister of Defence, and, when no action was taken, alerted the great Argentine dailies, *La Prensa* and *La Nación*. Then, in April, a Congressional Committee began investigations. Its report, in June, was sensational. If its findings were correct, they revealed the existence of a far-flung Nazi organization, with its headquarters in Montevideo and strong points elsewhere in the country, of German influences at work in Government Departments, of a Hitler Youth and a Labour Front, and of a Storm Troopers' Organization, and, still more dramatic, of a

plot to seize control of the state. This was the so-called Führmann plan. Arnulf Führmann was a German 'photographer'
reputed to be the Nazi liaison officer in the Río de la Plata
area, and from documents found in his possession it appeared
that a plot existed for a *coup d'état*, to be carried out with the
aid of Germans from Argentina and Brazil, the establishment
of a provisional government, and the organization of Uruguay
as a German agricultural colony.[107] These findings were taken
so seriously that a number of Nazi Germans were arrested;[108]
an Argentine expeditionary force was made ready at Concor-
dia; Brazil sent a quantity of small arms to Montevideo and
10,000 troops to the Uruguayan frontier; and the United
States despatched two heavy cruisers, the *Quincy* and the
Wichita to Montevideo.[109] Cordell Hull authorised the American Minister, Edwin Wilson, to make a statement which he
himself had drafted, that it was the avowed policy of the
United States to 'co-operate fully, whenever such co-operation
is desired, with all of the other American Governments in
crushing all activities which arise from non-American sources
and which imperil our political and economic freedom'.[110]
And though Uruguayans had always resisted conscription,
they showed themselves eager to enrol for short periods of
military training.

V

But what did 'full co-operation' mean? American anxieties
over the defence of the western hemisphere had become increasingly acute. Apart from the danger of a Nazi *coup d'état* in
one or another of the republics—a danger which neither
Washington nor London was inclined to discount—the question now was how far could the western hemisphere itself be
defended in the event of a total Nazi victory in Europe, and,
what the Army and Navy planners did not rule out, the
surrender of the French and British fleets?[111] Roosevelt did
not minimise the danger. The British fleet and the French
army, he said on 23 May, had been the buffer which for
decades had protected the United States and its way of life.[112]
If they were removed, America would be directly menaced;
and, on the eve of the epic evacuation of the encircled British

and French armies at Dunkirk, he told Lord Lothian that it was essential that the British navy should be treated not as a British but as an empire possession, never to be surrendered, adding the curious observation that, if the King were compelled to leave England, it would be better if his temporary capital were formed at Bermuda instead of in Canada, since the American republics might 'be restless at a monarchy being based on the American continent'![113]

It is true that by the spring of 1940 the United States had concluded agreements with all the Caribbean countries for the defence of their ports and airfields, and that United States military and naval representation not only in Central but in South America had been greatly increased, though it was by no means large.[114] To the relief of the United States, moreover, Colombia, by June, 1940, had eliminated most of the German personnel from the Scadta Airline, which operated within three hundred miles of the Panamá Canal, and Scadta itself was merged into a new company, Avianca, in which the Colombian Government shared an interest with Pan American Airways.[115] But of still greater concern were the great 'bulge' of Brazil and the island of Fernando de Noronha, where the French and Italian airlines had constructed landing fields and radio stations. Roosevelt, at the end of April, directed that urgent conversations should be held with Brazil over the security of this area; and, on the recommendation of General George Marshall and Admiral Harold Stark, his proposal rapidly broadened into a plan for secret conversations with most of the republics in order to determine which of them were willing to receive or lend aid to the others in case of need, and whether they would be prepared to make available their existing bases for land, sea and air forces. If and when any of them agreed, joint staff conversations should be held.[116]

The proposals for these exploratory conversations were made through diplomatic channels, and, on the whole, were favourably received, though the Argentine reply, perhaps not surprisingly, was cool. Cantilo asked the American Ambassador what assistance the United States thought she could give to Argentina if both France and Britain were defeated, adding that the best method of hemisphere defence was to assist the Allies—remarks not easy to counter. But even Argentina was prepared to discuss the defence of her coasts.[117] Accordingly, early in June, United States army or navy liaison officials were sent to the Latin American capitals, arriving, as in Chile, disguised as tourists.[118] Their discussions were reasonably satisfactory, though the United States was left in no doubt that her sister republics needed arms and supplies and could not afford to buy them. Brazil, despite Vargas's flirtations with Germany, declared that she would co-operate fully with the United States, though the arming of the country was a 'preliminary question'. Mexico expressed her readiness to engage in staff conversations in Washington. Chile declared that if the United States were attacked, or a third country which the United States wished to defend, she would assist her. Argentina alone was evasive, stating on 29 June that she was pursuing a course of strict neutrality and saw no danger to the American republics in the near future.[119] Two days earlier General Marshall and Admiral Stark had laid it down, with Roosevelt's approval, that until December, 1940, at any rate, the United States army would be unable to undertake any operations for the defence of South America south of the latitude of Venezuela unless mobilization and selective service were made effective at once. Incredibly enough, Ambassador Spruille Braden revealed this to a Colombian official. But the Latin American states, particularly the southern ones, were, in fact, well aware that the United States in the summer of 1940 could do little to defend them.[120]

Meanwhile agitation had been growing in the United States for the acquisition of additional bases in the Caribbean for the defence of the Panamá Canal. The Chiefs of Staff were prepared to advocate the occupation of British, French and Dutch possessions in the western hemisphere. Roosevelt, for his part, had long considered the idea of placing them, or such of them as might be endangered, under a Pan American trusteeship.[121] And the danger itself was brought home when the British, determined to run no risks, but to the indignation of Cordell Hull, landed marines in May on the Dutch islands, with their important oil refineries, of Aruba and Curaçao and informed the United States also of a rumour that Germany was planning to invade the Guianas with a force of 6,000 men, transported, so it was said, in ships then in Brazilian waters.[122] This may have been nonsense, though the American forces hurriedly made plans to counter such a move. But American anxieties about the fate of European colonies in the western hemisphere and American desires to turn the Caribbean into an American lake were not nonsense. Roosevelt, on 24 May, demanded that emergency plans should be drawn up for the occupation of the colonies to prevent them from falling, in one way or another, into German hands; and, while the army and navy were working on these, the State Department drafted for Congressional approval a declaration that the United States would not recognize any transfer, and would not acquiesce in any attempt to transfer, any geographic region of the hemisphere from one non-American power to another, and that if any such transfer or attempt at transfer should appear likely the United States would, 'in addition to other measures', immediately consult with the other American republics to determine upon the steps to be taken to safeguard their common interests. This declaration was approved by the Senate and communicated to Germany and Italy on 17 June, and on the same day invitations were sent out for a meeting of American Foreign Ministers at Havana at the earliest possible moment.[123]

VI

The Panamá Conference had met under the sign of neutrality, the Havana Conference, which opened on 21 July, met under the sign of defence. At Panamá the Germans had sought to gain admission as observers. As the Havana meeting drew near they sought not so much to observe as to intimidate and to bribe, playing on the hypnotic effect in Latin America of German military victories and potential economic strength. In Central America the German Minister, Dr. Otto Reinbach, had already told Guatemala that Germany regarded her adhesion to the Uruguayan protest against the invasion of the Low Countries as a hostile act; and, despite a tart rejoinder, on 1 July he formally warned the Central American states against taking any action at Havana detrimental to German interests—a démarche so *contraproducente* that he thought it wise to withdraw his note. Similar advice was given to Bolivia and Uruguay.[124] On a different tack the German representatives in Latin America were instructed to emphasise that the great advantages offered by trade with Germany would be considerably increased by the powerful economic expansion of the Reich which was to be expected after the end of the war.[125] Business houses in Chile were assured that Germany would be able to accept orders for October;[126] promises of armament contracts, railroad equipment and a steel mill were made to Brazil;[127] and the German Ambassador in Argentina, who maintained close relations with the ultra-nationalists and whose funds for bribing influential persons and for propaganda had been increased, was indefatigable in extolling the great prospects for trade after the war.[128] The air, meanwhile, in the aftermath of the Uruguayan affair, had been, and remained, thick with reports and rumours of Nazi subversive activities, of stores of arms and munitions discovered in Argentina and of a *Stützpunkt* near the naval base of Punta del Indio,[129] of an influx of Germans into Bolivia by way of Siberia,[130] of an attempted coup d'état, with Nazi assistance, in Chile,[131] and, so President Calderón Guardia declared, of the danger of a similar attempt in Costa Rica,[132] as well as, of course, the alleged projected attack on the Guianas.

It was, therefore, in an atmosphere of apprehension that the representatives of the American republics gathered at Havana, though apprehension was somewhat tempered by relief as a result of the British attack on the French capital ships at Oran and Mers-el-Kebir on 3 July (an action, incidentally, to which Roosevelt had given his prior approval),[133] by relief, also, that there had been no invasion of Britain and at the magnificent resistance of the British air force as the Battle of Britain began on 10 July. Cordell Hull, with an impressive array of officials, headed the United States delegation. Dr. Cantilo had intended to represent Argentina but, with the illness of President Ortiz, named Dr. Leopoldo Melo (the Argentine representative at the Panamá meeting) in his place. Brazil sent the Secretary-General of the Foreign Ministry, though of Dr. Aranha's support for the success of the Conference there was not the slightest doubt. 'We go there as American states', he said in a curious phrase, 'but if we fail to agree we will come away as Africans'.[134] The critical situation of

Chile dictated the appointment, not of her Foreign Minister, but of her Socialist Minister of Development, the sympathetic Oscar Schnake. Uruguay was represented by Dr. Manini Ríos, who had led her delegation at Panamá and was shortly to become Minister of the Interior, and Perú by her Minister of Justice.

Not too much importance should be attached to the absence of several of the Foreign Ministers, given their anxieties at home. There had been similar absences at Panamá. But reservations had certainly been felt, and some of the republics, more particularly the more southerly, were torn between fears of a Nazi-dominated and autarkic Europe and an America dominated by the United States, between anxiety to retain their freedom of decision should the United States enter the war and anxiety to maintain a common front, or, as Dr. Cantilo had phrased it, between 'continental solidarity' and 'liberty of action'. Argentina, he announced on the eve of the Conference, would oppose any military pacts,[135] and Chile declared that she stood for 'Democracy, Peace and Neutrality'.[136] Yet all, or nearly all, of the republics were well aware of the dangers, territorial, ideological and economic, which threatened the hemisphere should Britain collapse and the British fleet fail to provide them with the naval defence they needed against possible aggression.

As at Panamá, there were three major subjects for discussion: neutrality, under which would be considered the recommendations of the Inter-American Neutrality Committee and the problem of subversive activities; the protection of the peace of the western hemisphere, which included the problems of hemisphere defence and the situation of the European colonies; and economic co-operation. Important as was this last, the economic proposals put forward by Cordell Hull, though agreed to in principle, were referred to the Inter-American Financial and Economic Advisory Committee in Washington for further study.[137] Nor did neutrality occupy much of the delegates' time,[138] though Fifth Column activities were dealt with in a number of resolutions. These called for common action to put down subversive activities abetted by foreign governments, groups or individuals, for the exchange of information about them, for rigorous supervision of the entry of foreigners, for the prohibition of political activities by diplomatic and consular agents or by other foreigners, and for the prevention of the organization within the territory of one state, of rebellion or disturbances in another. And, in a Declaration of Reciprocal Assistance and Co-operation, the major principle was affirmed that any attempt on the part of a non-American state against the integrity or independence of an American state should be considered as an act of aggression against all the signatories, who would consult together and any or all of them proceed to negotiate the necessary agreements for defence and assistance.[139]

But the most important, and the most delicate, question was the problem which had prompted the hasty summoning of the Conference—the danger that European territorial possessions in the Americas might be converted into 'strategic centers of aggression' against the hemisphere. The State Department had drawn up a draft convention and resolution on this question. It re-affirmed the traditional American opposition to the transfer of territory in the American hemisphere from one European power to another, but as a principle upheld by all the republics, not merely by the United States. It reserved the right of the American States to judge whether, even without a formal transfer, the political independence or freedom of action of the European possessions had been impaired, and, if necessary, to assume temporary measures of control by a collective trusteeship. The resolution, as distinct from the convention, provided for emergency action.[140]

The Argentine reaction to these proposals was cautious. In a private conversation with Cordell Hull Dr. Melo declared that, while he approved of the 'no transfer' principle, he was not prepared to go beyond it. The European territories in question, he argued, were remote from Argentina, to which his colleague, Felipe Espil, the Argentine Ambassador in Washington, added that to take them over would be an unneutral act with unpredictable results. Publicly, the Argentine delegation went further, suggesting that, on the principle of self-determination, the colonies should be allowed to decide their own destinies and to become, if they wished, independent.[141] This, incidentally, was much the same as the position adopted by Mexico at the time of the Panamá

Conference.[142] Chile, likewise accepting the 'no transfer' principle, was similarly opposed to hasty action.[143] But the Argentine stand was the decisive factor. It was clear however, that
Dr. Melo wished to avoid any open disagreement with the
United States.[144] Finally, Cordell Hull asked him to cable, on
Hull's behalf directly to Prèsident Ortiz, still the legal President of Argentina; and he had his reward.[145] The Argentine
delegation withdrew its objection. Brazil and Uruguay supported the United States.[146] Chile fell into line in order to
show her solidarity with the other republics;[147] and on 27 July
agreement was reached on two documents, one, the Act of
Havana, to go into effect immediately, the other a Convention
requiring ratification by the various Governments.

The Act established an Emergency Committee composed of
one representative from each country. It was to meet at the
request of any signatory to the Act and assume the administration of any region attacked or threatened, and, as a matter
of urgency, any or all of the republics (in effect the United
States) could take action without waiting for the Committee to
meet. The Convention provided for the creation of an Inter-
American Commission for Territorial Administration which
would take over the functions of the Emergency Committee[148]
until the colonies in question were in a position to govern
themselves or be restored to their former status. Both the
Dutch and the French Governments had appealed to Argentina not to approve these measures, and France subsequently
protested to the United States.[149] Britain remained unmoved.
Argentina once again reserved her claim to the Falkland
Islands, Guatemala to British Honduras, and both Argentina
and Chile to Antarctica. The Conference adjourned on 30
July, having agreed to re-convene in due course at Rio de
Janeiro. It had been something of a triumph for Cordell Hull.
As the British Minister to Cuba observed, little had been
expected and rather more had been achieved. The necessity
for co-operation had been brought home to the republics, and
Argentina's opposition to the United States had not been as
strong and as sustained as had been feared.[150]

Neither the Act nor the Convention of Havana was ever
enforced. The French island of Martinique was indeed a
potential danger point. There the French High Commissioner

in the Antilles, Admiral Georges Robert, was loyal to Vichy and the custodian of $250 millions of French gold, a small force of naval vessels, and an aircraft carrier with 106 planes on board.[151] The British navy, on 4 July, took the precaution of instituting what was in effect a blockade of Fort de France, and the United States, two days later, sent a naval force to watch the British and ensure that no hostilities occurred.[152] An agreement of sorts was patched up between Rear-Admiral John Greenslade of the United States Navy and Admiral Robert in August, which had the effect of immobilising the French forces, and the British naval units were withdrawn though the United States continued to maintain an active surface and air patrol. But, in view of the attitude of the Vichy Government, Greenslade had to pay a further visit to Robert in November, when 'he used language that a sailor understood'.[153] Threatened by a bombardment and an occupation, Robert agreed not to move any French naval vessels without notice, nor to part with the gold and the planes. These conditions he observed, though on more than one occasion the United States did in fact prepare to occupy Martinique.[154] Hull had no liking for, and not much trust in, the stiff-necked Admiral Robert, but he was mortally offended by the action of the equally stiff-necked General de Gaulle in seizing the islands of St. Pierre and Miquelon off the coast of Newfoundland in December, 1941, and refusing to surrender them. It was, he thought, a direct violation of the Monroe Doctrine and the Havana Agreements.[155] De Gaulle was never forgiven.

III

FROM NEUTRALITY TO WAR

I

Two shadows had overhung the Havana Conference. One was the spectre that Germany might win the war, and this, in the eyes of many observers, was a possibility, indeed a probability, but not yet a certainty. The other was the question whether the United States would intervene. That, too, was a possibility, if not yet a probability and very far indeed from a certainty.[1] President Roosevelt's declaration at Charlottesville on 10 June that the United States would 'extend to the opponents of force the material resources' of America and at the same time speed up the use of those resources so that 'we ourselves in the Americas may have equipment and training equal to the task of any emergency and every defense', was still the limit of American commitment, though, as the Secretary of the Interior, Harold Ickes, wrote on 2 August: 'It seems to me that we Americans are like the householder who refuses to lend or sell his fire extinguisher to help put out the fire in the house that is next door, although that house is all ablaze and the wind is blowing from that direction'.[2]

But in the months after Havana slowly but surely aid to Britain and hemisphere defence became more and more intertwined. The Ogdensburg Agreement of 18 August, which established a Canadian-American Permanent Joint Defense Board, was itself a major step in the movement of the United States away from neutrality, for though Canada was an American state, she was also a belligerent. A second, still more striking, was the 'Destroyers for Bases' agreement of 2 September. By this the United States made available to Britain fifty old-age destroyers (which Churchill had asked for in May and again in June and July)[3] and Britain granted to the United States 99-year leases of naval and air bases in the Bahamas, Jamaica, St. Lucia, Trinidad, Antigua and British

Guiana, and, as a 'free gift', in Newfoundland and Bermuda. Even the isolationists—and there were many of them—found it difficult to condemn so favourable a bargain. After all, they wanted the bases, and Cordell Hull hastened to assure the Latin American states that their purpose was the common defence of the hemisphere and that they would be available to all, though in fact they were developed and used by the United States alone. It was Britain, not Latin America, that was denied their use, on the ground that this would imperil the sanctity of the 'neutrality zone'. 'As between offending America's Latin American neighbors and at the same time inviting Axis activities in the Neutrality Zone, and wounding the British, the Administration clearly regarded the latter as the lesser evil'.[4] But if Britain had to swallow a little of her pride, the transaction was as important to her as to the United States. In Churchill's words, it was a 'decidedly unneutral act', which would, 'according to all the standards of history, have justified the German Government in declaring war' upon the United States.[5] A fortnight later the President signed the Selective Service Bill. In November he was re-elected for a third term, and when, on 29 December, in his Address on National Security, he not only called for massive re-armament but declared that the United States must become 'the great arsenal of democracy', one of the questions that overhung the Havana Conference had been partially answered. The United States had moved from neutrality to non-belligerency.

A majority of the American people were by now convinced that the future security of America depended upon the survival of Britain, though they were not yet prepared to go beyond all aid to Britain short of war. And Britain had survived. The *Luftwaffe* had failed to destroy British morale. Hitler's invasion plans had gone awry. But the 'mortal danger'—in Churchill's words—which threatened the country through the mounting losses of merchant shipping in the Atlantic approaches, the gravity of Britain's financial plight as her dollar resources melted away, her enormous requirements in ships, 'planes, machine tools and armaments of every kind, and, as Churchill frankly admitted, the approach of the time when she could no longer pay for them in cash, all this was known to the President, his official family, and his military advisers before the end of 1940.[6] The answer was the great Lend-Lease Act, introduced into both Houses of Congress early in January 1941 and signed by the President on 11 March. Britain had been compelled to furnish for the world to see, not only a schedule of her dollar assets, but of her other overseas assets too, and the Administration had been 'fertile of suggestions to the British for stripping themselves bare'[7], before H. R. 1776, 'An Act Further to Promote the Defense of the United States', was passed and instantly acted upon by the President. With the huge appropriations at once made available for supplies of all kinds, as well as its provision for the communication of defence information, it came to Churchill as 'a draught of life'[8], and for Britain, as for Churchill, that is what it was.

Lend-Lease did not provide immediate assistance to Britain, hard-pressed in the Battle of the Atlantic. But other measures did.[9] American shipyards were opened for the repair of British naval vessels. In April the Red Sea and the Gulf of Aden were declared to be non-combat zones and therefore not prohibited to American shipping, which could thus replace British in carrying supplies round the Cape to the British forces in the Middle East. Also in April the President drew a line down the middle of the Atlantic, at longitude 25° east, to define the limits of the western hemisphere, which thus included most of Greenland—indeed the President claimed it all—and, with the consent of the Danish Minister in the United States, Greenland was placed under American protection. The sphere of operations of the so-called Neutrality Zone naval and air patrol in guarding the North Atlantic sea-lanes was now extended to Greenland and the meridian line[10], and the patrol itself was enlarged in May by the transfer of units from the Pacific Fleet.[11] In a broadcast address on 27 May, delivered in the presence of the entire Latin American diplomatic corps, the President proclaimed an unlimited national emergency, declared that the control by Germany of any of the 'island outposts of the New World' in the Atlantic would place portions of the western hemisphere in immediate jeopardy but that to dominate the Atlantic Hitler would first have to conquer Britain, and revealed that American patrols had been strengthened and extended in order to safeguard the needed convoys of supplies to Britain. In July the protection of one of these islands outposts, Iceland, by agreement both with its new republican government and with Britain, was taken over by American from British forces.[12] Whether Iceland could, or could not, be considered a part of the western hemisphere was beside the point. It was an outpost of defence both of America and Britain.

Successively, between March and the end of July, the United States seized Axis and Danish shipping lying idle in American ports and requisitioned them for her own (and British) use, froze German and Italian assets (and, later, Japanese), closed German and Italian consulates, pledged American aid to Soviet Russia when, on 22 June, Hitler turned his armies against her, established an Economic Defense Board,[13] issued a Proclaimed or Black List (disliked, but not universally condemned, in Latin America) of some 1,800 persons and firms in Latin America trading with the Axis, and, in the meantime, tightened up her export-licensing and export priorities control system. In August the President and Churchill met in Placentia Bay off Argentia, Newfoundland, and signed the Atlantic Charter—a statement of peace aims by a belligerent and a non-belligerent; and in November the provisions of the Neutrality Act which forbade the entry of American merchant vessels into combat zones were repealed and the ships allowed to be armed. Inevitably, acts of violence, 'the shooting war', with attacks on American merchant vessels and destroyers, had already occurred. Roosevelt would seem to have expected, and indeed hoped for, an 'incident' which would justify him in not merely waging war but declaring it, and he used the episode of the 'attack' by a German submarine on the U.S.S. *Greer* on 4 September to announce a new policy, promised at Argentia, of escorting British convoys between America and Iceland and shooting at sight.[14] But the finale of American neutrality was written not in the Atlantic but in the Pacific, and not by Germany but by Japan with the sudden attack on the Pacific Fleet at Pearl Harbour on 7 December. Four days later the United States was at war not only with Japan but with Germany and Italy.

II

At the time of the Havana Conference, though the American intelligence services had received reports of a possible Japanese attack on Hawaii, these had caused only a momentary concern.[15] It was the Nazi, not the potential Japanese, threat to the western hemisphere that pre-occupied the Administration. Uruguay had provided, or had seemed to provide, an alarming example of the dangers of Axis subversion; and it was plain that, with their limited air, naval and military forces, the Latin American republics in general were in no state to repel external aggression even if they could contain threats to their security from within. The Havana Conference itself had interrupted the secret, exploratory military and naval staff conversations which the United States had begun with almost all the Latin American states,[16] and these were now renewed on a more formal basis. The aim was to secure a clear undertaking from all the republics concerned that they would be prepared to co-operate with each other in rallying to the cause of hemisphere defence whether the threat came from within or without, and would make their land, sea and air bases available to the United States if her assistance was required.[17] Once again the Governments consulted made their needs for armanents crystal clear, and Argentina, doubting the ability of the United States to defend herself, let alone to come to the aid of a country 6,500 miles away, rebuffed United States overtures and preferred to look to defensive arrangements with her immediate neighbours.[18] But by the end of the year agreements of one kind or another had been concluded (though not necessarily ratified) with every Government approached except Argentina.

It was, of course, almost impossible for negotiations of this kind to take place without a spate of rumours; and of these the most potentially damaging was that the United States was seeking to acquire bases in Latin America as she had acquired them in the British West Indies. Spreading like wildfire from one country to another, such a rumour came like manna from heaven to German and other anti-United States propaganda. In Colombia, for example, the Government was accused of disposing of the national territory for thirty pieces of silver.[19]

In Brazil Dr. Aranha hastened to declare that no American nation needed to offer bases to another since, if attacked, the Americas would share all they had.[20] In Chile President Aguirre Cerda denied that Chile had ever contemplated the leasing or construction of bases, and no situation, it was said in the press, could justify a transfer of national sovereignty.[21]

The Chilean statements seem to have been inspired by the report of an American journalist published early in November to the effect that Uruguay had reached an agreement with the United States for the establishment of bases in Uruguay available to all American nations[22]—a confirmation, so it appeared, of Argentine fears of the erection of an 'American Gibraltar' in the estuary of the Río de la Plata.[23] Dr. Guani categorically denied that there was any intention of permitting the establishment of foreign bases on Uruguayan soil. All that was intended, he said, was the construction of naval and air bases by the Uruguayan authorities themselves, bases which any American nation would be able to use in case of need.[24] He also declared that no step would be taken without consultation with Argentina.[25] Sumner Welles, on behalf of the State Department, denied that the United States had ever sought to obtain the lease or cession of bases in Uruguay.[26] President Ortiz, still capable of asserting himself in Argentina, issued an emollient statement to the effect that the Americas must form a single unit for defence against foreign aggression,[27] and the Argentine Foreign Minister, now Dr. Julio Roca, declared that the Uruguayan and Argentine Foreign Offices were in close consultation.[28] The two Foreign Ministers in fact met at Colonia early in December with immediate results which were satisfactory to everyone—to everyone, perhaps, except those implacable enemies of the Uruguayan Government (of which, nevertheless, they formed a part),[29] the Herreristas. The Herreristas, placing the worst possible interpretation on the rumours (in which they were supported by General Franco's Spain), attacked President Baldomir, President Roosevelt and Dr. Guani with extreme bitterness. One of the Herrerista Ministers resigned, and, to the indignation of the Uruguayan press, the party moved a vote of censure on Dr. Guani in the Senate. At this Sumner Welles issued a further and stronger statement. The 'interpellation' of Dr. Guani, however, proceeded, but mostly to the discredit of the Herreristas. While the Senate declared that it could not tolerate the construction of any bases which implied a diminution of Uruguayan sovereignty, the Chamber of Deputies expressed its approval of Dr. Guani's policy, and President Baldomir declared that he would go forward without compromising either the sovereignty or the stability of the country and that Montevideo was a most suitable site for a base.[30]

The bases controversy illustrated the delicacy of United States relations with Latin America. It cleared the air, however, and removed, or allayed, fears that the United States was seeking to duplicate the arrangements made with Great Britain in the West Indies, in British Guiana and in Newfoundland. And not only did the United States obtain, except in Argentina, the military staff agreements, at least in principle, which she sought, she was able, again with the consent of the governments concerned, to arrange for Pan American Airways, through a new subsidiary, the Pan American Airports Corporation, to enlarge or construct air fields on the West Indies and South American routes from the United States to north-eastern Brazil, though not till July, 1941, did President Vargas formally authorise *Panair do Brasil*, also a subsidiary of Pan American, to reconstruct and re-equip a number of airfields in north-eastern Brazil.[31]

Still further to improve military relations Latin American army Chiefs of Staff were invited to the United States, partly to see for themselves the progress of United States rearmament. They were welcomed by President Roosevelt with the resounding declaration that the defence of the Americas was a matter of 'one for all and all for one'.[32] General Góes Monteiro, however, returned, according to one report, 'in high dudgeon' because he felt that insufficient honour had been done to him[33]—his disgruntlement was due, more probably, to the failure of the United States to supply armaments; and the army chiefs were followed by the naval chiefs in May, 1941. More Latin American officers were enrolled in United States service schools; and the number both of service attachés and service missions in Latin America was increased. By the end of 1941 the army was represented by attachés or missions in all the republics. Requests for armaments were a source of embarrassment. What the Latin American states could afford to buy and the United States legitimately sell from surplus stocks was limited. And it was modern weapons in considerable quantities, not old equipment, that the republics wanted. To examine and report on their requests a joint Army and Navy Board on the American Republics was established late in 1940. In March, 1941, after detailed appraisals and policy discussions it recommended an allocation of $400 million for army and navy material to be supplied within a three-year period or longer, and, in order to bring the republics within the scope of the Lend-Lease Act, the President, in April, certified that the defence of the Latin American republics was vital to that of the United States. The second lend-lease appropriation act in October authorised the allocation of funds for Latin American armaments.[34] Meanwhile the first Latin American Lend-Lease Agreement had been signed with the Dominican Republic in August, and six other agreements followed by the end of the year.[35] But very little military equipment had been provided for the Latin American nations by the time of the attack on Pearl Harbour, nor could it have been provided given the state of the United States armaments programme and the British and Allied requirements.

Axis military missions, on the other hand, had been eliminated, and so, to all intents and purposes, had Axis-controlled air-lines. This was a major step forward in hemisphere defence, effected partly by the expansion, with federal funds, of the services of Pan American Airways and Pan American Grace, and partly by the provision of financial and technical assistance to those countries which had relied on German-operated lines. In Colombia the German employees of Scadta had been discharged by June, 1940. But Colombia was exceptional. It was not till April, 1941, that *Lufthansa Perú* was expropriated, not till May that *Lloyd Aéreo Boliviano* was nationalised, and not till September that the planes and property of Sedta (*Sociedad Ecuatoriana de Transportes Aéreos*) were requisitioned.[36] In Brazil Axis influence was eliminated from the Varig and Vasp lines by August, 1941, and the trans-Atlantic service of Lati (*Linea Aérea Transcontinentale Italiana*) was forced to close soon after Pearl Harbour. Condor, the largest of the German air-lines, which had given good service to Brazil, was progressively Brazilianised after the United States entered the war and became by August 1942 the *Serviços Aéreos Cruzeiro do Sul*.[37]

III

President Roosevelt and his advisers had well understood at the time of the Havana Conference that hemisphere defence rested as much on economic as on political and military foundations. Various expedients had been proposed to deal with the problem of export surpluses and declining prices and to strengthen the Latin American economies, and some practical steps had been taken. But though exports from Latin America to the United States had increased, there had been a far greater increase in exports from the United States to Latin America, and, by the end of 1940, not merely was Latin America left with a large passive balance of trade from the United States but only a few crumbs of economic aid had yet fallen from the United States table.[38]

This situation changed dramatically in 1941. On the one hand a stream of financial and other assistance, intended for defence, development, communications, currency stabilisation and the like, began to flow from the United States southwards. On the other the progress of United States rearmament and her Lend-Lease and purchasing programmes acted as a powerful stimulus to Latin American production and raised the level both of exports and prices. The United States needed strategic and critical materials, materials, that is, essential for national defence in time of war or the expectation of war. She wished, also, like Britain, to prevent them from reaching the Axis powers. Latin America could supply a vast range of materials, ranging from antimony and asbestos to zinc and zirconium and from cinchona bark to quebracho wood; and of these valuable materials it was known that the Lati air-line flew quartz crystals, platinum, mica and industrial diamonds to Germany and that Japanese purchases ranged far and wide, some of them, until Hitler's invasion of Russia, intended for Germany by way of Vladivostock.

Already in June, 1940, the Reconstruction Finance Corporation, which had begun stock-piling in 1939, had been authorised to create new agencies for the purchase of strategic materials. These were the Rubber Reserve Company, the Metals Reserve Company and the Defense Supplies Corporation, and the contract signed by the Metals Reserve Company in November for the acquisition of Bolivian tin[39] was followed in 1941 by a series of agreements for the purchase, among other strategic and critical materials, of Brazilian rubber, manganese, nickel, chromite, quartz crystals and mica, Bolivian tungsten, Mexican antimony, copper, graphite, lead, mercury and tungsten, Chilean copper, antimony and manganese, Peruvian lead, zinc, copper, antimony and vanadium, and Argentine tungsten. Some of these were pre-emptive arrangements. Others took account of British and American commercial purchases. As a result the demand for some products, formerly in surplus, threatened to exceed supply, and for others, including a number of agricultural and forest products, it was greatly enlarged. At the same time the Latin American countries were encouraged to institute, if they had not already done so, export controls of important commodies, such as the United States was itself applying to articles and materials essential for national defence.[40]

Some crops, of course, still presented considerable problems. Though the Inter-American Coffee Agreement[41] led to a general rise in the value of coffee, substantial stocks had to be destroyed. The American public still ate bananas, at higher prices, when shipping shortages allowed them to become available. Of other agricultural and pastoral surpluses, Britain bought hides and meat from Uruguay and Brazil, together with Brazilian cotton. She took all the meat she could get from Argentina and considerable quantities of cereals, hides and skins.[42] Nevertheless, Argentina was compelled to use maize for fuel. Britain also continued her purchases of Venezuelan oil and Dominican sugar, together with some Cuban sugar,[43] Peruvian molybdenum and limited amounts of Peruvian cotton. But the extent of the United States programme—the United States proposing to take the exportable surpluses of Uruguyan and Argentine wool, hides and skins and of Chilean nitrates—made it possible for Britain, towards the end of the year, to limit such of her purchases as were purely pre-emptive, designed, that is, to prevent the supply of materials to the enemy while assisting the Latin American countries concerned, to the buying of wool in Brazil, Uruguay, Chile and Perú; and, in line with the co-ordination of British and American purchases, Britain agreed to buy, at an enhanced price, the whole of the 1942 sugar harvest in the Dominican Republic and Haiti, while the United States took the entire Cuban crop.[44]

Further to assist the Latin American economies the Export-Import Bank made credits available for the building of roads, particularly the Pan American highway, for the acquisition of transport equipment and machinery, and for development projects. Currency stabilisation agreements were concluded with several countries, including Brazil and Mexico. The Inter-American Development Commission[45] established national councils in each of the Latin American states. Intra-Latin American trade again increased, Brazil doubling her admittedly not very large exports to her South American neighbours and concluding further agreements with Argentina. And the resolutions and agreements of the Conference of the River Plate countries, held early in 1941, illustrated a desire not only for the creation of regional markets but for a closer co-ordination of economic interests and an improvement in communications, more especially in the shape of railway links between Argentina and Bolivia and Brazil and Paraguay.[46] Finally, in October, a trade agreement was at last signed between the United States and Argentina. It contained no drastic innovations. Fresh meat was still excluded on sanitary grounds—a long-standing Argentine grievance—from the United States. But the duties on canned corned beef, linseed, coarse wool, hides and many other products were reduced, at least to Argentine satisfaction if not to that of farming interests in the United States, and Cordell Hull had reason to be gratified by this further addition to his Reciprocal Trade Agreements programme.

The reverse side of this picture of comparative prosperity was the replacement of export surpluses by import and shipping shortages. Shipping problems had first been considered by the Maritime Conference held in Washington in 1940[47] and were referred to the Inter-American Financial and Economic Advisory Committee. In February, 1941, the United States set up a committee of its own to co-ordinate the shipping requirements of the Central and South American trades with the supply of tonnage, and at the end of March United States coast guard patrols, on the orders of the Treasury and in view of reports of actual or impending sabotage, took custody of all Axis-controlled shipping lying idle in American ports. Chile had already attached three Danish freighters at Talcahuano, Perú a Danish vessel at Callao, and in March and April a number of other republics from Costa Rica and Mexico to Venezuela and Perú seized German and Italian freighters, tankers and merchant ships, their crews attempting to scuttle, burn, or otherwise damage them, sometimes successfully, sometimes not. The Act of Congress authorising the President to requisition idle foreign merchant vessels was signed on 6 June. Meanwhile, on 26 April, the Inter-American Financial and Economic Advisory Committee had recommended that foreign flag vessels immobilised in the ports of the Americas should be appropriated and utilised in such a manner as to promote the defence of the economies of the republics as well as the peace and security of the continent, and this recommendation endorsing actions already taken met with general approval as well as the warm concurrence of Britain. It was formally adopted in August.[48] Brazil, incidentally, had already enlarged her *Lloyd Brasileiro* fleet by buying fourteen ships from the United States[49] and Argentina preferred, not to requisition, but to buy sixteen Italian ships in her harbours.[50]

But the shortage of freighters and tankers remained grave, and, combined with the increasing concentration both of Great Britain and the United States on war production and the resulting export contractions, faced the Latin American countries with serious difficulties in obtaining supplies of industrial and consumer goods—aluminium, tin plate, iron goods, rolling stock, machinery, building materials, chemicals and fuel. The United States sought to alleviate this situation through her system of export controls by allocating supplies in such a way as to give priority to requirements for national defence, essential public services and such national development projects as the Brazilian steel plant.[51] Britain could do little or nothing; and when, in 1942, German submarines began to operate in the Caribbean and Gulf of Mexico, there were also shortages of food stuffs in many of the Caribbean countries. Panamá and Venezuela were only two examples.[52]

IV

Politically the evolution of United States policy from neutrality to non-belligerency and from non-belligerency to all-out-aid to Britain had been watched in Latin America with mixed feelings of approval, concern and apprehension. The Ogdensburg Agreement and the Destroyers-for-Bases Deal in August 1940 were generally regarded as logical and desirable and as much in the interests of hemisphere defence as of Britain, and the fact that the bases were, theoretically, available to all American nations gave especial satisfaction. 'What better defence for America', asked the government newspaper in Mexico, 'than this great step taken in the interests of continental security?'[53] In Argentina and Chile, on the other hand, there was a tendency to argue, correctly, that Washington had acted on its own responsibility, that the arrangements had no connection with the Havana agreements, and that the United States must bear the responsibility for any untoward results,[54] while in Colombia El Siglo, published by Dr. Laureano Gómez, the leader of the Conservative party, violently denounced what it described as the irregular entry of Canada into the Pan American Union and condemned the Anglo-American deal as illegal, ill-timed, and improper.[55] A month later Japan's adherence to the Axis, while it added to Latin American anxieties, strengthened a feeling on the long, ill-defended Pacific coast as well as on the almost equally unprotected Atlantic sea-board that now, more than ever, the defence of the hemisphere was one and indivisible. 'No combination of dictator countries of Europe and Asia will stop the help we are giving to almost the last free people fighting to hold them at bay', said Roosevelt in his 'all for one and one for all' radio address of 12 October. 'Let no American in any part of the Americas question the possibility of danger from overseas'; and the enthusiasm with which Roosevelt's re-election for a third term was greeted in November testified not merely to his personal popularity but to the political confidence he had inspired. However critical the feelings towards the United States which had been generated over the years, and however violent the anti-Americanism of the extreme nationalist right and the extreme communist left throughout Latin America, Roosevelt, by his eloquent appeals both to idealism and realism and by his studious courtesy to his neighbours, had touched the hearts and minds of the Latin American peoples and gained their trust in a way which no other North American statesman had ever done.

It is difficult to over-estimate the importance of this trust as the United States continued to move away from a common policy of Pan American neutrality to one of intervention, Roosevelt himself constantly reiterating the argument that aid to Britain, albeit short of war, was the surest safeguard of the western hemisphere and that his every move was designed to prevent the advance of Hitlerism from the old world to the new. But for him the approval generally accorded in the Latin American press from Cuba to Chile of the great Lend-Lease Act and the conversion of the United States into the 'arsenal of democracy' would almost certainly have been less marked. The divisions of opinion which had been evident in the months after Havana, divisions which reflected class and party lines as well as geographical,[56] were still apparent in 1941, El Siglo even going so far as to talk of a struggle between Hispanic and Anglo-Saxon America.[57] But though disquiet and even resentment at the unilateral policy pursued by the United States, and fears of its consequences, were not confined to conservative ranks, the main stream of opinion flowed strongly in favour of the United States. Even the violent reversal of the 'Satanic Pact', as the Soviet-German agreement had been called in Latin America, and the promise of United States aid to Russia, were received with remarkable equanimity. No Latin American state had maintained diplomatic relations with the USSR since 1935, and only in Chile, Colombia, Costa Rica, Cuba, Mexico and Uruguay did the Communist parties, none of them large and all of them quarrelsome, enjoy legal recognition. The Communists, indeed, were the whipping boys of politics, and to the parties of the Right Communism was a more deadly enemy than Fascism.

The Pact had sown confusion in Communist ranks, and so did its reversal. Less was heard of 'Yankee imperialism' and more of Russian patriotism and the need to defeat Nazism. But any losses which pro-Allied opinion suffered on the round-abouts as the result of this *volte-face* were made up upon the swings by the arrogance of German diplomacy in Latin America, by the fears of Axis subversive activities, and by the horror felt at Nazi excesses in Europe. The words of Churchill on 22 June, which Roosevelt echoed with the statement that 'any defense against Hitlerism, any rallying of the forces opposing Hitler-ism . . . will hasten the downfall of the present German lead-ers, and will therefore redound to the benefit of our own defense and security',[58] carried conviction, even though the new ally was the old enemy, Russia.

Government-to-government relations with the United States, of course, were by no means all smooth. There were particular problems and difficulties in particular areas and particular circumstances. The possibility of an Axis victory, moreover, was ever present to Latin American minds, and the argument of German power was potent. Nevertheless, the United States and Latin America, despite the growing isola-tion of Argentina and the anxieties of Chile, travelled a similar road, and while Latin American relations with Germany in general deteriorated, 'defensive' Pan Americanism reinforced political solidarity in the western hemisphere. Reserves were inevitable, and, naturally enough, were more marked in the larger and more southerly states of South America, remote by sea and air from the United States, than in the smaller coun-tries of Central America and the Caribbean. For these the United States was increasingly their life-line. Economic self-interest and internal and external security alike dictated a strong interest in Caribbean defence, though in some of these states there were deeper currents of feeling too. All co-operated in the military conversations initiated by the United States both before and after the Havana Conference, and all, when the moment of decision came, declared war on Japan on the day after Pearl Harbour, and on Germany and Italy three or four days later, Nicaragua and Haiti, for good measure, including Bulgaria, Hungary and Rumania before the end of December.[59]

V

In Cuba, the most important of the island republics, Colonel Fulgencio Batista, 'that extraordinarily brilliant and able figure', so Sumner Welles described him,[60] had been elected to the Presidency, amid some genuine enthusiasm, in July, 1940, though for the last six years he had been the strong man of Cuban politics,[61] and the island had been ruled as much from the mansion which, as Commander-in-Chief, he had built for himself (though hardly out of the proceeds of his military salary) and from his military headquarters at Camp Columbia as from the presidential palace.[62] His power rested on an army which, though comparatively small, he had democratised and cherished. But, in a land of great poverty among the labouring classes and callous indifference to their sufferings among the rich, he sought also the support of the urban and agricultural workers. On assuming the Presidency in October 1940 he boasted, not without a measure of justification, that the revolutionary cycle which had begun with his own and his fellow sergeants' revolt in 1933 had run its course.[63] He could point not only to a long list of reforms in education and public health and to the ambitious plans he had formulated for a more equitable distribution of the island's wealth, better working conditions, higher wages, the re-organization of agriculture and mining, and the distribution of state lands to squatters,[64] but to the fact that he took office as a constitutional President to inaugurate a new and socially advanced Constitution. This remarkable document abolished discrimination of race, sex, class and colour, provided for a minimum wage, a 44-hour week, paid holidays and compulsory social insurance, for everything, indeed (according to its critics), except the elimination of mosquitoes. It created also a Prime Minister and a semi-parliamentary system. And if Batista assumed office as a constitutional President, he did so also as a professed enemy of totalitarianism and a warm protagonist of collaboration with the United States and of Pan Americanism.

This was the policy of common sense. Opposition to it came from two sources—the Falangists on the far right and the Communists on the far left. With her large and wealthy Spanish 'colony', Cuba had become the stronghold in Latin America of the *Falange*, that is, the *Falange Exterior* in alliance with the *Falange Español*. The *Falange*, however, commanded but little respect in government circles or among the public at large, and when, in 1940, its chief in Cuba visited General Franco and returned as the Spanish Consul-General, so hostile was the campaign against him that he was finally declared *persona non grata*. The Communists were well-organized and ably led. They had supported Batista and were represented in Congress. They were, of course, anti-American and anti-imperialist until the German invasion of Russia compelled them to execute a *volte-face* and they then embarrassed the British Minister with unwelcome attentions.[65]

But Batista had not admitted the Communists to his cabinet, and he and his ministers were well aware, as was responsible opinion in general, that Cuba's fate was bound up with that of the United States and that none but the United States could provide the economic assistance necessary to support the island's economy. Very rationally Batista followed the United States step by step, suppressing the *Partido Nazista Cubana*, agreeing to allow the United States to make use of Cuban territory not only for the defence of both countries but for that of the entire hemisphere,[66] and in January 1941 forbidding all totalitarian propaganda manifested in whatever form.[67] Significantly enough the passage of the Lend-Lease Act was greeted as a triumph for democracy, of which Roosevelt was the paladin, and in April a special meeting of the Senate was convoked in his honour.[68]

Cubans were by now becoming convinced that the entry of the United States into the war was merely a matter of time. In June Batista assured the American Ambassador that should the United States enter the war Cuba would instantly follow her example.[69] The Italian and German consulates were closed in August, together with the rooms of the *Auxilio Social*, the most important Spanish and Falangist benevolent society. The Spanish press and commercial attachés were declared unacceptable in October because of their Falangist activities. In November, by which time the United States and Cuba had agreed on the enlargment of the perimeter of the Guantánamo naval base and the improvement of the Camagüey air port,[70] a resolution of both Houses of Congress authorised the President to place the armed forces, the waters, railways and air fields of the island at the disposal of the United States for common defensive and offensive action.[71] On the 23rd Batista declared that when the United States became a belligerent Cuba would be the 'first Spanish-speaking nation' to be at her side and, shortly afterwards, referred to Churchill as 'the supreme leader of freedom in Europe'.[72] The declarations of war followed in a few days and their reception from Congress, students, merchants and the professional classes was all that could be desired.

The policy of common sense had meanwhile paid good dividends in preserving the economic and political stability of Cuba under the Batista régime, corrupt and inefficient as that régime was. In January 1941 the Export-Import Bank authorised a credit of just under $12 million to finance the production of an additional 400,000 tons of sugar[73] to tide over the crisis produced by the loss of European markets and in the interests of social stability. Once Cuba had settled her long-standing debts to American contractors who had been engaged on public works in the nineteen-twenties, a further credit of $25 millions was authorised in May for agricultural diversification and public works,[74]though it did not win the approval of the Cuban Congress till towards the end of the year and only a small portion had been utilised by the end of Batista's first term. Under the Lend-Lease Act Cuba was allocated some $7 million worth of military equipment in November. In December a Supplementary Trade Agreement reduced the United States duty on Cuban sugar, and negotiations were completed in the following January for the purchase of the entire 1942 sugar harvest.[75] War declared, Batista himself obtained, besides the strong support of the United States, a Law of National Emergency which freed him, at least temporarily, from the ineptitudes and factionalism of the new parliamentary régime. The British Minister, in reporting on Cuban-United States relations, struck a somewhat sour and sinister but not wholly unjustified note. 'The present Cuban Government . . .', he wrote in January, 1942, 'has been bought by the United States Government, who, in the form of eventual intervention, may have to pay a high price, both morally, in view of the Good Neighbour Policy, and materially in men and money, to safeguard the Cuban outposts to the Panama Canal'.[76] The idea of intervention in the nineteen-forties may seem ludicrous enough, even had the Roosevelt Administration been unable to obtain its desired ends by its economic policies.[77] But the idea had not been ludicrous ten years earlier and it was not ludicrous twenty years later.

As in Cuba, so in Haiti and the Dominican Republic there had been changes in the Presidency. In Haiti President Sténio Vincent, who had been in office since 1930, resigned, to the general surprise, in April 1941, ostensibly on the ground of ill-health.[78] He was succeeded, amid some disorders, by his Minister in Washington, Elíe Lescot, who was a friend of Sumner Welles and a warm partisan of the Allied cause. Lescot roundly declared in his inaugural address, what his predecessor had well understood, that Haiti's lot was bound up with the United States,[79] so much so indeed that the Head of the recently arrived United States Military Mission was made a 'technical' member of the President's cabinet.[80] But there was also a deeper spring of action. The members of the educated mulatto class, whose fount of culture had been France, were strongly nationalist in character. They had been suspicious both of United States interference and, with good reason, of aggression from the Dominican Republic. But they could have no sympathy with Nazi Germany, whose racial doctrines they found wholly abhorrent. President Lescot expressed a genuine feeling when he declared in January 1942, after Haiti had become a belligerent, 'the cause with which we are associated is the cause of the black man, of whom Haiti is the eldest daughter in this hemisphere'.[81]

No such sentiment animated the Dominican Republic. There President Jacinto Peynado had died in March, 1940, to be replaced by the Vice-President, Dr. Manuel Troncoso de la Concha, a former Rector of the University. But the new President, like the old, was merely a *roi-fainéant*. Supreme power remained with Generalissimo Trujillo. Perhaps the most remarkable features of his policy had been his offer to the United States, in December, 1939, of the full use of Dominican territory for the purposes of continental defence,[82] and the grants of land which he made in 1940 and 1941 for the settlement of European refugees, both Jewish and non-Jewish, near the Sosúa coast, actions calculated, perhaps, to enhance a somewhat tarnished international prestige. He also made a point of visiting President Lescot, and though it would not have been surprising had he felt, unlike his Haitian colleague, a degree of admiration for a European dictatorship on a grander scale than his own, he never wavered in the prudent conviction that his sheet-anchor was friendship and co-operation with the United States.

In both countries the major aim of the United States was to ensure their political and economic stability, as well as such co-operation as they could give in promoting hemisphere defence. The termination of United States control of the Dominican Customs in 1941, an event celebrated in Ciudad Trujillo by a salute of twenty-one guns and a *Te Deum* in the cathedral, and a similar but not quite so far-reaching agreement with Haiti,[83] each had their effect. Both countries received modest appropriations of Lend-Lease aid in the autumn of 1941 for the acquisition of armaments and munitions,[84] and while, under the Pan American Airport Development Programme, Haiti opened a new air-field at Chancerelles, the Dominican Republic completed another at Villa Duarte.[85] Haiti benefited by coffee sales to the United States, the Dominican Republic by British purchases (in agreement with Washington) of her sugar.[86] Each received substantial Export-Import Bank credits for road-building, public works and the like. The announcement in December, 1940, that the Bank had made a further $1 million available to the Dominican Republic in addition to £2 millions in June was greeted, if not by a *Te Deum*, at least by the sounding of sirens.[87] No demonstrations of this or any other kind accompanied the Republic's entry into the war, but, in the opinion of the American Minister, it met with the spontaneous approval of all sections of public opinion, and, at his instigation, a number of Axis nationals were interned in the interior.[88] What was described as a 'unique spontaneity' of public approbation was reserved, however, for a movement to induce Trujillo to resume the Presidency (as he did) in 1942.[89]

In Haiti the Export-Import Bank financed the establishment in July 1941 of the *Société Haitienne-Americaine de*

Développement Agricole to promote the growing and marketing of rubber, spices, and oil-bearing and medicinal plants.[90] 'Uncle Sam', observed the *Christian Science Monitor*,[91] had 'virtually adopted orphan Haiti', and Haiti repaid him by allowing United States forces to be stationed in Haitian waters and by other concessions. She even offered to place her harbours, landing grounds and sea-plane bases at British disposal also.[92] If there were any lingering doubts that Haiti, because of her old French sympathies, might be inclined to support the government of Marshal Pétain and Pierre Laval, President Lescot, on a visit to the United States, blandly disposed of them. When asked whether there were any pro-Vichy influences in Haiti, he is said to have replied, 'Of Vichy I know only the water';[93] and while Lescot remained President his views were also Haiti's.

VI

The reactions in Central America to the attack on Pearl Harbour were very similar to those in the island republics. The newly elected President of Costa Rica, Rafael Calderón Guardia, had declared, in May 1940, that a German victory would mean the doom of democracy and liberty in America, that the United States was certain to enter the war when her preparations were more advanced and that the whole of America would follow, Costa Rica gladly contributing her grain of sand.[94] German influences in Costa Rica were strong —the President said in July that he had been threatened with a *coup d'état* and assassination by his political enemies with German support[95]—and German propaganda, directed from Guatemala, was extensive. The Minister of the Interior, however, confessed 'with a certain amount of boyish glee and administrative pride' that eighty per cent of it was 'quietly made to disappear' by the Post Office,[96] and the Government early took steps to eliminate from the public service both German nationals and Costa Ricans of German origin or sympathies.[97] Vigilance—and action—were enhanced in 1941. In March one Italian and one German ship were seized in Punta Arenas, though not before their crews had set them on fire,[98] the ships later being sold and their crews deported.

The Nazi leader, Karl Bayer, was expelled in April, with the assistance of the United States and the Canal Zone authorities.[99] The country declared its non-belligerency in July, when the President personally assured the British representative that Costa Rica would automatically enter the war when the United States did so.[100] A United States Military Mission was welcomed in August, German consulates were closed in September and arrangements completed in November for United States instructors to train a military police force of 15,000 men—the minute Costa Rican army consisted of some 600 officers and men.[101] A modest credit had already been secured for the supply of arms,[102] together with a loan of over \$4 million for the completion of the Costa Rican section of the Pan American highway. This loan had been greeted with relief in 1940 because it would provide employment and wages during a period of depression in the coffee industry— Costa Rica had lost the British market to Kenya. A further loan was made available in 1941 to finance the coffee surplus in excess of the export quota to the United States and the highway loan was at the same time re-negotiated on the ground that its terms were too onerous.[103] Clearly the United States was not immune from criticism in Costa Rica, where the press was free and the game of politics vigorously played. But criticism of the Axis was of a different order and, when the moment came, Costa Rica was the first American state to declare war on Japan, anticipating by a few hours the declaration of the United States.

There could be few doubts that Costa Rica's actions were dictated by genuine convictions. As for the dictatorial régimes of her neighbours to the north, all alike sought shelter under the umbrella of the Good Neighbour policy. President Hernández Martínez of El Salvador could unblushingly assert in October 1940 that democracy was light and dictatorship darkness.[104] In November President Somoza of Nicaragua declared that the very survival of the Central American countries depended on the United States, and, a year later, that every Nicaraguan solider was potentially a United States soldier,[105] and in Honduras, where the General Manager of the United Fruit Company was reputed to be the second most influential person in the country,[106] President Carías Andino, who was undoubtedly the first, was almost equally emphatic. What was more, he took the bold step in March 1941 of expelling the German *chargé d'affaires*, Christian Zinsser, on the ground of undesirable activities. Zinsser had the reputation of being one of the ablest Axis agents in Latin America, and it was a curious coincidence, according to report, that, after a visit from Zinsser, the German *chargé d'affaires* in El Salvador committed suicide and the consul at Tegucigalpa died of a heart attack.[107] Zinsser left for Guatemala, whence also, after some delay and some pressure from the British and United States legations, he was expelled, returning to Germany by way of the United States. German annoyance was such that the Secretary of the Guatemalan legation in Berlin was declared *persona non grata* in reprisal.

What the Central American states wanted from the United States was protection from subversion from within and economic assistance. What the United States wanted from Central America was, in the first place, internal stability, and this, apparently, dictated United States policy over the supply of arms,[108] minimal indeed before Pearl Harbour, though Lend-Lease arrangements were concluded with Nicaragua in October, 1941 and with El Salvador and Honduras in February, 1942.[109] Secondly, the United States wanted, and obtained, for the protection of the Canal Zone, the freedom of Central American territory and waters, not only in Costa Rica, where she had a military mission, but in Nicaragua and El Salvador, where United States officers directed the military academies, and in Honduras and Guatemala also.[110]

Guatemala had been the centre for the dissemination of Axis propaganda throughout the Central American isthmus. The violently pro-Nazi *Deutsche Zeitung für Guatemala* was published in Guatemala City, and Guatemala City was also the residence of the German Minister to Central America, though *chargés d'affaires* were appointed to other of the republics after the outbreak of war. German coffee-planting families, moreover, were well-entrenched in society and business. But German popularity, never very high, suffered a steady decline. President Ubico had been greatly irritated by the German reaction to Guatemala's adhesion to the Uruguayan protest against the invasion of the Low Countries and by German menaces on the eve of the Havana Conference.[111] It was notable that the semi-official newspaper, *Nuestro Diario*, became progressively more anti-German in tone; and Ubico had his own methods of keeping Germans—and others —under close surveillance. Indeed, the supervision of foreigners was said to be closer in Guatemala than in any other Central American country,[112] and it was not relaxed by the alleged discovery in December, 1940, of a plot against the President's life in which Germans were said, though on no very good evidence, to have been implicated.[113]

President Ubico had no intention of leaving the presidency, forcibly or otherwise, and it must be admitted that during his long occupancy of it he had done more to modernize his country than his fellow Central American dictators had done in theirs. In theory his latest term of office was due to expire in 1943. But, as the result of an 'eminently popular' movement[114] in the summer of 1941, it was prolonged for another six years—an application of the Central American doctrine of *continuísmo*, the practice, that is, of continuing a President in power by constitutional amendments or other devices. Meanwhile his view that his own and his country's safety lay in close co-operation with the United States had been steadily enhanced. Not only was Christian Zinsser, after some hesitation, refused permission to remain in Guatemala after his expulsion from Honduras, but in April also the printing of all Axis propaganda was forbidden, with the consequent demise of two pro-Axis newspapers. A United States officer was appointed as Director of the Polytechnic School or military academy.[115] Under the Pan American Airport Development programme work proceeded on the enlargement of the Guatemalan City and San José airports.[116] German consulates were closed; and though the black-listing by the United States of German coffee-estate owners, and the methods of dealing with them, caused irritation and ill-feeling, not only did Guatemala become a belligerent at the same time as the United States but a comprehensive agreement on measures for hemisphere defence allowed her the full use of Guatemalan airfields and their facilities, permitted military planes to fly over and land on Guatemalan territory without formal notification through diplomatic channels, and allowed bomber squadrons to be stationed at Guatemala City and San José.[117] Ubico had already announced that out of respect for the cause which Britain was defending he would suspend Guatemala's claims on British Honduras for the duration of the war.[118]

VII

The Central American countries, whatever their political complexions and their past resentments, had shown themselves not only willing but eager to co-operate with the United States in foreign policy and defence, and the staff conversations carried on with each of them had resulted in a ready compliance with United States wishes. No staff conversations were held with Panamá, a country which had no army. Instead, the conduct of all defensive and military arrangements for the protection of the Canal, 'the keystone in the defense of the western hemisphere' as the War Plans Division of the United States War Department properly described it,[119] was left to the general-in-command of the Panamá Canal Zone Department and the American Ambassador to Panamá, but in an atmosphere much less complaisant than that which surrounded discussions in Central America.

United States-Panamanian relations were now in part regulated by a Treaty of Friendship signed in 1936, though not ratified by the United States Senate till July 1939.[120] Under this treaty the United States had surrendered the right she had previously enjoyed to acquire any lands, whether in public or private ownership, outside the Canal Zone which, unilaterally, she might deem essential for the operation or protection of the Canal. Were some 'new unforseen contingency' to arise which made the use of such lands necessary, the two Governments would agree on appropriate measures; and Article 10 of the Treaty provided that in the event of any 'international conflagration or the existence of any threat of aggression' which might endanger the security of Panamá or the neutrality or security of the Canal, they would join in 'measures of prevention and defense'.

In the early 'thirties the Zone authorities had acquired from a private owner the lease, at the nominal rent of $1 a year, of a large tract of land near the beach at Río Hato, some sixty or seventy miles south of the Pacific locks of the Canal. It was used both for recreational and flying activities. But the army quickly realised its value as an operational base for all types of planes in all sorts of weather and, the rent having risen to nearly $5,000 as the field became converted to these more serious purposes, the Zone Department (which had also put men on the small islands of Taboga and Taboguilla in the Bay of Panamá) would have liked to buy it. Clearly a lease from a private owner was a very different matter from the sale of some 19,000 acres of the national patrimony. But Panamá, it appeared early in 1939, though unwilllling for the land to be sold, was prepared to consider a 999-year lease. For one reason or another, however, no action was taken, though the Río Hato field continued to be used and was indeed designated in April, 1940, as a 'Department Training Area'. Then, in July, 1940, the State Department submitted to Panamá the draft of a lease, not only for the Río Hato field, on which construction work was urgently necessary, but for other sites which the War Department wanted as auxiliary and emergency landing fields, aircraft warning stations, searchlight positions, access roads and the like. The lease was to be for 999 years and the United States was to have exclusive jurisdiction over military and civilian personnel within the designated areas except over citizens of Panamá.[121]

The United States draft arrived at a time when a change in the presidency was taking place in Panamá. Presidential elections had been held in May, resulting in the return, unopposed, of Dr. Arnulfo Arias, a Harvard medical graduate, a member of one of Panamá's ruling families, and the Administration candidate. He was elected unopposed because the rival candidate had fled into the Canal Zone, alleging that the methods of intimidation employed by the Government made free elections impossible. Dr. Arias, on the other hand, as President-elect, was reported to have declared that he regarded Panamá as an ideal democracy.[122] An ardent nationalist with a dynamic personality and an imperious cast of mind, he was inaugurated on 1st October. Less than three weeks later he presented to the National Assembly (composed almost exclusively of his own supporters) the draft of a new Constitution. This extended the Presidential term from four to six years, reflected a strong spirit not only of political but of economic nationalism, imposed severe racial restrictions on immigration, particularly of West Indians—the influx of Jamaican labourers to work in the Canal Zone had long been a sore point in Panamá—and denied citizenship to non-Spanish speaking negroes and some other races.[123] Approved by the National Assembly and ratified by a plebiscite, for which there was no provision either in the old or the new Constitution,[124] it went into force on 2 January—to survive till 1946. In the same month an order was signed for the deportation of the New Zealander who edited the English section of the *Panama American* newspaper, because of his attacks on 'totalitarian tendencies' in the Government.[125] Justly or unjustly, this was a charge constantly made against Dr. Arias at home and abroad, and, if a man is to be known by the company he keeps, he had only himself to blame for the suspicion that he was closer to Germany than to the United States or Britain in his sympathies.[126] He was notably friendly with the representatives of General Franco and local members of the *Falange* and a warm supporter of the somewhat suspect cult of *Hispanidad*.[127] On the other hand, the American Ambassador was of opinion that, in spite of all that had been said of the President's pro-totalitarian leanings, he knew of no act since Dr. Arias had been in office which would seem to substantiate such charges.[128]

On assuming the Presidency Arias had early complained of the continued occupation by the United States of the Río Hato field. But he showed no disposition to repudiate Panamá's treaty obligations, and while affirming that his country had passed the stage of 'foreign tutelage', affirmed also, both publicly and privately, his intention to co-operate in the defence of the Canal and the continent.[129] He made it perfectly clear also that 999-year leases were out of the question and so, when 900 years had been lopped off, were 99-year leases. Instead, he suggested leases of four or six years, Panamá retaining full jurisdiction in the leased areas except over military personnel, and receiving adequate financial compensation.[130] Finally he stated that if the United States assured Panamá that a threat of aggression endangering the security of the Canal existed and based her request for sites outside the Canal Zone on the need for the defence of the Canal, his Government would immediately make them available.[131] Cordell Hull, on behalf of the United States, gave the required assurances, emphasising, at the same time, the serious view which the United States took of the continued delay of Panamá to carry out her treaty obligations,[132] and on 5 March, 1941, Arias, in a manifesto to the nation, proclaimed that Panamá had acceded to the request of the United States for the use of a number of areas outside the Canal Zone for the installation of air-bases, searchlights and aircraft detectors on condition that the occupation of these sites would end so soon as the war was over, that Panamá would be given adequate compensation, and that she would exercise jurisdiction over civilians in the occupied areas.[133]

During the next few weeks the United States, having occupied and utilised the Río Hato site all along, took possession of the other sites she required. By the end of 1941 about forty sites had been occupied, the number rising eventually to over a hundred.[134] But the conditions which Arias had laid down in his manifesto took Cordell Hull by surprise, and his gratification was expressed in somewhat chilly terms. Nor was he best pleased by the presentation to President Roosevelt of a list of claims and problems, known as the twelve points, which Panamá wanted settled.[135] The negotiations which followed, both on the conditions governing the leases and on the twelve points, were prolonged. They were a source of much annoyance to the State Department, which regarded Arias as, at the very least, difficult and obstructive, and they were not finally resolved till May 1942,[136] long after Arias had ceased to be President, but on terms not too far removed from the general conditions which he had laid down.

Panamá, then, had conceded in March, 1941, though not without difficulty, the demand for base areas outside the Canal Zone, and it is perhaps pertinent to recall that the conditions governing the leases of the bases given to the United States under the Destroyers-for-Bases Deal also provoked bitterness and difficulties in the West Indies and elsewhere. Panamá had also permitted vessels of foreign nationality to be granted Panamanian registry. Such vessels, with cargoes obviously intended for the Allies, could then enter combat zones prohibited to United States shipping till November 1941. The Panamanian merchant marine, in view of the profits to be made by such adventures, had grown by leaps and bounds, and the United States Navy had placed low-angled guns on a number of American ships so registered.[137] On 6 October, Dr. Arias decreed that vessels under Panamanian registry should not be armed. On the following morning he left for Havana, ostensibly to consult an eye-specialist, though more romantic motives were ascribed to his visit. He travelled in great secrecy under the name of A. Madrid and without having secured the necessary permission of the Supreme Court (while the National Assembly was in recess) to leave the country.

Whether the President, who was, after all, the virtual dictator of an admiring and subservient Assembly, anticipated a *coup d'état,* of which there had been rumours, must be a matter of conjecture. But his enemies, of whom there were many, and who may or may not have been emboldened by the thought of United States sympathy, were swift to see their advantage. Some of them meeting with members of the President's cabinet, it was decided that as Dr. Arias had left the country without permission, he must be replaced, and on 9 October, after a series of elaborate manoeuvres designed to preserve at least the appearance of legality, he was superseded by Dr. Ricardo Adolfo de la Guardia, the Minister of Government and Justice.[138] Naturally the United States was accused in Berlin and suspected elsewhere of instigating this palace revolution, and Cordell Hull hastened to issue a denial that she was in any way implicated.[139] But Dr. Arias's deposition[140] was greeted with relief both in the United States and, generally, in Panamá—except by General Franco's friends and allies and the numerous Germans who had entered the country in 1938 and 1939. The decree prohibiting the arming of merchant vessels was rescinded. A number of pro-Axis officials and sympathisers with Dr. Arias were arrested. The youth organization which he had founded was disbanded. The Spanish Minister, who had said that Panamá was under the 'Yankee boot', was declared *persona non grata,* and, despite the continuing discussions over the leases and the twelve points, the relations between Panamá and the United States were transformed. Panamá's declaration of war against the Axis powers in December became a matter of course, signalised by popular approval and an immediate intensification of security measures.

VIII

By mid-December 1941 the three island republics and the six states on the isthmus of Central America had all declared war on Japan, Germany and Italy. All, on 2 January, 1942, signed in Washington the Declaration of the United Nations,[141] undertaking to employ their full resources, military and economic, against the members of the Tripartite Pact and to make no separate peace or armistice; and all, by implication, subscribed to the principles of the Atlantic Charter. The three larger states of the Caribbean area, stopping short of belligerency, led the way among the Latin American nations in severing relations with the Axis Powers, Mexico and Colombia between the 8th and 19th December, Venezuela on the last day of the year.

In Venezuela General Isaías Medina Angarita had succeeded General López Contreras in the Presidency on 5 May, 1941.[142] Medina had been Minister of War. An *Andino* from the State of Táchira, as every Venezuelan President had been since 1899, he had pledged himself to continue López Contreras's social and economic policies, directed to the diversification of the economy, the development of industry and agriculture and the promotion of education, and he had promised also his whole-hearted collaboration in the defence of the western hemisphere, since 'nations living together must stick together.'[143] As the official candidate, his election by Congress —there was no popular election of the President—was a foregone conclusion. But the facts that López Contreras, who had supported a constitutional amendment reducing the presidential term from seven years to five, had no intention of trying to succeed himself, that a rival candidate, Rómulo Gallegos, a former Minister of Education and one of Latin America's most distinguished novelists, had been allowed complete latitude,[144] and that on 13 September a Law of Public Order gave legal recognition to political parties—all testified to the continuing liberalisation of political life. It was under this law that the clandestine *Partido Democrático* was re-organised as *Acción Democrática*, with Gallegos and Rómulo Betancourt, both to become Presidents of Venezuela, among its leaders. Betancourt had belonged to the 'generation of '28', the student generation which had rebelled against Gómez and had suffered for it, Gallegos to its mentors, and Betancourt had also been forced into hiding and residence abroad during the régime of López Contreras.

This slow unfolding of political life—too slow for *Acción Democrática*—had been accompanied by a rising tide of economic nationalism, with the foreign oil companies, of which Standard Oil of New Jersey and Royal Dutch Shell were the most important, as the principal targets of criticism. The oil industry had brought benefits to Venezuela. It had provided the major part of the Government's revenues. In 1940, when production was falling, because of the closure of European markets and a shortage of tankers, it still accounted for over 90 per cent of Venezuelan exports. The shortage was remedied in 1941, through the action of the United States, and output reached a record height. But despite the wealth which the oil industry had brought and was still bringing to Venezuela, it had resulted in an extraordinary disequilibrium in the country's economy. An agricultural country, Venezuela imported the half of her food stuffs. The cost of living was high, the standard low. Venezuela was in danger of finding herself in the position of King Midas, who had plenty of gold but nothing to eat,[145] and though there was no attempt at expropriation on the Mexican model, the demand that a greater share of the oil companies' revenues must remain in the country for productive purposes became increasingly insistent. The oil, in the current phrase, must be 'sown' to produce a more diversified economy.[146] Neither the State Department nor the Foreign Office, though they did not always see eye to eye, were unsympathetic to this view. Both held that the companies would be wise to make concessions, and both were anxious that nothing should arise to curtail the vital supplies of oil to Britain. This concern perhaps hastened also the conclusion in February 1942 of a long drawn-out negotiation for the partition of the oil-bearing submarine areas outside the limits of territorial waters between Trinidad and Venezuela; and, the Admiralty wishing to instal anti-submarine defences across the northern entry to the Gulf of Paria both in British and Venezuelan waters,[147] Britain further agreed to cede the small island of Patos, claimed by Venezuela but regarded by Britain as a dependency of Trinidad.

Venezuelan fortunes were so bound up with oil, most of it destined for the support of the Allied cause, that her neutrality was, in a sense almost nominal.[148] But, till the end of 1941, it was rigidly applied with the support of 'every influential element in the country'.[149] Venezuelans were unpleasantly conscious of their long, inadequately defended coastline and of the vulnerability of the bar at the entry to the Maracaibo oil field, and such was their caution that the Administration even refrained from public comment on President Roosevelt's statement of policy towards the belligerent powers, confining itself to expressions of approval of the idea of Pan American co-operation; and the press, though sometimes more outspoken, followed much the same line as the Administration. But there were limits. The Government presented a strongly worded protest to Germany and Italy over the sabotaging by their crews of three Italian tankers and one German freighter at Puerto Cabello, and Germans, Italians and their property were attacked by hostile crowds;[150] and rigid as the neutrality policy was, the bias of Venezuelan sympathies, traditionally more Francophile than Anglophile, in favour of the Allies was never in real doubt. Government and people, moreover, were well aware that the nearer the United States moved to war, the more difficult would neutrality become.

Despite complaints of the damage inflicted by the American and British Black Lists, and despite a lingering fear of an undue dependency on the United States, co-operation with the United States remained the corner stone of Venezuelan policy. In March, 1941, a United States naval mission replaced a former Italian mission. In October an economic mission to the United States presented a detailed and comprehensive exposition of Venezuela's import needs, which was at once passed to the United States Supply Priorities and Allocations Board, set up in August, for action,[151] and in December ex-President López Contreras had only just completed talks in

Washington on defence plans and the supply of armaments
when the attack on Pearl Harbour took place.[152] The Venezuelan reaction was unhesitating. The President instantly expressed his country's sympathy and solidarity with the United
States. The funds of the nationals of all Axis and Axis-
occupied countries were frozen. A decree of 12 December
stated that American countries at war with a non-American
state would not be treated as belligerents, and would therefore
not be subject to the effects of Venezuelan neutrality legislation. Diplomatic relations with the Axis countries were severed on 31 December and the *exequaturs* of German and
Italian consuls thereafter cancelled. And while, almost on the
eve of Pearl Harbour, Venezuela had permitted United States
planes on patrol duty to fly relatively freely over Venezuelan
territory,[153] in January the President declared that he would
welcome United States technicians who came to lay down new
air-fields under the Pan American Airports Corporation
programme.[154] A Defense Agreement, with the Caribbean
Defense Command on 15 January went still further, the United States Army undertaking to furnish three fully-manned
batteries to protect oil installations along the Venezuelan
coast.[155] Venezuela's reservations about so revolutionary a
proceeding were perhaps lessened by her first real experience
of the 'shooting war'. British troops had been landed at Aruba
and Curaçao on 10 May, 1940, to protect the oil refineries and
port installations.[156] They were relieved in February, 1942, by
United States troops with the agreement of the Netherlands
Government in exile and the assent also of Venezuela, which
undertook to collaborate, so far as practicable, in safeguarding
the islands. In the same month a German submarine shelled a
shore refinery at Aruba and six light-draft tankers which
carried oil across the bar at Maracaibo were torpedoed.[157]
One of them, the *Monagas*, was sailing under the Venezuelan
flag, and three Venezuelans were among the missing members
of the crew.[158] The 'Battle of the Caribbean' had begun. As
sinkings increased in 1942 oil production again fell, to rise to
new and ever greater heights as the battle was won.[159]

Colombia had also followed a policy of strict neutrality. But
the Colombian Government, like the Venezuelan, realised the
close correspondence of its interests with those of the United

States. As early as July, 1939, President Eduardo Santos had emphasised Colombia's obligations as a 'sure and loyal neighbour' to defend the security of the Panamá Canal. No one, he had said, would be allowed to menace it, directly or indirectly from Colombian soil[160]—an assurance that he more than once repeated. The Scadta airline, which, in the United States view, posed a potential threat to the canal, was 'de-Germanised' in June, 1940,[161] though many German pilots and other employees still remained in Colombia at the end of 1941, to be interned either in Colombia or in the United States in the following spring.[162] Both before and after the Havana Conference military staff talks between Colombia and the United States were held in a friendly atmosphere, with results generally satisfactory to the United States, though President Santos was careful to make it clear that the task of guarding Colombian territories and waters must remain in the hands of Colombians themselves, even if assisted by United States technical advisers.[163] The Government, in the view of American observers, was somewhat lax in its attitude to possible Axis activities, and a reference by President Roosevelt in a broadcast on 11 September, 1941, to the existence of secret German air-landing fields in Colombia within easy reach of the Panamá Canal provoked indignant denials. There was resentment, too, at the United States Proclaimed List.[164] But President Santos's whole-hearted support of Pan Americanism and his readiness to co-operate with the United States, much as he preferred informal to formal arrangements, were well-understood. Informally, in the summer of 1941, he agreed to allow relatively free flight privileges to United States planes over Colombian territory—a privilege still further extended early in 1942.[165] The United States, for her part, was prepared to assist Colombia in her economic difficulties by the Inter-American Coffee Agreement, by a credit of $10 millions in May, 1941, from the Export-Import Bank for highway and railway construction, and, once an agreement had been reached for a settlement of Colombia's outstanding obligations on her foreign bond issues of 1927 and 1928, by a loan of $12 million, some of it for defence expenditures. And in July, 1941, the United States presented a draft lend-lease agreement, which was not approved, however, till March 1942.[166]

But Colombian attitudes and sympathies were bedevilled by the violence of party politics, by the internecine war conducted between the two great parties, the Liberals and the Conservatives, and by the passionate interest already evident in 1940 in the presidential election due to take place in May 1942. The Conservatives and the Liberals were divided on almost every issue, domestic and foreign. The intemperate language of *El Siglo*, published by Dr. Laureano Gómez, the leader of the Conservative Party, its virulent anti-Liberalism, Anglo-phobia and Yankee-phobia, were probably unmatched in any other respectable Latin American newspaper. *El Siglo*, for example, declared in May, 1940, that Colombia, which had lost Panamá at the hands of the first Roosevelt, was not going to be dictated to by the second. Washington, it asserted, was dragging Latin America into war. The world was threatened by Churchill with the indefinite supremacy of Great Britain. Marshal Pétain was a man of destiny. In the European conflict neither side had right on its side, but England—the conclusion seemed inescapable from *El Siglo's* general line—had perhaps less right than Germany. As for Pan Americanism, it was a delusion. What the United States wanted was America for the North Americans, whereas the true aim of Colombia should be not Pan Americanism but Pan Hispanism.[167]

This extraordinary farrago of invective and nonsense was varied from time to time by a word of praise for Britain and of condemnation for Germany; and it is difficult to determine whether Dr. Gómez, who undoubtedly disliked and distrusted the United States, was or was not a Nazi sympathiser, whether his belief in *Hispanidad* and a Nationalist Spain led him impercetibly into sympathy with Italy and Germany, or whether he merely employed any stick, including foreign policy, to beat his Liberal opponents.[168] Even among his supporters the usual, but not invariable, tone of his newspaper was more than many of them could stomach, and some, at least, thought that his opinions were neither Catholic nor Conservative but totalitarian and anti-democratic.[169] His pacifist and Catholic sympathies, violently opposed to Communism and Soviet Russia, should not be pushed, they felt, to the point where they became pro-Nazi doctrines. But despite such criticism, Dr. Gómez's leadership of his party remained, if not unchallenged at least not seriously in doubt. Ultimately he was to attain the Presidency, but not till 1949.

But it was not the Conservative views which prevailed in Colombia but the Liberal; and the opinions of Dr. Santos's paper, *El Tiempo*, were the exact opposite of *El Siglo's*. Not only did Dr. Santos and the Liberals believe that Pan American solidarity was the foundation of sound policy; they agreed also that a German victory in Europe would be a direct menace to America. London and Churchill, declared *El Tiempo*, were the bulwarks of liberty. It feared that without the direct intervention of the United States England might perish from exhaustion; and, holding with Roosevelt, that Britain was America's first line of defence,[170] it warmly approved of United States aid to Britain.

It is true that the Liberals were themselves divided between the supporters of Dr. Santos and those of his predecessor, Dr. Alfonso López. Dr. López was a left-wing Liberal, Dr. Santos a right-wing Liberal. But there was no fundamental difference on foreign policy between their followers, though López himself was critical of Santos and, before he attained the Presidency for a second time in August, 1942, somewhat ambivalent in his attitude towards the United States. But when the Japanese attack on Pearl Harbour took place, Liberals of all complexions supported the President in severing relations with Japan on 8 December and with Germany and Italy on the 19th, and so did the country at large. Colombia did not declare war, so Santos explained, because she was not a military power who could make the weight of her forces felt.[171] But she was, *El Tiempo* declared, 'with the United States to the end'.[172] Late in December non-belligerent status was accorded to those American nations which had declared war. The German Transocean news agency was closed. Special powers were given to the police to dissolve clubs and associations whose activities were contrary to public order and to place potentially dangerous persons under surveillance. And in January, 1942, controls, later extended, were established over the assets of Axis citizens and those of Axis-controlled countries.[173]

IX

The polarisation of politics was less spectacular in Mexico than in Colombia. The spectrum of political opinions was indeed wide. It ranged from such bodies as the Revolutionary Anti-Communist Party (P.R.A.C.), the *Unión Nacional Sinarquista*, and *Acción Nacional* (P.A.N.) on the Right to the Trotskyites and the Stalinists on the Left. The *Sinarquistas*, as their name implied, stood for 'order', opposed the United States, Protestantism, Liberalism and Communism, appealed to the religious and conservative instincts of the backward peasantry, more especially in a number of the western and central Mexican states, and were organised on militaristic lines.[174] *Acción Nacional*, formed in 1939, drew its strength from the middle and upper classes in the urban centres of the north and west of the country, opposed the concept of *Hispanidad* to that of Pan Americanism and condemned the Mexican Revolution as an 'inventory of ruin and disasters'. Both organizations had leanings towards the Spanish *Falange*, officially frowned upon in Mexico, which welcomed, instead, Spanish republican refugees. The Communists, vociferous and irresponsible, were divided among themselves but united in regarding the Pan American Union as an 'instrument of oppression'[175] and the war (till June 1941) as an imperialist war. They had reaped much popular and governmental hostility, particularly after the murder of Trotsky, to whom President Cárdenas had given refuge, by a Stalinist agent in August, 1940.

But these were peripheral parties. The dominant and deeply entrenched political machine was the Party of the Mexican Revolution (P.R.M.) which Cárdenas had consolidated on the foundations of the most powerful of Latin American labour unions, the C.T.M. or Confederation of Mexican Workers, its rural equivalent, the National Peasant Confederation (C.N.C.) the Army, and a less regimented urban 'popular' sector.[176] None of these 'sectors' was Communist, though there were Communists and fellow-travellers within them. But Cárdenas's remarkable presidential term was drawing to an end, and he had no intention of flouting the revolutionary slogan of 'effective suffrage and no re-election'. He proposed, instead, to leave politics and to retire, in Roman fashion, to his farm.

The year 1940 was, therefore, an election year in Mexico as well as in the United States. It was hardly likely that the official presidential nominee, General Manuel Avila Camacho, who had been Secretary of War and of the Navy, would fail to be elected. But he had a strong opponent in General Juan Almazán, an old-time revolutionary general, now wealthy and conservative, who was supported by the anti-government forces generally, including, oddly enough, Trotsky's one-time host, the far from conservative painter, Diego Rivera. The election itself, on 7th July, was marked by wide-spread interest and stained by violence and bloodshed, and, the *Almazanistas* charging fraud, a period of great tension followed in which there were well-grounded fears of civil war. But Almazán's bark was worse than his bite. His disillusioned supporters, vainly hoping for encouragement from the United States, lost heart, and on 1 December Avila Camacho was peacefully inaugurated. It was notable that Vicente Lombardo Toledano, the powerful (and controversial) Secretary of the C.T.M.,[177] the Archbishop of Mexico[178] and, last but not least, President Roosevelt,[179] all gave him their support.

With this event the long history of the Mexican Revolution entered a new phase—the phase of consolidation. Its advent could be discerned during the last days of Cárdenas, who severely rebuked the labour syndicates both in the national railways and in the nationalised oil industry for putting their own before the national interest, denounced the Communists, and threatened to declare a proposed oil strike illegal. It became explicit when Avila Camacho declared that the time had come to consolidate the achievements of the Revolution, to build on the gains already won, and to fortify Mexico's friendship with the United States.[180] The right-wing hoped for, and the left-wing feared, a complete break with the Cárdenas régime. But their hopes and fears were alike unrealised. Reforms were introduced into the land laws with the intent of giving to the peasant a definite, though limited, title to land and increasing the number of peasant proprietors. The Government took over from the workers the administration of the national railways, which had been in a state of chaos. Soldiers on active servive were forbidden to participate in the P.R.M. and judges of the Supreme Court were given life-tenure. The

Communists, the President declared, must travel alone. But there was no weakening in the stand taken over the expropriated oil companies, no radical change in the revolutionary programme of land distribution, no attempt to eliminate the system of collective cultivation so dear to Cárdenas's heart, no repudiation of the need for a directed economy. The workers still retained a say on the managing board of the railways, and the right to strike was not seriously curtailed. Constantly appealing for 'sacrifice and sobriety', the 'unknown soldier', as Avila Camacho had derisively been called, successfully steered a middle course between left and right and, more than any of its predecessors his régime deserved, by its close, to be called a régime of national unity.

The presence of Vice-President-Elect Henry Wallace at Avila Camacho's inauguration, and his enthusiastic reception,[181] were signs of that growing rapprochment between Mexico and the United States which, also, had characterised the last days of Cárdenas. Mexico, in the nineteen-thirties, had consistently opposed fascism in all its forms, German, Italian, Spanish. She had condemned German rearmament in 1935, had urged that sanctions against Italy in 1936 should include an oil embargo, and had protested against the invasion of Austria in 1938. But 1938 was the year in which most of the foreign oil companies were expropriated; diplomatic relations with Britain had been severed; and, as a result of the boycott of Mexican oil imposed by the companies, Mexico had been forced to look for markets in Germany, Italy and Japan.[182] It was perhaps not surprising that on the outbreak of war Mexican neutrality had been tinged with cynicism, while, in left-wing circles, whether Communist or not, the view tended to prevail that there was little to choose between one side and the other.

Roosevelt, shortly before the war had begun, had written to Cárdenas suggesting that 'all matters of difference' between Mexico and the United States should be resolved, and, negotiations with the oil companies having reached a stalemate, that the dispute itself should be referred to impartial arbitration.[183] But though Cárdenas was himself well-disposed and alive to the need of continental solidarity, he was alive also to the residual fears in Mexico of the United States and the fierce isolationism of organised labour. Nor did he favour arbitration of what he regarded as a domestic issue. Nothing came of Roosevelt's suggestion, and when, on 3 April, 1940, the State Department, in a formal note, renewed the proposal for international arbitration, there was a storm of protest in the Mexican press; the conventional attacks on the oil companies were renewed; arbitration was declared to be an insult to Mexican sovereignty and dignity; and the proposal was rejected.[184] At much the same time the Government had the satisfaction of announcing that a financial settlement had been reached with the Sinclair Oil Company,[185] thus destroying the companies' united front. As for the other American companies, of which Standard Oil of New Jersey was the largest, the Mexican Ambassador in Washington proposed early in June that Mexico and the United States should each appoint a commissioner who would jointly evaluate the remaining properties and determine the method of compensation.[186]

The matter so rested till the Mexican elections and their aftermath were over. Meanwhile, with the Battle of France, Mexican foreign policy had undergone a dramatic change. Already in May Cárdenas, seeing the writing on the wall, had proposed the introduction of compulsory military service — a measure endorsed by his cabinet in June and by Congress in August.[187] Early in June the Under-Secretary for Foreign Affairs, Ramón Beteta, had let it be known that Mexico would like to come to an understanding with Britain.[188] On the 9th Cárdenas broadcast an appeal to all the American republics for a united defensive front.[189] On the 10th he sent a message of sympathy to President Albert Lebrun condemning Italy's entry into the war, and on the 12th he ordered the expulsion of the German press attaché, Arthur Dietricht.[190] Lombardo Toledano, on the same day, in what was derisively called his 'New Testament', told the Confederation of Latin American Workers that it was the duty of all workers to fight Fascism and that their relations with the United States were daily growing more cordial,[191] though this pronouncement by no means implied that his suspicions of the United States and of 'democratic imperialism' were removed.

Faced with an increasingly difficult economic situation and

an apparent choice between a Nazified Europe and collaboration with the United States, Mexico did not hesitate. In conversations with United States Army and Navy staff representatives the Mexican Ambassador in Washington declared on 11 June that Mexico was 'prepared unreservedly to collaborate with the United States in plans for the common defense' and to develop air and naval bases at places chosen strategically 'not only from the purely national point of view but from the broader point of view of hemisphere defense', though he pointed out that the necessary basis for joint military action in an emergency was a general political agreement.[192] Conversations were renewed after the July elections, and though no formal agreements were entered into in 1940, it was a sign of changing times that Cárdenas in September formally repeated his belief in the necessity of friendship with the United States and, while attacking the oil companies for what he called their campaign of defamation, expressed his willingness to resume diplomatic relations with Britain since Mexico was 'spiritually on the side of the democracies'[193], and that the organ of the P.R.M. could observe in October that England had certain secret weapons — 'her men, women and children'.[194]

Given the importance of Mexico in hemisphere defence and her increasing sympathy for the Allied cause, the time was now fast approaching when the United States could no longer allow any difficulties between the two countries to remain unsettled, if they were capable of settlement.[195] Even before the new Administration had taken office Sumner Welles had spoken to the Mexican Ambassador in Washington of a comprehensive settlement of all outstanding claims and disputes which had accumulated over the years of the Revolution.[196] Both Avila Camacho and his new Foreign Secretary, Ezequiel Padilla, were strong protagonists of Pan American cooperation, and Avila Camacho, like the United States, was anxious to see Mexico's air and naval defences strenghtened.[197] There was talk in December of establishing a Joint Defense Commission, similar to the Canadian-American Commission, and in February, 1941, further air, naval and military conversations were begun in Washington.[198] To continue throughout the year, they were revealed by Padilla to the press and to the Senate in March when he forthrightly declared that Mexico would consider any aggression against an American country as an attack on herself, and his statements were re-iterated by the President in May, though, in reply to questions from Lombardo Toledano, Avila Camacho was careful to add that no secret agreements existed with the United States and that Mexico would never lease or cede any of her territory to a foreign power[199] — a plain reference to the United States' wish for naval bases. A flight agreement, however, allowing United States naval and military aircraft en route to the Panamá Canal to use Mexican landing fields for twenty-four hours became effective in April.[200] In the same month the Government seized ten Italian and two German ships lying idle in the ports of Vera Cruz and Tampico. In July it rejected as 'imperious and unacceptable' a German note protesting against Mexico's 'resigned acceptance' of the United States' Black List; it cancelled in August the *exequaturs* of all German consular officers in retaliation for the eviction of the Mexican *chargé d'affaires* at Paris and the shutting of Mexican honorary consulates in German-occupied territory; and it supported in November a Chilean protest against the execution of French hostages by the Germans.[201]

The conclusion, on 15 July, of a commercial agreement under which the United States undertook to buy the entire surplus output of eleven Mexican strategic materials[202] and to provide the greatest possible facilities for the export of those products most needed for Mexican industry, and on 19 November, after months of patient negotiation (and mounting exasperation in the State Department at the intransigence of the oil companies), of a comprehensive settlement of all outstanding problems, finally placed the relations between the two Governments on a firm basis of friendship and co-operation.[203] By a series of agreements the United States promised financial assistance to stabilise the Mexican peso, to buy Mexican silver in large quantities, to furnish loans and credits for the completion of the Mexican portion of the Pan American Highway, and to negotiate a trade treaty. Mexico undertook to pay $40 million in settlement of general and agrarian claims — the latter for expropriated land-holdings — of American citizens. As for the oil dispute, a joint commission of two experts was to be set up to value the expropriated properties and recommend the amount and method of compensation. The companies were recalcitrant to the last. But the State Department was now adamant. The experts' recommendations were made, and accepted on 19 April, 1942, much to the anger of the companies. Some slight modifications followed, but, with the settlement, [204] a long and difficult chapter in United States-Mexican relations was closed.

Exactly four weeks before the Mexican-United States agreements of 19 November were signed diplomatic relations between Britain and Mexico were resumed. The State Department had long urged such a resumption upon the British Government. Both in 1940 and in 1941 hints had been dropped by Mexican officials at home and abroad that Mexico would welcome it, and in March, 1941, Sr. Padilla went so far as to tell the British Consul-General that he would 'gladly see a renewal of diplomatic relations' and that Britain enjoyed the whole-hearted sympathy of the Mexican Government. Lord Halifax wrote from Washington in May that it seemed 'absurd when the Mexicans, whose natural sympathies are all on the side of the democracies, are offering us their friendship we should not take advantage of this'. The Ministry of Economic Warfare and the Department of Overseas Trade were strongly in favour.[205] But the Foreign Office long held back. It feared that a resumption of relations might have unfortunate effects on oil supplies from Venezuela and Iran and be regarded by them as a tacit acceptance of the principle of expropriation.[206] It hesitated to do anything which might impair the united front of the American companies and of Royal Dutch Shell, of which Mexican Eagle was a subsidiary, and it hoped that Mexico would yet agree to restore to the companies a measure of administrative control. But this was to live in cloud-cuckoo land. By the end of August the Foreign Office had begun to realise that its fears were exaggerated and its hopes were vain, and, understanding that the United States was about to reach a general settlement with Mexico which it would impose on the oil companies, it decided to wait no longer.[207] On 22 October an identical statement of the renewal of relations was made both in the British and the Mexican press and heartily welcomed in Mexico, though Bri-

tain reserved her position over the oil dispute. The new British
Minister (soon to be raised to the rank of Ambassador) presented his credentials on 6 February, 1942, when Avila
Camacho expressed his great admiration for Churchill and
the complete adherence of his government to the Allied
cause.[208] But it was not till September 1947, after seemingly
endless negotiations, that an agreement was reached for the
indemnification of Mexican Eagle, which had operated the
rich Poza Rica field. The debt was finally and completely
discharged by 1962.[209]

With this healing of old sores and with, also, the *volte face* of
the militant left in Mexico after the German invasion of Soviet
Russia, the way was open for complete collaboration between
Mexico and the United States, and it came at a vitally important moment in the history of both countries. On 7 December
1941, Mexico severed relations with Japan and on the 11th
with Germany and Italy, freezing also Axis funds. The cause
of the United States, declared the President, was the cause of
America; Lombardo Toledano telegraphed a message of support to President Roosevelt in the name of the workers of
Latin America; and the organ of the C.T.M. declared that the
time had come 'to work, to produce, to produce'.[210] On the
24th the Senate assented to a Presidential message opening
Mexican ports and airfields to United States military and
naval planes and on 12 January 1942 a Joint United States-
Mexican Defense Commission was at last established.[211]
Mexico, Avila Camacho explained to the new British Minister, felt unable to enter the war because of the unprepared
state of her army and the sparsity of her population. But she
was determined to do the next best thing and to place her
resources at the disposal of those who were fighting the
Axis.[212] Nevertheless her entry into the war was not long to be
delayed. It came on 30 May 1942 after Mexican tankers had
been sunk by German submarines; and Mexico was one of the
two Latin American states to send forces abroad. The 201
Fighter Squadron was ordered to Luzon in March 1945, and
from there took part in the bombing of Japanese installations
in the Philippines and in Formosa.[213]

IV

SOUTH OF THE EQUATOR

By the end of 1941 every American state north of the equator was either at war with the Axis powers or had severed relations with them. South of it no such action had been taken. Chile, on 9 December, had indeed seized the initiative among the Latin American states in asking for a consultative meeting of American Foreign Ministers, the United States making a like request on the same day and expressing the wish that the meeting should be held at the earliest possible moment. An agenda had been approved by the Governing Board of the Pan American Union; the meeting, in accordance with the decisions taken at Havana, was to be held at Rio de Janeiro; and the eight as yet non-aligned countries—Ecuador, Perú, Bolivia, Paraguay, Uruguay, Brazil, Argentina and Chile—preferred to await its outcome rather than to act individually and without general consultation. Each of these countries had its own pre-occupations, and two of them, Ecuador and Perú, had only recently been at war and were still in a state of suspended hostilities.

I

Ecuador, of course, lay not only below the equator but upon it. Her President, Dr. Carlos Arroyo del Río, had taken office in September, 1940, with the declared intention of putting an end to the 'political orgy' in which his country had so long lived.[1] After a stormy interval, in which at least three revolts had been attempted, between his election and his installation, the most sensational episode had been the breaking of the windows of the presidential palace during riots at Quito in January, 1941, riots mainly attributed to discontent among the working classes and to the supporters of one of the defeated presidential candidates, Dr. Velasco Ibarra.[2] But the President seemed to have survived less by the intrinsic strength of his government than by the dissensions among its opponents, and not only did his political position remain precarious, he was confronted with serious economic difficulties—a fall in cacao exports, due to the ravages of the witch-broom disease as well as the loss of European markets, a shortage of shipping, and financial stringency. The United States had provided help by a grant of credits from the Export-Import Bank to develop roads and railways and for agricultural research, and negotiations for further aid were in progress in 1941. Ecuador had everything to gain and nothing to lose by collaboration with the United States.

Governmental and popular opinion (if much meaning can be attached to the word 'popular') shared this view, except among entrenched conservatives. Nor was there any great liking for Germany, Italy or Japan. Japan, indeed, had long been a bug-bear on the Pacific coast and was especially obnoxious in Ecuador because Japanese textiles undercut Ecuadorean. Besides anti-Japanese demonstrations in June, 1940, there had been press campaigns against Japanese competition both in August, 1940, and in April, 1941. The press, much to the indignation of the Italian Ambassador, who made a formal protest in January, 1941,[3] had shown itself markedly unfriendly to Italy also, and though there had long been an Italian Military Mission, this left in November, 1940, to be replaced by Military Aviation and Naval Missions from the United States. As for Germany, Congress held so-called secret sessions in August and September, 1940, to investigate Nazi activities, more particularly those of the Transocean news-agency, the Sedta Air Line and the German College in Quito.[4] The Transocean offices were wrecked in January, 1941; the Director was expelled in June; and the agency itself was closed in December. Sedta, however, had given good service (as well as free rides). The Government was reluctant to disband it, despite United States pressure, but refused in July, 1940, to sanction an extension of its services to the Galápagos Islands,[5] and the line was eventually driven out of business in September, 1941, by the competition of Pan American Grace and the with-holding of American-controlled oil-supplies.

For the United States the prime importance of Ecuador lay in her relative proximity to the Panamá Canal and her owner-

ship of the Galápagos Islands. The islands, of which Albermarle, or Isabella, is the largest, are only some one thousand
miles south-west of Panamá, and their potential value for
radar-station sites, sea-plane bases and air-fields was obvious.
In 1940 and early in 1941 it was rumoured that the United
States was seeking bases in the islands and that Ecuador
would not be averse from granting facilities on them—
rumours officially denied in both countries. The State Department and President Roosevelt were well aware of the im-
policy, in the light of South American susceptibilities in general
and the delicate problem of Ecuadorean-Peruvian relations in
particular, of giving a handle to criticism.[6] Roosevelt, however, did make various proposals for establishing a sort of collective protectorate over the islands. That failing, a further suggestion was to make use of the Pacific Development Company
of Delaware, which, with the aid of federal funds, had been
seeking, since November, 1940, concessionary fishing and
mining rights from private owners on Albermarle Island. But
the owners, it appeared, held only a fraction of the land which
would be required, and by September, 1941, not only had the
Company's affairs become public but the Ecuadorean Secretary of Public Administration denied all knowledge of its
rights. Finally, late in 1941, the Navy Department having
already received permission in October to use the Galápagos
as a patrol base and to enter Ecuadorean ports, the State
Department began formal negotiations for a formal agreement
providing for naval facilities on the islands and a base on the
mainland as well.[7]

The attack on Pearl Harbour, which heightened Ecuadorean fears for the safety of the islands and put an end to State
Department objections that a Galápagos base would offend
Perú, was a clinching argument. President Arroyo de Río,
who had been given extraordinary powers for a second time
within the year, at once declared Ecuador's solidarity with the
United States. He also offered to allow the United States to
erect installations and make use of facilities in the Galápagos,
and an advance unit of a United States naval force was on its
way to them in a British steamer within a week. In January,
1942, moreover, work was begun on the construction of a joint
army and naval base at Salinas near the entrance to the

harbour of Guayaquil, though it was not till March, 1942, that the President announced that Ecuador was co-operating with the United States in its establishment, not till May that the facilities in the Galápagos became effective, and not till September that Ecuadoreans officially learned of their existence.[8]

Peruvian and Ecuadorean policies had moved on parallel lines. President Manuel Prado, representing the wealthier and more privileged classes in Perú, had assumed office in the same year as President Arroyo del Río. Personally popular, he had met with little active opposition. Even Apra, though it was still outside the law and its leader, Haya de la Torre, declared in July, 1940, that democracy did not exist in Perú (an incontrovertible statement), remained relatively quiescent, Haya de la Torre calling for an Indo-American Union of Defence in alliance with the United States and declaring that a Nazi victory in Europe would mean the end of civilization and liberty,[9] and President Prado proclaiming his support of United States policies and of inter-American co-operation.[10] As in Ecuador there was no love lost for the Japanese, and, as in Ecuador, and at much the same time, there were anti-Japanese riots in Lima and other cities. Though the *Limeño* aristocracy had long cultivated ties of friendship with the Spanish nobility and with Italy, neither Italians nor Germans had gained much popularity among the middle and lower ranks of society. Immigration was suspended in May, 1940. A new Naturalisation Law in June was intended to prevent the abuse of double nationality. The issue of identity cards was tightened up[11] and a Law of National Security in August forbade the diffusion of anti-democratic doctrines and the use of uniforms and signs.[12] By the end of the year the Italian mission for training the police had been dismissed and an Italian air-mission cancelled; arrangements were being made for the expropriation of the Caproni Airways Factory, though it was long before they became effective; and both Houses of Congress had demanded that the operational permit for *Luft-hansa Perú* should be withdrawn. By contrast, a contract for a United States Naval Mission had been renewed and another for a Military Aviation Mission signed. In April, 1941, the authorities attempted to seize five German ships loaded with cotton and petroleum. Three were set on fire by their crews. Two, belatedly pursued by Peruvian cruisers, escaped to sea, were intercepted by the Canadian auxiliary cruiser, *Prince Henry*, and were also fired by their crews. The Government promptly attached the funds of the North German Lloyd and Kosmos Companies, closed the Transocean news-agency, sequestrated the planes of *Lufthansa Perú* and seized its ground properties.[13]

Like Ecuador, Perú had been beset by economic difficulties —shipping and other shortages, market losses, rising living costs. She was mainly dependent on her exports of cotton, wool and sugar, deriving merely an export tax on petroleum and mineral exports. Chile had taken more Peruvian sugar and Japan large quantities of cotton at high prices, her trade increasing both in 1940 and 1941. But Britain, formerly a major customer, had reduced her cotton purchases in 1940 and still more in 1941, and her export restrictions were beginning to be severely felt at the end of 1941. The United States, on the other hand, bought more wool than usual and the Metals Reserve Company contracted in October, 1941, to buy Peruvian strategic materials, Perú agreeing to confine any other sales to countries of the western hemisphere, except for British purchases of molybdenum.[14] The British Minister, Courtenay Forbes, expressed the opinion, early in 1942, that Perú, in common with the rest of Ibero-America, would become 'largely dependent on United States charity for her economic existence.'[15]

Anxious to develop home industries, including a steel plant at Chimbote, and to press forward with road construction (she had completed her section of the Pan American highway)[16], it was inevitably to the United States that Perú looked for economic aid, and she did not look in vain. Aid (in the form of loans) had been made available in 1940,[17] and more was to be given in 1942. If doubts about such economic dependency remained, the attack on Pearl Harbour and fears for the country's safety silenced them. The Japanese colony in Perú was much larger than in Ecuador and the Peruvian coast line was equally exposed. The Government had already agreed to grant port facilities for United States naval patrol vessels and had been persuaded to improve an air-field at Talara, where the petroleum installations were unprotected.[18] In August the Chamber of Deputies (like the Ecuadorean Congress) had solemnly approved the Atlantic Charter, with its repudiation of all hegemonies and of territorial and other aggrandisement, and had invited American legislatures to form a united front in support of democracy and to intensify methods of defence.[19] On the day after Pearl Harbour the leading newspaper, *El Comercio*, whose owners, the Miró Quesada family, had long been suspected, rightly or wrongly, of being Nazi sympathisers at heart, declared that 'it is the part of the Latin Americans in this grave hour to make the United States feel the warmth of their continental solidarity; and to come to an agreement as to how to afford to the great republic of the north the most efficient material and moral support with the object of contributing to the triumph of the nation on which now depend the destinies of America'. The Government froze Japanese funds, established coastal patrols and strengthened guards on airports, and President Prado, like President Arroyo del Río, sent a personal message of sympathy to President Roosevelt, while the Minister of Foreign Affairs said that Perú would sever relations with Japan at once if she only knew what to do with her large Japanese population.[20]

What had gravely embarrassed the relations of the United States both with Ecuador and Perú, though Pearl Harbour helped to clear the air, had been the frontier dispute between the two countries. This concerned a relatively small area on the Pacific coast in the region of Tumbes and some 120,000 square miles of territory not fully explored east of the Andes and north of the Marañon, itself a main tributary of the Amazon. The dispute was of long standing and had defied many attempts at mediation or arbitration. Frontier incidents multiplied in 1940 and 1941 and in May, 1941, the United States, Brazil and Argentina offered their 'friendly services', though without prior consultation with the two disputants, in order to avert what Sumner Welles called 'the most serious element of danger today in the entire western hemisphere'. The offer, welcomed by Ecuador, but accepted by Perú only with far-reaching reservations,[21] coincided with the announcement that the United States was selling two coastguard cutters to Ecuador, a matter of little moment, but one which was followed in October by the seizure in New York of eighteen Douglas bombers which Perú had bought in Canada with British and American consent from the Royal Norwegian Government but which the United States War Department commandeered.[22]

Meanwhile war between Perú and Ecuador had begun in earnest on 5 July, each side accusing the other of responsibility for the conflict. The United States, which, of course, would furnish no weapons of any description to either party while hostilities were in progress, now found that far from being blessed as a peace-maker, she reaped nothing but odium, first in Perú, where President Roosevelt was actually hissed in the cinemas, and then in Ecuador. The one country was alive with rumours that the United States intended to sacrifice Perú to Ecuador at the price of the Galápagos Islands, the other contrasted the apathy with which she regarded 'aggression' against Ecuador with her war-like gestures in other regions of the world.[23] For Ecuador, with much inferior forces, the war inevitably went badly, and, though mediation was again offered, it was not till 2 October that the military commanders, in the presence of observers representing the mediators, agreed to a truce. So matters rested, Perú continuing to occupy not only disputed but undisputed Ecuadorean territory in a temporary stalemate. The mediating powers, now joined by Chile, renewed their efforts to secure a settlement during the Rio de Janeiro Conference of American Foreign Ministers in January, 1942, and a Protocol of Peace, Friendship and Boundaries was signed on 29 January. The territory on the Pacific coast was subjected to a Solomon's judgment, while of the vast area known as the Ecuadorean *Oriente* Perú was put in possession of by far the most valuable part, completely excluding Ecuador from riparian rights on the Marañon-Amazon river system. Ecuador ceased to be, in any sense, an 'Amazonian power'.[24] Washington was greatly relieved. Perú regarded the outcome as a definitive settlement. In Ecuador feeling ran high, and though the Protocol was accepted in 1942, it was denounced in 1960.

II

With no exposed coast-line unlike Perú and Ecuador, but isolated in the heart of South America, Bolivia might have been thought to be removed from the tides of inter-American, and still more of extra-American, conflict. But her stores of minerals, more especially of tin, but also of tungsten, antimony, copper and lead, necessarily involved her in international concern, and, cut off from the sea as she was, her central geographic position, her frontiers marching with those of five countries, could conceivably have made her a strategic pawn in an Axis game. With a long and violent tradition of political instability, she had only recently passed through an era of erratic, nationalistic and socialistic military rule, marked by strong authoritarian tendencies and the rise of left-wing nationalist movements. The German legation was over-staffed;[25] German propaganda had been and remained prolific;[26] and in April, 1939, a few months before his mysterious suicide, the then President, Colonel Busch, had appealed for Nazi support in establishing a totalitarian state.[27] Busch, dead, was to become a father figure in a new *Movimiento Nacionalista Revolucionaria* (M.N.R.), of which Víctor Paz Estenssoro, a Socialist deputy, was the effective founder, and which, modelled on national-socialist lines, was anti-semitic, anti-American, anti-'imperialist', and, initially at least, pro-Axis in outlook.[28] Under the provisional government of General Carlos Quintanilla, however, elections for both houses of the legislature and for the presidency had taken place in March, 1940, and, though there had been attempted *coups d'état* both before and after the elections, the country, much to the relief of the old oligarchy, had returned, however precariously, to 'democratic' civilian government with the installation of General Enrique Peñaranda in the Presidency in April.

Peñaranda's government, which had a substantial majority in the Senate but not in the Chamber, represented the parties of the right, centre and moderate left. Corrupt and inefficient as it turned out to be, however good its original intentions, it sought, as indeed its predecessors had done, to strengthen political and economic relations with surrounding nations, to improve both internal and external communications, and to foster the development of natural resources. The Foreign Minister, Alberto Ostria Gutiérrez, played a prominent part in the Regional Economic Conference of the River Plate countries in January and February, 1941,[29] negotiating also a number of conventions with Argentina, Uruguay and Paraguay. In particular Bolivia had agreed with Brazil in 1938 on the construction of a railway from the Brazilian city of Corumbá on the Paraguay River to Santa Cruz de la Sierra at the foot of the Andes—a section of what it was hoped would become a transcontinental line from Santos on the Atlantic to Arica on the Pacific.[30] A convention with Argentina was now designed to hasten the construction of a line, also to Santa Cruz, through Bolivia's oil-bearing region, from the Argentine frontier town of Yacuiba. Towards the European war the Government's policy was one of strict neutrality, but it professed also a firm belief in co-operation and understanding between all American nations.[31]

From an economic point of view co-operation with American nations meant, more especially, co-operation with the United States. In November, 1940, the Metals Reserve Company had signed a contract for tin-ores and concentrates not sold (as the greater proportion was) to the United Kingdom,[32] and thereafter the construction of a tin-smelter was begun at Texas City. On 20 May, 1941, in the face of intense Japanese competition, the Company arranged to buy the entire output of Bolivian tungsten over the next three years.[33] But Bolivia wanted more than markets for her metals. Even before Peñaranda's election a plan had been proposed to the United States, in December, 1939, for various kinds of aid, technical and financial; and the State Department had not been unsympathetic. But there was a difficulty. No compensation had yet been proposed for the seizure in 1937, during the era of 'military socialism', of the properties of the Standard Oil Company of New Jersey.[34] There was no question of the return of the Company's properties. Bolivian nationalism would not have tolerated this, nor did the State Department expect it. But the Department did hold that the Company was entitled to compensation. For its part, the Bolivian Government, according to the American Minister, Douglas Jenkins, was 'overwhelmingly' in favour, in December, 1940, of some kind of settlement, and in March, 1941, the Senate approved its attitude. The Chamber, however, adjourned in April without taking any action, and there were riots in La Paz at the mere suggestion of accommodation, together with violent opposition from the M.N.R.[35]

Meanwhile, compounding the danger that the Standard Oil dispute might become a 'festering sore'[36] in United States-Bolivian relations, German propaganda remained intense, and there had long been rumours of German 'immigrants' arriving through Perú by way of Siberia and Japan, of German sympathies among Bolivian army officers, of possible *coups d'état*, and of the establishment of a pro-Axis government.[37] In April Ostria Gutiérrez himself told Jenkins that the German Foreign Office was sending communications in the German legation's pouch (conveyed across the Atlantic, of course, by the Italian air-line, Lati) to Bolivian army officers and others from the Bolivian Military Attaché in Berlin, Major Elías Belmonte, formerly a Minister of Government during the Busch régime, and that the German Minister, Ernst Wendler, did his best to deliver them. In the opinion of Jenkins, opposition to the Government was being 'encouraged and assisted in every possible way by the Germans', who were bent 'on destroying American influence in this part of the world, if they can'.[38] Similar information of the abuse of the diplomatic bag was given by Ostria Gutiérrez to the British Minister, who was asked whether Britain 'could help in the matter', British assistance having earlier been sought to prevent Belmonte's return to Bolivia.[39]

There seems little reason to doubt that the Peñaranda régime, and certainly Ostria Gutiérrez, feared a totalitarian-minded *coup d'état* in 1941.[40] In May, after prolonged negotiations with the United States, it at last took action against *Lloyd Aéreo Boliviano*, whose headquarters were at Cochabamba, the second largest city in the country and a supposed centre of disaffection. The line was nationalised on 14 May[41] and its German personnel was dismissed a few days before the signing of the tungsten contract with the United States. A month later the President declared that 'rumours of Nazi activities were not unfounded' and the Chief of Staff that a 'frankly subversive spirit' was abroad.[42] Struggling with grave economic problems—food shortages, inflated prices and the like —the Government sought to strengthen its hand[43] by offering the Ministry of Economy to Paz Estenssoro himself. But the manoeuvre was unsuccessful. Paz Estenssoro resigned within a week. Then, on 18 July, Jenkins gave Ostria Gutiérrez a photocopy of what purported to be a letter from Belmonte to Wendler, dated the 9th June. Jenkins was careful to say that though the source from which the letter was obtained deserved every confidence, the State Department could not vouch for the authenticity of Belmonte's signature because it had never before seen it. The Bolivian Acting Chief of Staff and others familiar with the signature, however, had no hesitation in doing so.[44]

'Friends in the Wilhelmstrasse', ran the letter in part, 'tell me that from information received from you the moment is approaching to strike our blow to liberate my poor country from a weak government of completely capitalistic tendencies. I go much further and believe that the *coup* should take place in the middle of July. . . .' It declared that Cochabamba should be the focal point of the rising, that the tungsten contract with the United States must be cancelled and the tin contracts with Britain and the United States modified, that 'the surrender of our airlines to the interests of Wall Street' was an act of treason, that Bolivia needed work and discipline, and that Belmonte himself awaited the signal to arrive by air to begin the task of freeing first Bolivia and then the whole of South America from 'Yankee influence'.[45]

The Government acted at once. A state of siege was instituted on the 19th. The German Minister was declared *persona non grata* and asked to leave the country as soon as possible. A number of officers and civilians, several of them prominent members of the M.N.R., were arrested, imprisoned or exiled to Santa Cruz de la Sierra, Paz Estenssoro, however, enjoying parliamentary immunity. Belmonte was dismissed for 'treason', remaining in Germany in close touch with the Wilhelmstrasse till 1944, when he went to Spain.[46] Three M.N.R. or Socialist journals, *La Calle*, *Busch* and *Inti*, were suspended, though the ban on *Inti* was soon lifted, and the alleged Belmonte letter was published in the press. Naturally, but correctly, its authenticity was denied by Wendler, Belmonte and the German Foreign Office, and, during a series of acrimonious debates in the Chamber in late August and early September, it was denounced as a British forgery (which it was), carried out with the connivance of the Foreign Minister himself. Indeed, what Ostria Gutiérrez called the 'pro-Nazi' press accused him, so soon as opportunity offered, of manufacturing it personally. Given the disturbed state of the country, the state of siege was prolonged till late October. But the Chamber itself, early in September, voted in favour of an amnesty. The suspended journals re-appeared and the imprisoned persons were all, or nearly all, released.[47]

The supposed Belmonte-Wendler letter had in fact been skilfully fabricated by a member of the British Security Co-ordination Service (B.S.C.), an organization which had been set up in New York at the time of the fall of France by a remarkable Canadian, Willliam Stephenson, and which maintained close relations with the head of the Federal Bureau of Investigation, J. Edgar Hoover, and, later, with General William Donovan, who was in charge of the body which became the Office of Strategic Services.[48] The intelligence officer, H. Montgomery Hyde, had been sent to Bolivia early in May to investigate the rumours and reports, at which both Britain and the United States felt a natural concern, that Nazi elements in the country—and Belmonte—were planning a *coup* with the object of establishing a pro-Nazi military dictatorship, and to 'plan a counter-offensive'.[49]

Hyde, a barrister and historian, collected all the information he could in Bolivia, and making certain 'arrangements', returned to New York apparently convinced of the reality of German subversive activities, though not of the precise extent to which Belmonte was concerned in them. The nature of the 'arrangements' remains uncertain, but B.S.C. ensured that news of a sensational letter sensationally discovered should reach and stimulate the curiosity of the State Department and the F.B.I., and the outcome of the 'counter-offensive' was the forged letter, alleged (with 'cloak and dagger' embellishments) to have been stolen from a German courier.[50] Stephenson's London contacts, having been told of the existence of the letter, urgently asked to see the text and then said that the

Bolivian Government should be warned but that the whole matter should be discussed with the Americans who should be left to take what action they wished.[51] Accordingly, the letter was given to Hoover and a photostat copy was sent by the Department of Justice on 5 July to the Department of State. Sumner Welles read it to the Bolivian Minister in Washington[52] and, after a further photocopy had been delivered to Ostria Gutiérrez, publicly supported the actions subsequently taken by the Bolivian Government. He can hardly have known, at this point, that the letter was a forgery. Indeed, he is said to have believed the opposite.[53] Whether Roosevelt was aware of the truth when, in a world-wide broadcast on 11 September he referred (incorrectly) to the discovery of 'secret air-landing fields in Colombia, within easy reach of the Panama Canal' and to a recent endeavour 'to subvert the Government of Bolivia'[54], is an open question. But the State Department had been alerted to the facts by 22 July. The story had been told by another British Intelligence Officer, Frederick L. Stagg, to Spruille Braden, the American Ambassador to Colombia, with whom he was on familiar terms, and Braden immediately telegraphed the State Department, though not discounting the possibility that genuinely incriminating evidence might have been uncovered in La Paz.[55]

Ostria Gutiérrez had meanwhile begged for speedy economic help from the United States,[56] and his appeal was quickly answered. On 1 August the State Department put forward a plan for long-term economic collaboration between Bolivia and the United States, the details depending upon the report of an economic mission. An agreement was also signed on 4 September for the despatch of a Military Aviation Mission. The Italian Military Mission's contract was cancelled in October. In December armaments and munitions to the value of $11 millions, it was agreed, should be allocated to Bolivia under the Lend-Lease Act, and a few days later the economic mission, headed by a senior Foreign Service Officer, Merwin L. Bohan, arrived in La Paz.[57] By then the United States was at war. Bolivia on the 10th, declared that she stood solidly with the United States and her American allies and would not regard them as belligerents, and a new Foreign Minister,

Eduardo Anze Matienzo, explained that she had not severed relations with the Axis powers for fear of subversive activities with which the Government lacked the arms to cope.[58] But Axis citizens were placed under close supervision, the Transocean news-agency was closed, and in January the *exequatur* of the German consul at Potosí was cancelled. Finally, on 27 January, during the Rio de Janeiro Conference, a financial settlement was at last reached with the Standard Oil Company, Bolivia agreeing to pay the company $1,500,000, with interest from 13 March, 1937, for 'the sale' of all its rights, interests and properties.[59] On the same day an agreement was signed for the establishment of a Bolivian Development Corporation to be financed in part by credits from the Export-Import Bank,[60] and Bolivia, on the 28th, severed relations with the Axis. As *El Diario* had remarked on 9 December, the international crisis provided an opportunity for Bolivia to obtain from the United States all the aid she needed, though in this her reach may be thought to have exceeded her grasp.

III

If isolation had been thrust upon Bolivia, despite her frontiers with five surrounding nations, by the loss of her Pacific coastline in the War of the Pacific (1879–83), low-lying and also land-locked Paraguay had grown up in isolation. Like Bolivia, she had reaped a legacy of bitterness and frustration from the disastrous Chaco War, even though Paraguay, not Bolivia, had emerged victorious. In the aftermath Colonel Rafael Franco had launched his brief 'Liberating Revolution', intended, he announced, to be 'of the same character as the totalitarian transformation occurring in contemporary Europe', and General Estigarribia, who had become a dictator *malgré lui*, had embarked on an ambitious programme of reform and reconstruction—land reform, public works and, partly inherited from Colonel Franco, the development, assisted by credits from the United States, not only of internal but of external communications, with Brazil, Argentina and Bolivia. He had also endowed the country with a new Constitution, but died in an aeroplane accident three weeks after its promulgation.[61]

No Congress was in existence when Estigarribia died in September, 1940, and the cabinet installed his Minister of War, Colonel Higinio Morínigo, as Provisional President. 'Provisional' he was not. Despite promises that he would continue the policies of his predecessor and that elections would be held in accordance with the new Constitution, Morínigo turned for support to young and nationalist army officers, announced in mid-October that elections would be postponed till February, 1943,[62] and on the 30th November assumed the 'totality of power', set on one side the Chamber of Deputies, imprisoned or exiled members of the long-time ruling Liberal Party, including some of Estigarribia's former cabinet ministers, imposed a strict censorship of the press, and, borrowing some of ex-President Franco's clothes, spoke in terms of a 'new Paraguay', emphasising, as did his ministers, not only discipline, hierarchy and order but the farcical nature of democracy among an illiterate people.[63] Paraguay had returned to her old-time dictatorial traditions; and, while the news transmitted to the press emanated almost entirely from German and Italian agencies, the British representative noted how, with the change of government, a 'press campaign against democracy' began, 'in which, of course, the democracies, although not named, were included'. This, he said, 'was made possible by the appointment to the papers of Government interventors, all of whom were, if not pro-German, at least admirers of totalitarian technique'.[64]

Morínigo's rule was highly illiberal and authoritarian, and it was made yet more so by a Decree Law in July, 1941, which imposed a Draconian code for crimes against the State, the President and his Ministers, and for many other offences, by the establishment in August of a special tribunal for the trial of such offences, together with the institution of a Department of Press and Propaganda and a still more rigorous censorship. But the régime had had to contend with a long sequence of conspiracies and attempted *coups d'état*, beginning with an abortive rising in January, said, improbably, to be Nazi-inspired,[65] movements in favour of ex-President Franco, who had to be detained in Montevideo, a number of other plots, alleged or genuine, among army or navy personnel (the navy functioned on the Paraguay River), and labour and student disturbances. Nor was it devoid of ability. It included a number of able and energetic young men sincerely concerned with the regeneration of Paraguay, as, for example, the Foreign Minister, Dr Luis Argaña, and its achievements were not negligible. It proceeded, though slowly, with Estigarribia's agrarian reforms, and, more actively, with the road-building programme, designed, in particular, to improve communications with Brazil. While Dr Argaña visited Brazil in June, 1941, and Dr. Vargas Paraguay in August, ten conventions were signed and ratified providing, *inter alia*, for the provision of credits for the building of those sections of a railway which would link Concepción to Campo Grande in Brazil and thereafter to the port of Santos, and for a Paraguayan free port at Santos itself. Earlier, at the Conference of the River Plate countries in January and February, conventions were signed with Uruguay for the appointment of a mixed commission to study the establishment of a Paraguayan-Uruguayan financial consortium for the development of public works in Paraguay, and with Argentina and Bolivia relating to the use of the Pilcomayo River.[66]

Japan, in January, 1941, had signed a trade agreement with Paraguay for the exchange of Paraguyan cotton for manufactured goods. Argentina increased her Paraguayan imports, and Britain and the United States theirs. But Paraguay, unlike most Latin American countries, took no action whatever against Axis interests, though, with good reason, President Morínigo and Dr. Argaña were careful not to alienate the United States. Useful credits had been made available from the Export-Import Bank for agricultural purposes, highway construction, river-port works, air-port improvements and the like, and in September an allocation of $11 millions was awarded to Paraguay under Lend-Lease arrangements.[67] Skilfully balancing the interests of Brazil, Argentina and the United States, Paraguay, economically at least, was not faring too badly by the end of 1941. When the crunch came with the state of war between the United States and Japan, Morínigo and Argaña declared on 9 December that Paraguay would fully honour her obligations and on the 10th the Government formally announced that it would fulfil 'with absolute fidelity its international undertakings' in respect of the defence of the continent, expressed its solidarity with the United States, and supported Chile's proposal for the calling of a meeting of American Foreign Ministers.[68] Relations with the Axis having been severed at the time of the Rio de Janeiro Conference, further 'financial manna' descended from the United States for public health services, and for agricultural and industrial development, and in 1942 Brazil, too, extended credits for these latter purposes.[69]

IV

Brazil, in November, 1940, celebrated the tenth anniversary of Dr. Vargas's accession to power and the third of the establishment of the *Estado Novo*.[70] His dictatorship, almost 'absolute in form', was entirely personal — there was no *Estado Novo* party — but Vargas was a master of the arts of political manipulation and persuasion and employed a Machiavellian astuteness to contrive and maintain a delicate balance of interests, civilian and military, within his cabinet and between opposing forces, both international and domestic, outside it. Dependent as he was on the departments of police, censorship and propaganda, and, ultimately, on the armed forces, he was commonly portrayed, not without justice, as a paternal statesman devoted to his country, the development of its resources and the welfare of its people; and his personal popularity had increased rather than diminished. Such opposition as remained, or made itself evident, was concentrated, for the most part, among the old *Integralistas*, with a measure of German support. But the stability of his régime was unquestioned, and the months between the Havana Conference and the entry of the United States into the war were among the quietest that Brazil had known since the Revolution of 1930.[71]

They were months, too, of slow but steady economic progress, of recovery from the collapse of the markets of continental Europe, and increasing (though irregular) collaboration with the United States, while, in line with his policy of keeping in touch with the people, Vargas travelled thousands of miles, not only to the far north but, what none of his predecessors had done, to remote parts of the interior. 'Here I am in your country, Mr Interventor,' he said in Goyania, the newest of the State capitals, in August, 1940, 'to begin the march to the west'. This was the true path of Brazilian nationality. The country had grown longitudinally; it must now grow latitudinally. And in Manaus, near the confluence of the Negro and the Amazon, he spoke in October of the planned and systematic exploitation of the riches of the Amazon basin and of a conference of the countries which bordered it.[72]

The 'March to the West' was to be a slogan for the future.[73] But, as the draining of the Fluminense lowlands was one notable achievement of the Vargas régime, so also was the foundation in 1941 of the *Companhia Siderúrgica Nacional* and the Volta Redonda steel plant. This was a major step forward in the rise of the new industrial Brazil, a Brazil which, in Vargas's hopes, should become the industrial heartland of South America.[74] He had constantly looked to the enlargement of Brazil's South American market, and his efforts were now intensified. An Export-Import Department was added to the Bank of Brazil in May, 1941. Earlier in the year Brazil had assisted at the regional conference of the River Plate countries at Montevideo, intended to achieve a closer economic co-operation between them. In July and August Vargas not only set foot on Bolivian soil near Corumbá to meet the Bolivian Foreign Minister and a mixed Brazilian-Bolivian Commission, whose financial recommendations for the construction of the Corumbá-Santa Cruz railway he later approved; he also paid a state visit to Asunción to ratify a number of conventions between Paraguay and Brazil, among them the agreement to link Paraguay by rail (as well as Bolivia) to the port of Santos.[75] In November the Foreign Minister, Oswaldo Aranha, concluded a trade agreement with Chile, and both in 1940 and 1941 conventions were signed with Argentina to foster trade and complementary economic development. A shipping service was inaugurated to Venezuela by *Lloyd Brasileiro*. Canada, under an agreement negotiated in 1940, established a legation in Rio de Janeiro in September and a Canadian trade delegation followed in October.[76]

An increase in trade with South American countries and Canada was one element in the revival of Brazil's export trade in 1941. But this of course, could not compensate for the loss of European markets and the continuing decline of British trade, though Britain still bought Brazilian meat, foodstuffs, hides, and, as a good-will gesture, cotton, partly for her own needs, partly to keep Brazil's Special Account sterling in balance to meet payments for British imports, the service on the external debts, which had been resumed in 1940, exchange for current dividends and the like.[77] Nor were the substantial Japanese purchases of Brazilian cotton in the first half of the year more than a contributory element. The prime cause of Brazil's recovery was the great expansion of trade with the United States.

The establishment of the Volta Redonda steel mill had itself been made possible by a loan of $20 million (later increased to $45 million) from the Export-Import Bank and the raising of matching funds in Brazil. The agreement with the United States was signed in September, 1940, and put an end to simultaneous negotiations with Krupps in Germany.[78] The Inter-American Coffee Agreement of November, 1940, coming into effect in April, 1941, halted ruinous competition among the coffee-producing countries and assured Brazil a fair share of the North American market at enhanced prices. In May Brazil agreed to restrict, through the imposition of export licences, the export of certain strategic materials to the United States alone and the United States undertook to buy the exportable surpluses. Other strategic materials were added later, exports to Britain being permitted by way of the United States.[79] As a result mineral exports soared. Natually enough the general dislocation of international trade enhanced economic nationalism[80] and the drive for import substitution and economic self-sufficiency. But it was not only exports to the United States that increased, so also did United States imports. Brazilian orders for steel, machinery and other equipment for Volta Redonda were given special priority and the United States undertook to facilitate generally the shipment of materials needed for Brazilian industry.[81]

Strategically (as well as politically) Brazil's importance to the United States was, in the words of the American Chief of Naval Operations, 'perfectly enormous'.[82] The great Brazilian 'bulge', lying immediately below the equator and the mouths of the Amazon, stretched far into the South Atlantic. At its most easterly extension Natal and Recife are closer to Africa,

across the 'Atlantic narrows', than to the nearest island of the
West Indies. The 'bulge', and indeed the whole of the vast
extent of the Brazilian coast northwards from Rio de Janeiro,
an archipelago of inhabited islands rather than a continuous
area of settlement, were practically defenceless. For their protection Brazil had little more than an antiquated navy—the
first destroyer to be built in Brazil was launched in July,
1940—a small, fairly well-disciplined but much less well-
equipped army, the greater part of which was concentrated in
south-eastern Brazil, and an air-force devoid of modern combat planes. (There was no separate Air Ministry before January, 1941, and Vargas, much to the annoyance of the army,
placed a civilian at its head). So alarmed had the United
States been at this unprotected state that in May, 1940, fearful
of a possible Nazi invasion, she had hastily devised the extraordinary 'Pot of Gold' plan for an emergency expeditionary
force of 100,000 men to points between Belém and Rio de
Janeiro.[83]

The course of events in Europe in the summer of 1940
relieved these immediate fears, but not the anxiety to secure
an effective defence of the 'bulge', more especially since
French West Africa and Dakar were in Vichy hands. A double
chain of airfields was constructed by Pan American Airports
Corporation on the West Indian and South American routes
to north-eastern Brazil.[84] Plans for military co-operation,
which included the provision of air and naval bases in the
north-east, had been discussed even before the war began, and
army and navy staff agreements, which contained pledges of
mutual assistance, were concluded in the autumn of 1940.[85] In
July, 1941, Vargas issued a decree officially allowing Panair
do Brasil, a subsidiary of Pan American, to construct, enlarge,
equip or re-equip a number of airfields in the vital area
between Belém and São Salvador, though, with his oral permission and privately, not publicly, sites had been acquired
and construction work begun long before the decree was
issued. Indeed, Atlantic Airways Ltd., an *ad hoc* subsidiary of
Pan American, began in June to ferry aircraft and supplies
from the raw landing strips across the South Atlantic to aid
the British campaign in North Africa. The ferrying service
was to become the main purpose of the new sites, and the field

at Natal the principal air-base for this vital trans-Atlantic supply route. It was not, however, till after Pearl Harbour that Brazil allowed American marines, in the guise of technicians, to be stationed at Belém, Natal and Recife to safeguard what were virtually unprotected fields.[86]

The air-field programme was, ostensibly, a strictly civilian affair. In July, however, a Brazilian-American Joint Group of Staff Officers was set up in Rio de Janeiro, its members participating in a survey of the north-east and of the island of Fernando de Noronha, and the United States contingent preparing a defensive plan which included Belém, Natal and Recife as sites for major air-bases and supply installations. The Planning Group dissolved in October, but the Brazilian Chief of Staff, General Góes Monteiro, recommended the establishment of a permanent Joint Board for North-East Brazil to plan the construction of base facilities and co-ordinate defensive arrangements.[87] It was established in December. Meanwhile Recife and Bahia had been made available for the refreshment and upkeep of the United States Naval Patrol in the South Atlantic, and on 11 December the first United States Naval Air Squadron arrived at Natal to be welcomed by the Brazilian Army Air Force.[88] Finally, at the instance of the United States and the invitation of the Royal Netherlands Government Brazil agreed to take special measures of vigilance on her frontier with Dutch Guiana, or Surinam, and to send a mission to Paramaribo to concert defensive measures. The United States, for her part, sent troops, to be under Netherlands' command, for the protection of the valuable bauxite mines. A simultaneous announcement was made in Washington and Rio de Janeiro on 24 November, the American troops beginning to disembark in Surinam on the following day.[89]

These arrangements were not concluded without multiple difficulties and delays. The United States was primarily concerned with the north-east, the Brazilian general staff with the south-east, where the German and Italian communities were concentrated and where Brazil had long been haunted by illusory fears of Argentine attack from the border provinces of Misiones and Corrientes. Brazil was perfectly prepared to agree to the construction of military air bases in the north-east, financed by the United States Government. But she was not willing for American troops to be stationed on Brazilian soil. Indeed, in June, 1941, military manoeuvres in the north-east were cancelled in order to avoid the embarrassment of refusing to allow United States forces to participate in them, as had been wished. No Brazilian cabinet, Góes Monteiro had thought, could survive such a proposal, and Aranha had thrown up his hands in consternation at the idea.[90] Brazil, above all, wanted military equipment, munitions, armaments, now that German supplies were cut off, and these the United States was in no position to provide. (This was the reason why Brazil so bitterly resented the detention of the *Siqueira Campos*, with its load of armaments, by the British in November, 1940, and the United States pressed for her release).[91] Brazilian armament requests, indeed, rose from $180 millions in June, 1940, to $250 millions by January, 1941. The War and Navy Departments in the United States agreed in March on a programme making $100 millions of military and naval matériel available, with an initial credit (which Brazil did not take up) of $12 millions. But it was not till October that a lend-lease agreement allocating the $100 millions could be signed, and few supplies of any kind had been received in Brazil by the time of Pearl Harbour.[92]

It was not in Vargas's character to be driven into hasty action by the United States or to be other than cautious. 'We all feel', he declared on 7 September, 1940, 'that, if necessary, the American peoples will unite their soldiers and their arms to defend their sovereignty'.[93] In February he assured the American Ambassador that Brazil would be at the side of the United States if war was declared against her by any non-American country.[94] Similar assurances seem to have been given in May.[95] Yet on May Day Vargas sent greetings to Hitler and his best wishes for the prosperity of the German nation.[96] In June he left the German Ambassador with the decided impression that Brazil was 'the bulwark against the inclusion of South America in Roosevelt's anti-German policy',[97] and in November Vargas's brother, Benjamim, told the Ambassador, at the President's 'express direction', of Brazil's 'urgent desire' to 'continue on good terms with Germany', complaining of American pressure and explaining that the Surinam agreement was no more than an empty gesture.[98]

Whether or not Vargas was still hedging his bets or believed that he could still insulate Brazil from what was obviously becoming a world war, he pursued his Brazilianisation programme with vigour. A ban on the publication of newspapers in any language but Portuguese bore hardly on the German and Italian communities. So also did a prohibition against the teaching in foreign languages in primary and secondary schools. But English and American newspapers were affected too, and so, also, though in minor degree, were English and American schools.[99] The elimination of Axis airlines was a different matter. Vasp (*Viação Aérea São Paulo*), which was Brazilian-owned but had strong connections with *Lufthansa*, was persuaded by American pressure to dismiss its German personnel by August, and Varig (*Viação Aérea Rio Grandense*), which was partly Brazilian-owned, followed this example.[100] But Condor, a subsidiary of *Lufthansa*, and the pioneer of Brazilian air-services, and the Italian trans-Atlantic service, Lati, continued their operations. Both lines were suspected of spotting on behalf of Axis raiders and submarines and of monitoring the movement of British shipping in the South Atlantic—an explanation of increasingly heavy sinkings[101]— and Lati of transporting also such valuable commodities as industrial diamonds, mica and platinum. Both were placed on the United States Proclaimed or Black List in July, 1941, and Condor did indeed incur official censure from time to time for infringing Brazilian regulations. It was forced, by the curtailment of oil-supplies, to suspend operations in November between Buenos Aires and Santiago, and all applications to extend its services were refused.[102] But no other action was taken against either line until the United States was actually at war with Germany and Italy.

The excuse, so far as Lati was concerned, was that Brazil had no other means of communication, except by cable, with her representatives in Europe, and, for Condor, that it was an essential as well as the oldest part of the Brazilian airways system. But Pan American agreed in November to open an alternative service to Lisbon and Portuguese West Africa, and on the day that the United States declared war on Germany and Italy Cordell Hull asked that steps be taken to close Lati at once. Brazil agreed. By Christmas all Lati's facilities had been closed, its oil supplies cut off, and orders issued for its expropriation.[103] The British Security Co-ordination Services, which had achieved so spectacular a *coup de théâtre* in Bolivia,[104] may also have had a hand in the elimination of Lati, forging, apparently, a letter purporting to be written from Lati's Italian president to his general manager in Brazil and referring to Vargas and the Brazilians in highly offensive terms. Surrounded by an aura of carefully contrived authenticity, a copy was finally delivered into Vargas's hands, with immediate and gratifying results.[105] As for Condor, it too came under the ban imposed on Lati, but, shortly afterwards, 'de-Germanised' and re-organised, flew again as a purely Brazilian enterprise.[106]

With the attack on Pearl Harbour Brazil at once declared her solidarity with the United States. Given the economic relations between the two countries, the lend-lease agreement, the airfields programme, and the naval arrangements, it was the least she could do. But Dr. Aranha hastened to call in all of the Latin American representatives in Rio de Janeiro to tell them that an attack on the United States was an attack on all the Americas, that Brazil had taken only the first steps, and that there were many others to come. He thought, the American Ambassador reported, that it would be well worth while trying to get unanimity of action for these.[107] He had taken a similar line on a recent visit to Argentina and Chile when, both in public and private, he had declared that Brazil would not be a party to any special South American defence bloc and that she proposed to co-operate fully with the United States. 'We will not remain neutral if an American nation takes part in the war', he had told the Argentine Press. 'Nations must either save themselves united, or perish in the face of the enemy'.[108]

The declaration of solidarity, of course, involved no specific commitments. But it had been endorsed by a united cabinet, Góes Monteiro taking a decided stand in favour of the United States, and it was followed by decree laws freezing the funds of non-American belligerent nations, though British banks were subjected to a merely nominal control, and declaring Brazil's neutrality in the war between Japan and the British Empire (except Canada) and the Netherlands—a decree which Aranha subsequently alleged had been issued by mistake![109] It was followed also by action against *Sindicato* Condor and Lati. But Vargas still sent his private secretary repeatedly to the German Embassy with 'protestations of good intentions and distorted accounts of diplomatic pressure from Washington'.[110] He was now, perhaps, lagging behind rather than leading Brazilian opinion. And though Aranha's views and policy admitted of no doubt, the evidence suggests that not till the New Year and the eve of the Rio de Janeiro Conference did Vargas finally make up his mind that Brazil must stand or fall by the United States with the material inducements that stand offered and the prospects it afforded of pre-eminence in South America. He never intended to do too much too fast and without corresponding advantages. These he was to obtain in 1942. Having broken with the Axis on 28 January, Brazil was to become a belligerent in August, and, in 1944, the only Latin American state to send an expeditionary force to Europe.

V

As a buffer state between Brazil and Argentina, and smaller than England and Scotland combined, Uruguay had always to pay a cautious regard to the opinions and attitudes of her two over-mighty neighbours, each of which was jealous or fearful of the other. She had nevertheless shown from the outbreak of the war a resolute independence of judgment. The reception given to the crew of H.M.S. *Ajax* after the 'Battle of the River Plate' and the 'spiritual reaction of the people of Uruguay' to the invasions of Scandinavia and the Low Countries, to Italy's 'stab in the back', and the fall of France, had amply demonstrated their strong anti-Nazi and anti-Fascist sympathies, feelings which were enhanced by the disclosures in June, 1940, of Nazi activities in Uruguay itself and of the so-called Führmann plot against the State.[111] Only among the Herreristas, that is the 'official nationalist' wing of the *Blanco* or conservative party, whose parliamentary importance was out of all proportion to their popular support, were contrary opinions expressed. Their leader, Senator Herrera,[112] was, to all appearances, the counterpart in Uruguay of Dr. Laureano Gómez in Colombia, ambitious for power, a bitter opponent of President Baldomir, in touch with extreme nationalists in Argentina, and, if his paper, *El Debate*, was any guide, more fearful of the United States than of Nazi Germany. But Herrera out-Heroded the Herreristas. They admitted his leadership for domestic, partisan reasons, mainly connected with the burning issue of constitutional reform (of which the President put forward a preliminary plan in July, 1940), but not all of them could swallow his extreme anti-United States and, though perhaps not altogether genuine, pro-German views.[113]

The Herreristas were not the only 'nationalist' group. There was another wing of the *Blanco* party, the 'independent nationalists', of a quite different complexion but who—such were the intricacies of Uruguayan politics—had long abstained, like the so-called 'Batllista' wing of the *Colorado* or liberal party, from participating in elections;[114] and these, like the President, his courageous Foreign Minister, Dr. Guani, and Dr. Pedro Manini Ríos, who became Minister of the Interior in August, were firm supporters of the United States and the democratic cause. Herrera might deride the disclosures of June, 1940. But the principal organs of the press and the great majority of the Uruguayan people were at one in their condemnation of Nazi activities and their fears of a victorious Germany. While the press applauded the military preparations of the United States and President Roosevelt's successive moves to aid beleaguered Britain and to strengthen hemisphere defences[115] (as well as his re-election for a third term), eight Nazi suspects, who had been arrested in June but released, were re-indicted in September, charged with subversive activities, and, to German anger, ultimately sent to prison.[116] Despite the virulent opposition of the Herreristas and Argentine disquiet, the President and Dr. Guani, who had welcomed military conversations with the United States, showed themselves perfectly willing to provide air and naval facilities for the United States if required, Dr. Guani emphasising that any bases for this purpose would be 'directed, maintained and controlled' by Uruguay and would be placed at the disposal of any American state in an emergency under conditions established by the Government.[117] Uruguayan sovereignty would not be impaired. And Dr. Guani was sustained both by the Chamber of Deputies and by public opinion.

Neither in 1940 nor in 1941 had Uruguay's economy greatly suffered by the war. Britain indeed refused clearance of German machinery essential for the great Río Negro hydroelectrical scheme—the United States came to its rescue in 1942—but agricultural exports flourished. In December, 1940, the Export-Import Bank had approved credits of over $7 millions for materiél for national defence and for industrial projects,[118] and while Britain, formerly Uruguay's best customer and source of supply, took large quantities of meat, the United States, hitherto a much less important market, enormously increased her imports of wool, hides, canned beef and linseed. Uruguay enjoyed a greater prosperity than she had for years and ended 1941 with a large export surplus.

Nothing immediately resulted from the bases proposals in late 1940. The material resources were lacking. Dr. Guani had to be content with somewhat inconclusive defence discussions with the Argentine Foreign Minister at Colonia in December. But a Commission was appointed to draw up plans for an air-port or air-base near Carrasco Beach—a project long mooted—1,000 acres being set aside for this purpose in January, 1941; and the proposal for an aero-naval base was revived later in the year. Exasperated beyond measure by the tactics of the Herreristas, both participants in and critics of his government, the President, with doubtful legality, demanded in March the resignation of the three Herrerista members of his cabinet, replacing them with *Colorados* of his own complexion. A new draft Constitution was prepared, certainly not to the liking of the Herreristas, and the Government boldly went ahead with its pro-Anglo-American foreign policy. Two Danish and two Italian ships were seized in April and an Italian protest was rejected; and when, amidst a recrudescence of anti-Nazi activity, a new pro-Nazi journal, ironically named *Libertad*, appeared on 31 May, not only did some newsboys refuse to deliver it, but university students burnt it; the paper's life was short, and in June its editor, Alejandro Kayel, a deputy, was, with unanimous approval, suspended from the

Chamber. On the 20th the Government announced, as it had done in 1917, during the first World War, that it would not treat as a belligerent any American country which, in defence of its own rights, found itself at war with nations of other continents; and, on the following day, it invited all American republics to adopt the same policy. 'The Government of Uruguay' said Sumner Welles, 'has once again lighted the way towards a constructive and practical co-operation between all of the American republics at this moment which is more critical than any which has transpired since the achievement of their independence'. But though Brazil agreed with the proposal, Argentina did not. Nor were the replies of Chile, Perú and Colombia favourable. The proposal was allowed to drop.[119]

This was not so with the project for an aero-naval base, for which a site was proposed at Laguna Negra, to the north-east of La Paloma, the deepest of the lagoons which fringe the Atlantic coast of Uruguay, and somewhat less offensive to Argentine susceptibilities than a base at Punta del Este or Montevideo. A contract for the construction of air and naval bases was actually offered to a British firm.[120] Under the Land-Lease programme, moreover, a loan of $17 million had been negotiated for the purchase of essential war materials and armaments.[121] This was approved by the Chamber of Deputies in October and by the Senate in December. The Chamber, in October, had also appointed a committee to investigate subversive activities. In November, it called on all American republics to protest jointly to Germany against the execution of civilian hostages in occupied countries, and, with the attack on Pearl Harbour, the country took an unequivocal stand. Uruguay, Dr. Guani declared, must identify herself without reserve with the cause of the United States, even though she was in no position to lend military aid. The Government declared that the United States would not be treated as a belligerent. The Chamber of Deputies sent a message of solidarity to the United States House of Representatives. The Senate condemned the act of aggression to which the United States had been subjected.[122] German and Japanese credits were frozen and, within a few days, Uruguay had engaged to treat as non-belligerents all American states at war with the Axis powers. After the Rio de Janeiro Conference and Uruguay's severance of relations with Italy, Germany and Japan, the privilege of non-belligerency, with the concomitant freedom of Uruguayan ports, was also, on 5 February, 1942, extended to Great Britain.

VI

Uruguay would have preferred to keep in step both with Brazil and Argentina. But this was to prove increasingly difficult and finally impossible. Argentina, at the outbreak of the war, had adopted a policy of strict neutrality, a rather legalistic neutrality, but not markedly different from that of the other republics. But President Ortiz and his Foreign Minister, Dr. Cantilo, had made no secret of their frank sympathies with the democracies.[123] In April and early May, 1940, indeed, they had travelled further than Washington in proposing that the American nations should substitute non-belligerency for neutrality.[124] Even in the dark days at the end of May the President had expressed his fullest confidence in the ultimate victory of the Allies,[125] and the German Ambassador, in June, was by no means satisfied with the state of German-Argentine relations.[126]

The army, to be sure, had been German-trained, and the British and German Ambassadors were at one in reporting its pro-German proclivities.[127] Of the higher-ranking officers, some, such as General Bautista Molina, whom Ortiz retired, and General Basilio Pertiné, who, though also retired, was president of the *Círculo Militar*, or officers' club, were outright Nazi sympathisers. But these were not the views of the Minister of War, General Carlos Márquez, and there is little evidence that the rank and file of the army, whatever their professional admiration for the clock-work precision of German military operations in the spring of 1940, were moved by any other considerations than a resolute determination to preserve their country's neutrality at all costs.[128]

Ortiz and Castillo may have come under army pressure as a result of their non-belligerency proposal. With its failure, both re-affirmed the traditional Argentine policy of neutrality.[129] They had also been subjected to civilian criticism. Argentine opinion was not wholly on the side of the democracies, let alone of Pan Americanism. Fascist and ultra-nationalistic doctrines had their appeal to arch-conservatives, to upper-class young men-about-town, to right-wing intellectuals and others who sought to rehabilitate the reputation of the greatest and worst of Argentine tyrants, Juan Manuel de Rosas— Rosas Clubs were founded—and to the medley of men and doctrines embraced in the *Alianza de la Juventud Nacionalista*, headed by General Molina, as well as to other nationalistic groups such as the younger *Afirmación Argentina*, presided over by the fascist-minded ex-governor of Buenos Aires Province, Dr. Manuel Fresco. But there was no united nationalist movement, and nationalism, as such, had little to do, except among the extremists, with Fascism or Nazism: its sources were indigenous. Even outside the extreme nationalistic ranks, however, the news of British reverses evoked echoes of satisfaction or semi-satisfaction. Given the entrenched nature of British interests in Argentina, 'twisting the tail of the financial lion', as the British Ambassador, Sir Esmond Ovey, put it, had formed 'a popular method of appeal to the electorate'.[130] The British, he thought, were not, and never would be, 'deliriously popular', except among a very small section of the community; and, as the Foreign Office noted, some of the British concerns in Argentina were 'more or less deservedly unpopular': British beneficiaries had not bothered enough about the Argentine goose that laid the golden eggs.[131]

Nevertheless, the majority of Argentines, if they feared that Britain would lose, hoped that she would win. The great metropolitan newspapers, *La Prensa* and *La Nación* were, and remained, firm in their democratic sympathies, and, be it added, their admiration for President Roosevelt; and the formation in June, 1940, of *Acción Argentina*, a non-party organization to fight fascism, which included Socialists, Radicals and Conservatives, the termination of the German military mission (though little progress had been made in plans for military co-operation with the United States),[132] and the alarm raised in June and July by reports of Nazi activities in the territory of Misiones, all pointed to what were, after all, the dominant trends in public opinion. But the public mind was confused. The barometric pressure tended to move up and down according to events in Europe. And confusion was compounded when, because of the increasing gravity of his diabetic illness, the President found himself constrained, on 3 July, to delegate his executive functions to his Vice-President, Dr. Ramón Castillo, thereby injecting a new element of uncertainty into public life. Ortiz and Castillo each owed their position to ex-President Justo, still a power behind the scenes and not devoid of further presidential ambitions. But President and Vice-President were poles apart in temperament, outlook and convictions. Ortiz, though he had re-affirmed Argentine neutrality, remained 'an excellent friend of England and democracy'.[133] Castillo, more determinedly neutral, was more reserved in his sympathies and more certain than uncertain of an Allied defeat. Ortiz, a one-time Radical, had sought to purify politics and to restore democratic practices, and, under him, the Radicals had emerged from the political wilderness to gain control of the Chamber of Deputies. Castillo, an ultra-conservative, believed that Radicalism—the label was, of course, a misnomer—and, for that matter, Socialism (though Socialist influence was almost wholly confined to Buenos Aires) must be held in check by every possible means and that power must remain in the hands of the conservative oligarchy who were the beneficiaries of the Revolution of 1930.[134] It is difficult to resist the conclusion that his foreign and domestic policies were alike subordinated to this end.[135]

There was, however, no immediate break with the President's programme, and, indeed, Ortiz, on his sick-bed, was still capable, on occasion, of exerting his authority. He had, moreover, received an overwhelming vote of confidence in Congress on 24 August.[136] But in order to put an end to the difficulties of the Vice-President in governing with a cabinet not of his own choosing, it was obviously desirable that he should be allowed to appoint a new one; and early in September he did so. More to the right than its predecessor, it nevertheless commanded a good deal of respect, containing as it did an ex-Vice-President, Dr Julio Roca, as Minister of Foreign Affairs, and, as Minister of Finance, Dr. Federico Pinedo, who had held the same post in 1933. Both men were strong supporters of the Allied cause. Roca was so notoriously pro-British that he was compelled to lean over backwards to maintain the appearance of impartiality, even going so far as to ban the showing of Charlie Chaplin's famous film, 'The Great Dictator', in December in order not to offend the Italian population, and emphasising Argentina's concern to preserve a 'jealous and vigilant peace'[137]—a concern wholly in line with traditional policy but not unassociated, perhaps, with the views of the army on the one hand and the knowledge, on the other, that the United States, by her own admission, was not capable of defending Argentina should peace be broken.[138]

Roca had made it a condition of accepting the Foreign Ministry that Castillo should continue to follow the policies of Ortiz, and Castillo, on more than one occasion, affirmed his intention of doing so.[139] But though, in October, he declared that the era of 'patriotic fraud' was at an end,[140] the provincial elections which took place in Santa Fe in December and in Mendoza in January proved exactly the opposite. Outraged by this return to electoral fraud and convinced that no redress was to be had, and no fair play to be expected, from the Government, the Radicals, though by no means united, used their majority in the Chamber to bring the Government's legislative programme to a standstill.

An immediate casualty was the budget—the 1940 budget having finally to be re-enacted by decree for 1941. A second was Dr. Pinedo's 'economic revival' plan. Economic as well as political uncertainty dogged Argentina. Though Britain continued to buy large quantities of meat and smaller, though substantial, amounts of hides, skins, wool and wheat, and was negotiating further extensive purchases, Argentina had lost almost the whole of her markets in continental Europe and was confronted with huge surpluses of wheat, maize and linseed. She suffered also from a scarcity of tonnage, rising freight rates, the soaring prices of British manufactures, uncertainty of deliveries and shortages of coal and other essential imports. Dr. Pinedo proposed to meet these problems by federal purchases of agricultural surpluses, the expansion of industry, especially the manufacture of products which could not be imported from abroad, and a programme of low-cost housing. These projects would be financed by the mobilisation of the banking resources of the country and the attendant use of United States loans. Sterling balances would be used to buy up British investments, including the railways. From areas, such as the United States, whose exports were not paid for by imports, the import of non-essential goods would be severely restricted. Finally, trade with neighbouring countries and the inter-change of non-competitive products were to be encouraged by every possible means.[141] The Pinedo plan aimed, therefore, at the salvation of the rural economy, the growth of industry, the creation of employment, the expansion of intra-Latin American trade, and the reduction in the rôle of foreign capital.

The plan was approved by the cabinet in November and by the Senate in December, at a time when, as the result of a mission headed by Dr. Raúl Prebisch of the Central Bank, the Export-Import Bank of Washington approved the increase of a hitherto untouched loan of $20 million to $60 million and the United States Treasury authorised a stabilisation loan of $50 million.[142] It was warmly welcomed by the *Unión Industrial Argentina* and severely criticised by *La Prensa*. But, whatever its merits or demerits, it was left hanging in the air by the Chamber of Deputies. Pinedo, on 14 January, resigned. Nor were the loans negotiated by Dr. Prebisch ever ratified. The Government had to use the banking resources of the country to buy agricultural surpluses and to finance expenditure which could not be met by the Treasury in the normal way. It was fortunate, however, in that war-time circumstances came to its partial relief—the conclusion of commercial treaties and the growth of trade with other Latin American states, heavy British purchases, and, above all, a phenomenal increase, as a result of the United States purchasing programme, in the value of exports to the United States leading to the conversion of an import into an export surplus. At last, moreover, a Reciprocal Trade Agreement was signed with the United States in October,[143] though it long remained unratified.

Pinedo's resignation was followed on 24 January 1941 by that of Roca, who complained publicly that the legislative stalemate made his work impossible, leaving in suspense a vast plan of commercial treaties, credit operations and defensive arrangements[144]—the agreements concluded with Uruguay at Colonia in December[145] were examples. Privately, he denounced Castillo for the deviousness of his policies, warning him that they might lead to revolution.[146] Finally, early in February, Dr. Ortiz himself took a hand, issuing a manifesto in which he severely criticised Castillo, dissociated himself from his policies, and called for unity and co-operation among all political leaders.[147] But he made no attempt to resume his functions. The Conservative Senate insisted on appointing a Committee to investigate his health and its report, in April, confirmed that the President was almost totally blind and beyond the hope of recovery. There was talk of forcing his resignation.[148] But Dr. Ortiz remained President *de jure* till his death in July, 1942, his influence inevitably diminishing, and Dr. Castillo the President *de facto*.

One result of this executive and legislative *impasse* was an abortive nationalist-military conspiracy headed by General Molina.[149] Another was the closing of the ranks of the Conservative cabinet (and of the oligarchy) under the aegis, it was thought, of ex-President Justo.[150] Since Roca's resignation the Minister of Justice, Guillermo Rothe, an amiable nonentity, had been Acting Foreign Minister. But on 13 March Dr. Castillo appointed both a new Finance Minister, Dr. Carlos Acevedo, and, a new Foreign Minister, Dr. Enrique Ruiz-Guiñazú, formerly Ambassador to the Holy See, though he was not sworn in till June, after making a semi-royal progress to Washington, Bogotá, Rio de Janeiro and Montevideo. Sumner Welles (who had reason to be prejudiced) described him as 'one of the stupidest men' ever to hold office in Argentina; the British Ambassador found him 'practically impossible to speak to in the sense of discussing any serious subject'; Dr. Alberto Gainza Paz, the sub-Director of *La Prensa*, frankly called him an '*idiota inflado*';[151] and it has been said of him that he 'coupled his limited international experience with a certain enthusiasm for the Hispanist version of Fascism' and appeared to regard Madrid as the 'capital of the West'.[152]

These are harsh judgments. But Dr. Ruiz-Guiñazú, at the time of his appointment, was something of an unknown quantity,[153] and his elevation and that of Dr. Acevedo (a former Finance Minister) appeared to herald a return to more normal conditions. A still more hopeful sign was the decision of the Radicals early in May, moved in part by an unfavourable reaction of public opinion, to substitute 'constructive opposition' for parliamentary intransigence. But disillusion quickly followed. Socialist and Radical leaders, the great newspapers, and *Acción Argentina*, in a monster *cabildo abierto*, or open meeting, had clearly demonstrated the strong current of opinion in favour of the democracies and close Pan American co-operation. But when Congress re-convened, at the end of May, Dr. Castillo's message to it, with its frigid reference to the war, came as a cold douche. Nothing could have been in greater contrast to President Roosevelt's proclamation of a state of unlimited national emergency on the previous day. Nor did Dr. Ruiz-Guiñazú's actions on his assumption of office relieve the misgivings felt at the Government's international as well as its domestic policies. He rejected on 27 June the Uruguayan proposal that an American nation entering the war, in defence of its own rights, should be treated as a non-belligerent, and, according to Dr. Gainza Paz, was 'intensely pleased with himself at having scotched this measure';[154]and throughout the rest of the year the Castillo régime clung to the same rigidity of policy it had previously shown, more timorous in its foreign aspects (for fear of a German victory) than in its domestic, and apparently undisturbed by the dangers of an Axis controlled Europe and determined to yield nothing to the opposition at home.

In February *La Prensa* had begun the publication of a series of articles on foreign unassimilated groups, particularly the Germans, in Misiones, where a Government enquiry into Nazi activities had been made in December. In May the extent of Nazi infiltration in Argentina, and the neglect of the Goverment to stop it, was raised at the Radical Party Convention by a Deputy, Raúl Damonte Taborda, and in June the Chamber of Deputies, having listened to bland re-assurances from the Minister of the Interior,[155] appointed a Committee under Damonte Taborda's chairmanship to investigate anti-Argentine activities. Its proceedings, aided by search-warrants from sympathetic judges,[156] both offended the German Ambassador, who protested against police raids, organized by the Committee, on Nazi organizations—the head of the Press Office of the German Embassy fled the country at the end of August in order to escape arrest by the Committee—and embarrassed the Government, which asked for written promises not only from the German Ambassador but from the British to refrain from propaganda. In view of General Molina's Nazi associations it also banned the recently organized 'Supreme Council of Argentine Nationalism'.

The Committee's findings were contained in five reports issued between late August and late November and caused an immense sensation, notwithstanding Damonte Taborda's well-known political partisanship and the fact that much of the substance of the reports had already become public knowledge. They purported to show that there existed in Argentina a regimented foreign community subject to strict military discipline and a terrorist secret police; that the National Socialist Party, banned in 1939, simply operated under another name; that German community funds and German bank accounts were manipulated by the German Embassy, which spent enormous sums and had more employees than the British and American Embassies combined; that the newspaper, *Pampero*, which claimed to be Argentine, was heavily subsidised as also was the Transocean news-agency; that Buenos Aires was the centre for German propaganda throughout South America; that Nazi political and racial doctrines were taught in German schools; that large numbers of Germans had infiltrated into official positions and into the labour movement; and that the Federation of German Trade Unions was the German Labour Front in disguise.[157]

Shortly before the publication of the third report, Damonte Taborda accused the German Ambassador, Edmund von Thermann, of being the director of more than half a million Germans organized as Storm Troopers throughout South America and on 15 September the Chamber of Deputies by a vote of 78 to 1 censured him for abusing his diplomatic privileges, and asked that he should be declared *persona non grata* and that German charitable, social and labour organisations should be dissolved and their leaders deported. The Ambassador reacted angrily. Dr. Castillo, on the 21st, dissociated the Administration from statements made in the Chamber. The Argentine Ambassador in Berlin had already disavowed the Committee and Ruiz-Guiñazú had in effect apologised to von Thermann while asking him 'in all friendliness' whether it might not be desirable for him to be given another post or extended leave—a suggestion rejected by the German Foreign Office. As for the Chamber's requests, Argentine caution, despite public concern, prohibited Argentine action.[158]

Dr. Castillo's position, however, was by no means easy. The War Minister, General Juan Tonazzi, and ex-President Justo were much disturbed by the revelations of the Committee. On the other hand, almost so soon as the Committee had been set up, a group of junior officers had issued a manifesto attacking both it and the Administration.[159] Castillo found himself 'walking a tight-rope' between those army officers, 'who favoured a German victory abroad and saw no threat in Axis activities within Argentina and those officers like the War Minister who saw a danger in both'.[160] Late in September there was again a military conspiracy in which officers of the Air Force were implicated but which was suppressed through the energetic action of Justo. Not much information appeared about the movement in the press. But El Mundo described it as 'anti-democratic',[161] and there was no doubt whatever that the Chief of the Army Air Force was pro-German. The intention, it would seem, was to force the Government to take a still more authoritarian line in both external and internal policy, if not to seize control of it. But though the coup was averted and the Chief of the Army Air Force removed, the disaffected officers were treated with great leniency.[162] Early in October, moreover, a delegation of officers presented Castillo with a virtual ultimatum. From the accounts available,[163] its demands included the dissolution of the Radical-controlled Municipal Council of Buenos Aires, which was in fact disolved by executive decree on 10 October; the disbandment of Acción Argentina, whose meetings were prohibited in November; and the maintenance of strict neutrality, which Castillo had no intention of abandoning. And with no prompting whatever, he once again condoned gross irregularities in provincial elections, this time in Catamarca, San Juan and Buenos Aires. On 16 December, eight days after the attack on Pearl Harbour, he proclaimed a state of siege, suspending constitutional guarantees and curtailing the freedom of political expression. He even prohibited a mass meeting to affirm the adhesion of the Argentine people to the cause of democracy and to pay homage to Roosevelt—a meeting at which the American Ambassador was to have read a personal message from Roosevelt. 'We don't want anyone', Castillo remarked, 'to speak ill of anybody'.[164]

It casts an interesting light on the Government's frame of mind that at this very moment an Argentine mission headed by a Rear-Admiral and a Brigader-General had arrived in the United States for discussions on defensive co-operation and Lend-Lease aid. A year earlier, Dr. Roca, then Foreign Minister, had indicated that Argentina would be disposed to renew talks on defensive measures 'as soon as the military requirements of her government' became more clearly established. No further steps, however, were taken until after the passage of the Lend-Lease Act. Then, in April, Sumner Welles had a conversation with the Argentine Ambassador, and, in July, Norman Armour in Buenos Aires presented Ruiz-Guiñazú with a memorandum detailing the intention of the United States to provide Lend-Lease aid to the American republics, stating the understanding that Argentina was disposed to renew the staff conversations broken off in 1940, and suggesting that a military-naval mission might be sent to Washington to reach agreements which could be approved by both governments. After much hesitation and despite the reservations of Ruiz-Guiñazú, the Argentine cabinet decided to accept the invitation on the somewhat specious understanding that the question of military co-operation was not linked with the supply of military and naval equipment. Not till 27 November, however, did the mission leave Buenos Aires, and, before talks could begin, the United States was at war.[165] In the event they led nowhere. Argentina, apart from Panamá, which was a special case, was the only Latin American country not to receive Lend-Lease aid. By February and March, 1942, she was making unofficial approaches to Germany for the supply of arms.[166]

With the attack on Pearl Harbour the Castillo-Ruiz Guiñazú policy was put to its eleventh-hour test — the twelfth hour was to be struck at Rio de Janeiro in January, 1942. According to Armour, Castillo had assured him in December that Argentina would comply with her continental obligations and that the United States could count on her full support.[167] On the 9th the Government announced that it would not treat the United States as a belligerent in the war with Japan and, on the 13th, in the war with Germany and Italy. President Ortiz, Acting-President Castillo, and ex-Presidents Justo and Marcelo T. Alvear all sent friendly messages to Roosevelt, and Justo was reported to have said that Argentina ought to help the United States in every possible way, even if it meant war.[168] On the 10th *La Prensa* declared that aggression against one American state was aggression against all and *La Nación* that none could remain netural. By contrast, Ruiz-Guiñazú on the 11th, and Castillo, on the 15th, assured von Thermann that Argentina would adhere to her policy of neutrality towards Germany and Italy, Castillo adding that the forthcoming Conference of American Foreign Ministers at Rio de Janeiro could not come to any binding decisions such as a declaration of war or the breaking of relations.[169] On the next day he instituted the state of siege, muffling (but not wholly stifling) the views even of *La Nación* and *La Prensa*. President Vargas of Brazil, like Acting-President Castillo of Argentina, had tried to keep his lines open with Berlin. But while Vargas decided that he must stand or fall with the United States, Castillo took a different view. Neutrality, he thought was the best and safest policy. Neither he nor Ruiz-Guiñazú believed in military alliances or measures of pre-belligerency. They doubted an allied victory. Nor did they wish to stand alone. The Foreign Ministers of Chile, Perú and Paraguay all passed through Buenos Aires on their way to Rio de Janeiro, and at a luncheon which he gave them on 7 January Ruiz-Guiñazú spoke of the need to preserve America for the peace, work and hope of mankind, of the 'brotherhood of the southern republics' and of 'regional harmony'. But if this was an attempt to form a southern bloc, it met with no sympathetic response. 'In America', said the Chilean Foreign Minister, Juan Bautista Rossetti, 'there are no distinctions between North, Central and South. There is but one brotherhood—that of all the American peoples'.[170] Rossetti went on his way to Rio de Janeiro alone. So did the Peruvian and Paraguayan Foreign Ministers. And so did Ruiz-Guiñazú.

VII

Chile, as Rossetti left for Rio de Janeiro, was in the throes of a presidential election caused by the sudden death of President Aguirre Cerda, whose celebrated Popular Front Government had finally dissolved in January, 1941. Faced by continual strikes, rising living costs, administrative incompetence, Conservative opposition and internal dissensions, it had miraculously survived for two years and twenty-one days. But in January the differences between its constituent parties proved at long last to be irreconcilable. The Radicals, the most moderate as well as the largest of the parties, but embracing a wide variety of opinion, quarrelled among themselves and with the Socialists, the second largest party, and the Socialists repudiated the Communists, who, though not represented in the Government, were the fifth in the hierarchical order. Finally, Radicals, Socialists and the Confederation of Labour all resumed their freedom of action.[171] Given the vertiginous rapidity with which Chilean parties combined and flew apart, the name 'Popular Front' continued to survive abroad and even to some extent in Chile, more particularly when the parties of the Left and Centre obtained a clear majority in both Chambers in the March Congressional elections. But Government was no longer a coalition but the government of the President relying on his personal authority and on *ad hoc* alliances.[172] There were hopes of the Front's official revival when the Communists switched their tactics after Soviet Russia had become the ally of Britain. But on 10 November the President resigned, to die a fortnight later. Senator Gerónimo Méndez, the President of the Radical Party, became Provisional President, and elections were called for 1 February, 1942. At a critical time in inter-American relations, Chile was plunged into the convulsions of a presidential campaign which was to result in a substantial victory for Sr. Juan Antonio Ríos, one of the leading Radicals, and the candidate of the Left, over the irrepressible Carlos Ibáñez, supported by the *Vanguardia Popular Socialista*, the Conservatives and the Liberals.

Internationally, there was little doubt where the preponderance of Chilean sympathies lay in 1941, though they were clouded by fears about the outcome of the war and of its extension, especially in the South Pacific. The President himself was a democrat and an ardent admirer of Roosevelt.[173] Of the old Popular Front parties the Radicals, and, still more strongly, the Socialists, led by Oscar Schnake, the Minister of Development, and by Marmaduke Grove, the General Secretary, had shown themselves increasingly partisans of the democracies and of collaboration with the United States. The Radical Socialists took much the same line when their leader, Juan Bautista Rossetti, whose attitude had been somewhat ambiguous, became Foreign Minister in June and hastened to assure the British Ambassador of Chile's strict neutrality and the American of her desire to collaborate with the United States.[174] The Communists executed a right-wing turn when the U.S.S.R. was invaded and the Confederation of Chilean Workers even asked for a severance of relations with the Axis.[175] On the Right the rupture between Germany and Russia tended to increase sympathies for Germany in conservative and clerical circles,[176] and so distinguished a paper as *El Mercurio* could refer to 'those cordial sentiments of friendship which unite Chile to the Government of Germany'.[177] But such leading Conservatives as Sr. Miguel Cruchaga Tocornal were firm believers in co-operation with the United States, and the *Falange Nacional*, a liberal offshoot of the party, under the presidency of Sr. Eduardo Frei Montalva, was both anti-Communist and anti-Nazi.

These sentiments were not universal. The activities of the Nazis, supported by the Communists until the invasion of Russia, were perfectly open. But though Germany was becoming increasingly unpopular, even the danger of subversive movements among the German communities, more particularly in southern Chile, in the area between Temuco and Puerto Montt, was regarded with comparative indifference. The antics of González von Marées and his *Vanguardia Popular Socialista* were one thing—he himself was arrested in May on a charge of involvement in an attack on Radical Party headquarters, sent to a lunatic asylum, but released after one day. The danger of any real Fifth Column subversion was quite another. Aguirre Cerda could not bring himself to believe in it.[178] In August, however, the Government was forced to recognise that subversive activities did exist. A number of

Germans were arrested in the region of Puerto Montt and a judicial enquiry was begun at Valdivia. Metal badges showing a sun with a large swastika rising over a Chilean landscape, rifles and cartridges were discovered; documents were impounded; and further arrests, including that of the manager of the Banco Germánico in Santiago, were made in September. The Senate debated the question of Axis activities at length in October and a bill was introduced into the Chamber with the intent of repressing them. But its progress was slow. By the end of the year, when the presiding judge of the Court of Appeal in Valdivia signed a report which described the organization of a Chilean Nazi party, uniformed, run on military lines, with its own police and judicial system, and directed by the Commercial Counsellor of the Germany Embassy, no action had been taken.[179]

Discoveries such as these, even when discountenanced, as they tended to be, by the Minister of the Interior, whose own anti-Nazi sentiments, however, were perfectly clear,[180] strengthened rather than weakened the desire, on which nearly all sections of opinions were united, to preserve neutrality. Chileans might have a genuine sympathy for the democracies, a genuine admiration for President Roosevelt, a genuine desire for Pan American solidarity, and a genuine anxiety about continental defence. But they were hard-headed, cautious and independent,[181] and they had no desire for defence to be converted into offence, or to be dragged into a war which would leave their long coast-line exposed to hit-and-run attacks from the Far East. Chile had accepted, in April, 1940, an agreement for a United States Military Aviation Mission. She had entered, before the Havana Conference, into staff conversations with the United States and had promised, somewhat vaguely, that if the United States were attacked Chile would assist her. After the Conference, she had welcomed the invitation extended to Latin American Chiefs of Staff to visit the United States. But she had also shown great sensitivity over the question of United States bases,[182] and while, early in 1941, she had gone so far as to seize Danish ships in Talcahuano harbour, she had rejected in March a proposal for the establishment of a United States naval observers' office at Punta Arenas. She had also been somewhat offended at not being invited to join with the United States, Brazil and Argentina in mediation in the Peruvian-Ecuadorean dispute in May.[183] Economically, she had sought to mitigate the effects of the war by fostering trade with her neighbours, negotiating commercial treaties with Argentina, Brazil, Perú and Bolivia and despatching trade missions. Both in 1940 and 1941 she had also sought assistance from the United States not only in the form of Export-Import Bank loans to enable the Chilean Development Corporation to buy hydro-electrical and railway equipment, but in the purchase of her nitrates and copper,[184] and in August, 1941, she had agreed in principle to the sale to the United States of her strategic materials.[185] But in 1941, as in 1940, neutrality remained her watchword, though Oscar Schnake, looking across the Pacific, asked the question, 'Can Chile remain neutral by her own wish as an independent nation?' and supplied the answer, just so long as it suited the conqueror.[186]

The appointment of Rossetti as Foreign Minister had a distinctly favourable effect on Chilean-United States relations. He immediately took steps to force the German consul at Valparaíso, who had been guilty of infringing Chilean laws, to leave the country. In July he declared that if the territorial integrity and independence of the American nations were attacked, Chile would contribute to the common effort.[187] He made no difficulty in October in agreeing to an American request that ships of the United States navy on patrol duties might use the ports of Antofagasta and Valparaíso for fuel and supplies,[188] and Chile, like Uruguay, favoured a joint Pan American protest in November against the German execution of French hostages.[189] On the other hand, like Argentina, she had rejected in July the Uruguayan proposal to regard as non-belligerent any American nation at war with a non-American state, and a basic Lend-Lease allocation presented to her in the same month of $50 millions provoked such prolonged discussion and concern that no agreement had been reached by the time that the United States entered the war.[190]

One object of Chilean policy at this time, for which she wanted American support, was the defence of the Magellan Straits, the alternative route to the Panamá Canal from the Atlantic to the Pacific. The Straits had been neutralised under the Argentine-Chilean Treaty of 1881, but Chile, fearing that shipping in them might become liable to Japanese attack, sought Argentine consent to their fortification. Having in November, 1940, suddenly announced the annexation of Antarctica between 53° and 90° degrees of longtitude, thus cutting across both British and Argentine claims, she had reached an agreement on these with Argentina in March, 1941. But a favourable settlement of the Straits question eluded her. It appeared to have been reached in December. But appearances were deceptive,[191] and Argentine recalcitrance, it may be thought, was hardly calculated to win Rossetti's approval, in opposition to Brazil, of that regional southern bloc which Dr. Ruiz-Guiñazú sought to promote.[192]

Rossetti seems to have been disliked by his colleagues in the Council of Ministers.[193] He did not belong to the powerful Radical party or to the Chilean élite—he was the son of an Italian grocer.[194] But with the death of President Aguirre Cerda shortly before the attack on Pearl Harbour, his influence became, for the moment, decisive. According to Claude Bowers, the American Ambassador, in an account clearly derived from Rossetti himself, it was at his instigation and under the threat of his resignation that the Chilean Government acted without delay on the news of the Japanese attack. Non-belligerent status was granted to all American nations which were at war. Measures were immediately taken to protect mines and industries in American ownership and to secure the uninterrupted flow of strategic materials; and Rossetti not only asked for a meeting of American Foreign Ministers, he authorised Bowers to say that Chile was in complete accord with the United States and would fulfil her obligations as to 'common continental defense'. He was pledged to Aranha, Bowers reported, to put Chile at the side of Brazil and the United States.[195]

But though Platonic expressions of Pan Americanism abounded in Chile, beyond these measures the Government was reluctant to go. Chile, declared La Nación, could not afford the attitudes of belligerency. She was too exposed and too ill-defended;[196] and La Nación spoke for Chilean opinion in general. The press lamented the inevitable loss of Japanese trade and foresaw serious economic consequences. And not only the press but the public, members of the armed forces and of Congress, and Rossetti himself feared the possibility of Japanese attack.[197] In order to be able to counter these fears Rossetti even asked for a signed protocol, for secret use if necessary, to the effect that the United States would support Chile if she were attacked by any nation outside the hemisphere—a request which Sumner Welles regarded as redundant, though authorising Bowers to deliver a signed communication repeating specific promises of military assistance made in the past.[198] Ecuador and Perú, of course, also had exposed coasts. But Ecuador and Perú were nearer to the United States, whose defensive shield could be cast over them. Chile remembered her vital power plants for the great mining establishments such as at Tocopilla, her oil and water storage tanks, the nitrate recovery plants, and the nitrate and copper ports on her northern coast. She would argue that it was more important for the Allies to be certain of the supply of Chilean —and Bolivian—minerals exported from Chilean ports than to have the purely moral support which was all that Chile could contribute to the Allied cause by a rupture of relations with the Axis or a declaration of war.[199]

V

UNITY OR UNANIMITY?

Under the Declaration of Reciprocal Assistance and Cooperation for the Defense of the Nations of the Americas adopted at
the Havana Conference in July, 1940, a consultative meeting
of American Foreign Ministers became almost automatic so
soon as an act of aggression had been committed by a non-
American against an American state. Long before the attack
at Pearl Harbour, indeed before the passage of the Lend-
Lease Act itself, the State Department had begun to consider
whether such a meeting was not desirable in any event, given
the unilateral direction of United States policy away from Pan
American neutrality towards belligerency. But, concerned at
this drift as some of her southern neighbours were, the United
States could not find sufficient support for a meeting. Nor was
Sumner Welles, at any rate, sure that it was desirable.[1] With
the sudden attack on Hawaii on the morning of 7 December
opinion was instantly transformed. That evening Cordell Hull
informed the other American republics that the United States
had been subjected 'to acts of unprovoked aggression' perpetrated 'under conditions of the most infamous treachery', and
asked for an expression of their views. On the 9th both the
United States and Chile notified the Governing Board of the
Pan American Union, of which Hull was chairman, of their
desire for a consultative meeting,[2] and on the 10th the Department of State put forward an agenda for the Board and its
member states to consider.

The response was immediate. The Latin American countries were deeply stirred. The United States had not taken
America into war. War had come to America. By the evening
of the 11th all of the republics except Bolivia, Cuba, Mexico
and Nicaragua, whose accord soon followed, had expressed
their agreement to the proposed meeting, though Honduras,
curiously enough, thought it unnecessary.[3] The Ecuadorean
Foreign Minister had remarked, somewhat pathetically: 'An

Asiatic nation attacks the United States and the hemisphere is with you. Perú, a former friend and neighbor, attacked Ecuador and we bleed partially because of our wounded and dead, partially because of the violation of a principle',[4] and while Ecuador wanted her differences with Perú to be discussed at the conference, Perú did not. Chile proposed that the meeting should be held at Santiago, not at Rio de Janeiro, where the Foreign Ministers had agreed, at Havana, to meet next, and Costa Rica, Guatemala and Venezuela proposed Washington. But the United States, very wisely and much to Brazilian satisfaction, insisted on Rio de Janeiro, not unmoved by the fact that there the chairman of the conference would be the Brazilian Foreign Minister, Dr. Aranha, and alive also to the psychological effect of the meeting taking place in the capital of Brazil.[5] Canada, though hitherto she had held aloof from the Pan American system, suggested that she, too, might be invited to attend, but gracefully accepted President Roosevelt's reasoning that, under existing inter-American arrangements, this would not be possible.[6]

The agenda, approved on the 17th, was divided into two parts. The first, entitled 'The Protection of the Western Hemisphere', was concerned with measures to curb alien activities dangerous to the peace and security of the hemisphere, the exchange of information about the presence of undesirable aliens, and the consideration of measures which might immediately be undertaken 'for the development of certain common objectives and plans which would contribute to the reconstruction of world order'. The second part looked to the strengthening of 'the economic solidarity' of the American republics. It instanced the consideration of measures for the control of exports in order to conserve basic and strategic materials, to increase the production of such materials, to furnish each country with essential imports, to maintain adequate shipping facilities and to control prejudicial alien financial and commercial activities.[7] There was no official proposal in these early days that the eight as yet non-aligned states should sever relations with the Axis powers, but much unofficial discussion and speculation. In Brazil Aranha had given what the American Ambassador, Jefferson Caffery, called 'pep talks' to all the Latin American representatives at

Rio de Janeiro, speaking 'very seriously' and saying that 'this is the fight of all the Americas'[8]; and Sumner Welles, who was to lead the American delegation, early sought Aranha's views about the possible 'formulation of a common continental policy' and also on the attitude which Chile and Argentina might take over a severance of diplomatic relations with the Axis 'as part of a continental security policy'.[9] Brazilian reports were re-assuring. 'You can tell Welles', Aranha told Caffery, 'that I shall be whole-heartedly with him at the conference on every question except one; and that is the blacklist. The British handle their blacklist in such a way as not to offend us. Your publication of the blacklists *et cetera*, has caused me personally no end of trouble'.[10] But the attitude of Argentina, more particularly in view of the declaration of a state of siege on 16 December and the measures taken under it to stifle, though not wholly successfully, expressions of Argentine opinion, a report that at a cabinet meeting Ruiz-Guiñazú had argued against any closer co-operation with the United States and in favour of the strictest possible neutrality, and the rumour that he intended to have discussions with the Foreign Ministers of Chile, Paraguay, Bolivia and possibly Perú on their way to Rio de Janeiro in order to secure their support of the 'Argentine position'—in the event the Bolivian Foreign Minister flew direct to Rio de Janeiro—caused much concern.[11] So, to a lesser degree, did the possible attitude of Chile, Rossetti, the Foreign Minister, sending messages to Welles that he wished to see him before the conference opened, and Hull and Aranha urging him (and Aranha exerting his influence in Perú, Paraguay and Bolivia as well) to take no hard and fast line before that date.[12] Welles was sufficiently confident to tell Lord Halifax late in December that he expected the Conference to take the kind of action desired by the Allies and that he did not think that the Argentine Government would relish being in a minority of one.[13]

One 'kind of action' was exemplified in a draft resolution which the United States circulated on 1 January, 1942, to a number of American Foreign Ministers. It referred to 'the concerted plans for world conquest on the part of the Governments of Germany, Italy and Japan', now suddenly 'placed in execution against the Western Hemisphere' through the 'treacherous attack committed by Japan upon the United States' and by the declaration of war immediately following by all three of the Axis powers, and declared that the American republics 'for the purpose of protecting and preserving' their 'freedom and integrity' could no longer maintain relations 'whether political, commercial or financial' with Germany, Italy and Japan.[14]

The Dominican Republic had gone further, Generalissimo Trujillo suggesting to Haiti that the two countries propose that all the republics should declare war jointly.[15] Coincidentally this at first was also the opinion of the United States Chief of Staff, General Marshall, and of Admiral Stark, who would have preferred a declaration of war to a severance of relations,[16] and the Joint Intelligence Sub-Committee of the Chiefs of Staff in London (whose opinion, of course, was not asked) was inclined to take the same view though the Latin American Department of the Foreign Office was doubtful.[17] Welles, for his part, was rightly certain that it would be impossible to persuade all the Latin American states to join in the war as belligerents. He also differed from the Army and Navy Departments, but got his way through the support of Roosevelt, in advocating the establishment of an Inter-American Defense Board, consisting of military and naval representatives of each of the republics, meeting in Washington but without executive responsibilities.[18]

Welles and the American delegation, which included Wayne Taylor, the Under-Secretary of Commerce, Warren Lee Pierson, of the Export-Import Bank, and Carl Spaeth, of the Board of Economic Warfare, arrived at Rio de Janeiro on the 12th, three days before the Conference opened and two before the beginning of the German submarine campaign on the Atlantic coast of North America. Hull had felt unable to leave Washington. But it had been agreed on the eve of Welles's departure that the prime object of United States policy should be to obtain a joint declaration on the part of the American republics to break off relations with the Axis[19], and in a later exchange of telegrams, after Welles had seen Ruiz-Guiñazú for the first time, it was also agreed that it would be preferable to allow Argentina to proceed alone rather than to accept a compromise formula.[20] Ruiz-Guiñazú had arrived on the 14th. His efforts to induce his Chilean, Peruvian and Paraguayan colleagues to support the 'Argentine position' had failed.[21] But Argentina, significantly, had agreed to take over the representation of Italian interests in Mexico and Central America.[22] She had protested vigorously against the signing of the Declaration of the United Nations of 1 January by nine Latin American states which had already, and without prior consultation, declared war, observing that 'there is a certain contradiction in inviting us to participate in the study and adoption of measures of common defense at the same time that nine countries proceed without prior exchange of views in defining in absolute form their double position, intracontinental and extracontinental, with the consequent risk and responsibilities of a state of war'.[23] And Ruiz-Guiñazú even argued that an attack in the mid-Pacific on Asiatic possessions of the United States did not itself constitute an attack on the Americas.[24]

Rossetti also arrived on the 14th, though not in company with Ruiz-Guiñazú. His was an embarrassed position. Presidential elections were due to be held in Chile in a fortnight's time. The status of the existing government was provisional, and Rossetti was well aware that he might not be Foreign Minister for long. In the opinion of Bowers, the American Ambassador, he was 'miles ahead of nine tenths' of Chilean politicians of all parties, including bitter enemies of Germany and warm friends of the United States, in wanting complete co-operation with the United States. But he had 'iron-clad instructions' not to break with the Axis, such was Chilean alarm over the country's vulnerability to attack.[25] Japan, of course, was far distant. But, as the Foreign Office in London had learnt from a secret source, and as the Chilean Ambassador in Tokyo had told his government, Japan was confident in December of securing command of the sea in the South Pacific, when she could resume normal trade with South America, especially with Chile and Perú;[26] and the fear of such supremacy and the consequent threat to Latin America worried both the Admiralty and the Foreign Office.[27] Chileans read with alarm newspaper reports of blackouts and alleged plans for evacuation on the west coast of the United States.[28] On the very eve of the Rio de Janeiro Conference

Japan began the invasion of the Netherlands East Indies, and it is not likely that Chile would have had the hardihood two days later to reply, as Aranha robustly replied in effect, 'So what?', when the Italian Ambassador warned him that if Brazil severed relations with the Axis, Japan would declare war on Brazil, implying that difficulties would follow with the Japanese colonies there.[29]

Of Aranha's stand, like that of Dr. Guani, the Foreign Minister of Uruguay, there was no doubt. He had been active behind the scenes before the Conference convened in lobbying other non-aligned states;[30] he made every effort to force an early settlement of the Peruvian-Ecuadorean dispute outside the Conference rooms so that the Conference should not be embarrassed; and he had the powerful support of President Vargas. On the 10th Vargas had called together his cabinet and his military and naval chiefs and told them that he had reached the decision that, in the highest interests of Brazil as well as because of her prior commitments, 'Brazil must stand or fall with the United States'. Both General Dutra, the Minister of War, and General Góes Monteiro, the Chief of Staff, had declared that Brazil's ability to defend herself was very limited. Nevertheless, Vargas told Welles, they had acquiesced; and, once the Conference had begun, Vargas used all his great influence, so Welles reported, to induce the Chilean Government to agree to an immediate severance of relations with the Axis, not only interviewing Ruiz-Guiñazú also, but.sending a personal message to Acting President Castillo in Argentina.[31]

Yet Vargas's address of welcome at the opening of the Conference on 15 January was caution itself. He said nothing about a break in relations, but contented himself with praising President Roosevelt, affirming Brazil's intention to defend her territory, and emphasising the importance of economic collaboration, remarks which earned the commendation of the Italian Ambassador himself.[32] The speech of Sumner Welles did not. Welles declared that 'the security of the three-hundred millions of people who inhabit the Western Hemisphere' and the independence of each of the countries represented at the Conference would be determined by whether the American nations stood together or stood apart. He denied

that the United States had made any suggestion or any request as to the course which any other American government
should take. He referred to a 'holy war' and to a 'ruthless and
barbarous foe', to the danger of Axis activities in the hemisphere, to the problems of economic warfare and economic
defence, and to the necessity that 'the united voice of the free
peoples of the Americas must be heard' when peace was
made.[33] Dr. Aranha called for 'common action' and 'continental organisation' to protect America from the fate of Europe,
and Dr. Guani, on behalf of Uruguay, declared that he was
prepared to support a resolution providing for a rupture of
relations with aggressor countries and would propose that any
State defending an American nation should be considered as a
non-belligerent.[34] It was left to the Mexican Foreign Minister,
Ezequiel Padilla, however, in an impassioned oration, not at
the opening of the sessions but on 23 January, to refer to the
'luminous spirit, heroically haughty and full of faith' of England and to the 'subjugated peoples' who yet kept alive the
flame of hope.[35]

Welles himself almost studiously avoided any reference to
the struggle which Britain, the Commonwealth and Empire
had been waging virtually alone. 'In line with the [State]
Department's general policy of not acting jointly with the
British in matters pertaining to the other American republics',
he had told the American diplomatic and consular officers in
Latin American in August, 'care should be exercised that such
co-operation is not in the nature of joint action'.[36] And, with
Pan Americanism rampant, Sir Noel Charles, the newly
appointed British Ambassador to Brazil, wondered whether
the fact that the United States was now a belligerent and an
ally had almost escaped notice. Charles had made a point of
calling on Welles in Washington, and had been impressed.
But he was only able to exchange the barest courtesies with
him on two formal occasions in Rio de Janeiro.[37] Welles, of
course, was extremely pre-occupied. But it could hardly have
been made plainer either at Rio de Janeiro, or while the
preparations for the Conference were in hand, that the State
Department had no wish for Britain to play any political part
in 'the rallying of Latin America'. Late in December Lord
Halifax had told Welles that Britain was 'anxious to give any

help' that she could to the United States 'in the evolution of
South American policy and to do nothing which might run
counter to it'. Again, early in January, Halifax was instructed
that Britain would be prepared 'favourably to consider any
suggestions for positive action' which the State Department
might think useful and, in particular, any specific action likely
to bring about an improvement in the Argentine situation.
But to these approaches Laurence Duggan, the Department's
Adviser on Political Relations, replied politely but negatively,
and, in the opinion of some members of the Foreign Office,
evasively.[38]

During the Rio de Janeiro Conference itself, Wayne Taylor,
of the Department of Commerce, who happened to be an old
friend of a member of the British Embassy's staff, Philip
Broadmead, spoke to Broadmead of an alleged impression
among certain Latin American delegations that Britain was
indifferent to the independent attitude which the Argentine
Government was supposed to be going to adopt. He was then
told of what had passed at Washington and of Britain's continued willingness to help. But when he was asked to ascertain
Welles's views, he did not hesitate to say that it was useless to
try to get Welles to make suggestions since he was fun-
damentally opposed to asking the United Kingdom to help
the United States in any American problem. Taylor, for his
part, wondered whether Britain could not 'rub into' the
Argentines the fact that they would find themselves in shipping
difficulties if they held aloof—a view which Adolf Berle, then
an Assistant Secretary in the State Department, apparently
shared —though the Foreign Office knew, and the Foreign
Office knew that the Argentines knew, that, for supply
reasons, Britain could not afford to send fewer ships to
Argentina.[39]

It could, of course, be argued, and was argued in the
Foreign Office, that there was nothing particularly unreason-
able on the part of the United States in wishing to maintain
independence of leadership in Pan American affairs and to
reserve responsibility in this sphere for herself; and, indeed,
that the promotion of Pan American co-operation, for which
Welles stood, required that there should not be too apparent a
collaboration with Britain. But it was also questioned whether

Welles's 'marked intention', as Sir Noel Charles put it, 'to keep non-members of the Pan American Union out of the orbit of the Conference brought any real advantage to the United States, while, again in Charles's opinion, it did raise a feeling of surprise in a number of Latin American delegates, especially when it was fully realised that the United States was opposed to the presence of Canada.[40] As for economic affairs, in these as in other matters, the Foreign Office was anxious to secure the fullest possible co-ordination of Anglo-United States war-time activities in Latin America as elsewhere;[41] and the Ministry of Economic Warfare, on January 1, had suggested a number of detailed measures which it would have liked to see put forward. None was adopted. The United States took the view that it would be impossible to secure more than general recommendations at the Conference and the United States delegation later argued that most of what the Ministry wanted had in fact been covered by these recommendations.[42]

With the organization of the Conference for business under Dr. Aranha's chairmanship, two Committees were formed, one for the Defense of the Continent, of which Dr. Aranha was also chairman, and one for the Economic Solidarity of the Hemisphere, over which Sr. Padilla presided. Each appointed sub-committees, and within a few days more than eighty projects or proposals had been tabled. But everything at the outset was subordinated to the major question which all anticipated and some feared—the question of a rupture of relations with the Axis. The critical resolution was presented on the 16th by Dr. Gabriel Turbay, the Colombian Ambassador in Washington, in the names of Colombia, Mexico and Venezuela. It proposed a joint severance of relations, political, economic and financial, with the Axis powers in terms very similar to those of the proposal circulated by the Department of State on 1 January.[43] The delegates of the three countries had seen Ruiz-Guiñazú and had told him that under no consideration would they recede from the position they were taking and that they had the support of every nation of the continent except Chile and Argentina. Welles had also seen him and had found him 'wavering and vacillating' and obviously much shaken by the strong line taken by the other

delegations and by public opinion in Brazil. 'I am now beginning to believe' wrote Welles, 'that the Argentine Government
may decide to come along mainly because of the firm attitude
taken by President Vargas and Aranha . . .'[44]

At this point the Axis took a hand, the German, Italian and
Japanese Ambassadors all writing to Aranha on the 16th and
17th, the German Ambassador stating bluntly, and his two
colleagues in more veiled fashion, that if Brazil broke diplomatic relations, she could anticipate a state of war. Aranha
was unmoved,[45] and so, apparently, was Vargas. The decision
of his government, he told Welles, was final, but it implied,
inevitably, that Brazil would soon be actually at war. He had
assumed a great responsibility on behalf of the Brazilian
people, more particularly because of the meagre results of his
efforts to obtain at least a minimum of war supplies from the
United States—a statement which moved Welles and
Roosevelt to action. 'Tell President Vargas', Roosevelt telegraphed on the 19th, 'I wholly understand and appreciate the
needs and can assure him flow of material will start at once.'[46]

The issue was now joined. By the 18th Ruiz-Guiñazú was
reported to be 'in a state of panic', such was the pressure that
had been brought to bear upon him by Vargas, Aranha,
Welles and others, and fearful that Argentina would be completely isolated and deprived even of Chilean support, since
Rossetti was known to have sent urgent messages to his Government asking for full authority to accept the joint resolution.
Seeking a way out, he suggested that an additional article
should be added to the resolution to the effect that any republic which felt it impossible to break relations at once could
adhere to it later and that meanwhile Argentina would submit
two further proposals, first, that the American Republics condemned the attack on the United States and reaffirmed their
decision to lend assistance to her, and, secondly, that each
would negotiate with the United States the form in which such
assistance should be given and would enter into bilateral or
multilaterial conventions necessary for the defence of the continent. Welles was not sympathetic; and while he was careful
to avoid saying anything which could be used as a complaint
that the United States was bringing economic or financial
pressure to bear on Argentina, he did ask members of his

delegation to make it clear to Raúl Prebisch and other members of Ruiz-Guiñazú's team that the economic and financial assistance which the United States could give to the American republics would necessarily be limited to those nations which were whole-heartedly and effectively co-operating with the United States in the defence of the hemisphere.[47] Finally, after a four-hour meeting on the 21st between Aranha, Ruiz-Guiñazú, Rossetti, the Peruvian Foreign Minister, Alfredo Solf y Muro, and Welles, agreement was reached upon the text of a revised joint declaration. The vital clause was the third. It declared that the American Republics 'in the exercise of their sovereignty and in conformity with their constitutional institutions and powers', provided that these were in agreement, could not 'continue their diplomatic relations with Japan, Germany and Italy', since Japan had attacked and the others had declared war upon a nation of the continent. The Argentine Government, Welles reported early on the morning of the 22nd, had officially accepted this text and the Chilean Foreign Minister had also accepted, though with the proviso that he must obtain the official approval of his Government.[48]

This was a very substantial modification of the original resolution. In Washington Hull and his colleagues wondered, as well they might, what meaning was to be attached to the phrase about constitutional institutions and powers, provided these were in agreement. It looked, they thought, very like a loophole,[49] as indeed it was. But all speculation was quickly ended. The Acting President of Chile accepted the text. But no sooner had Castillo read it in Buenos Aires than he flatly repudiated it—to the dismay of the entire Argentine delegation. The Conference was plunged into confusion. The immediate reaction was that Argentina must be left to go her own way.[50] But Vargas, Aranha, and the Foreign Ministers of Bolivia and Uruguay all pleaded that they should not be forced into a position of open antagonism with Argentina, and that if a rupture took place within the American family, their countries would be the ones to suffer. Argentina and Chile, too, they added, would become the *foci* of Axis subversive activities directed against neighbouring states, and in Brazil the army would be both alarmed and probably restive.[51] In the end, after prolonged and agitated discussions during

which, Welles later recorded, 'formula after formula was
brought up only to be rejected', an agreement was reached on
23 January for which Aranha as much as Welles and Ruiz-
Guiñazú had a large share of responsibility.[52] It declared that
the American republics 'following the procedure established
by their own laws within the position and circumstances of
each country in the actual continental conflict, recommend
the rupture of their diplomatic relations with Japan, Germany, and Italy, since the first of these states has attacked and
the other two have declared war upon an American
country'.[53] This, with trivial amendments, became the Resolution on the Breaking of Diplomatic Relations adopted by
the Conference. 'Yesterday', Welles declared in a broadcast
on the 24th, 'the governments of 21 American Republics,
officially and unanimously proclaimed that they jointly recommended the severance of relations' with the Axis. 'For the
first time in the history of our hemisphere joint action of the
highest political character has been taken by all of the American nations acting together without dissent and without
reservations'.[54]

The news of the compromise resolution reached Hull on the
evening of the 23rd, not from Welles or the State Department,
but in a broadcast to which he was listening in his apartment.
He was furiously angry, and in a telephone conversation with
Welles through the White House connection, spoke 'more
sharply' than he had 'ever spoken to anyone in the Department', accusing him of changing the Department's policy
without consultation and of accepting an agreement which
was 'the equivalent of a surrender to Argentina', and ordering
him to disavow it. Roosevelt, who had been listening in, then
joined the conversation, and it was Roosevelt who pronounced
the verdict. Welles was the man on the spot; a decision had
been taken; it must stand.[55] In a long telegram to Roosevelt on
the next day Welles described the concern of his Brazilian,
Uruguayan and Bolivian colleagues at the prospect of an open
breach with Argentina, declared that in the opinion of Aranha
and of the Foreign Ministers of Mexico, Perú and Venezuela
as well as of the heads of the Colombian, Cuban and Bolivian
delegations, the resolution, as approved, was stronger and
more satisfactory than the one Castillo had rejected, and

asserted that had Argentina and Chile 'been forced out of the united line-up, before this Conference closed the United States would have been attacked from one end of the continent to the other for having broken the united American front . . .'[56]

As it was, Perú severed relations with the Axis powers on 24 January, Uruguay and Paraguay on the 25th and Bolivia on the 28th. There had been a flurry of activity behind the scenes in Brazil. General Góes Monteiro had written to General Dutra, the Minister of War, opposing a break, and Dutra, on the 27th, had sent the letter to Vargas with a supporting letter of his own, arguing, as Vargas himself had argued, that a break would mean war, that the Brazilian armed forces were ill-equipped and that it would be wiser to wait until Brazil was in a position to provide loyal co-operation with the United States.[57] But Vargas had received from Welles the personal assurances of Roosevelt; Aranha declared that he himself would resign if Brazil did not fulfil her promises and would tell the world why; and Vargas, though keeping Aranha waiting till the last minute, stood firm.[58] At the end of his closing speech at the final session of the Conference on the evening of the 28th Aranha made the dramatic announcement of the rupture of relations between Brazil and the Axis and also of the settlement of the dispute between Perú and Ecuador, for which negotiations had been taking place concurrently.[59] On the following day Ecuador became the nineteenth American state to break with the Axis. Both Perú and Bolivia had received threatening letters from Japan, but took them in their stride, though President Peñaranda of Bolivia expressed fears of attacks on Bolivian mines by carrier-based Japanese aircraft.[60] Chile had apparently been told that she would not be attacked if she remained neutral, but Rossetti, in a strange mixture of contradictions, told the plenary session on the 24th that 'without the slightest shadow of a doubt' Japan would at once attack Chile, sought renewed assurances from Welles of immediate help from the United States, and told him that Chile was prepared to break off relations without further delay.[61] In fact Chile maintained her neutrality and Argentina hers. Castillo, indeed, had never contemplated any other course. As for Ruiz-Guiñazú, when the plane carrying him and the Argentine delegation home was forced to make a crash-landing in Rio harbour, Aranha was reported to have remarked: 'The plane was not overloaded . . . It was simply Ruiz-Guiñazú's conscience that was heavy'.[62]

To the extent that a major political resolution had been watered down, that a compromise formula had been substituted, and that Argentina and Chile failed to break with the Axis, Hull's judgment, that the united American front had been broken,[63] was plausible. What he failed to grasp, or what Welles had failed to make clear to him, was what the consequences might have been had the compromise been rejected. Welles's own view, expressed both in 1944 and 1950, was that Brazil, in such an event, would have felt it impossible to break relations and that 'the policies of other republics bordering upon Brazil might have been modified accordingly.' By his own account, he expressed this view in the memorable three-cornered telephone conversation with Hull and Roosevelt, though it was not so explicit in his telegram to Roosevelt on the following day.[64] But unanimity was not unity; and, since human frailty and obstinacy are infinite, there would be a high price to pay for this fact in a confrontation between Argentina and the United States. Nothing of this was apparent in Welles's own description of the Conference after that confrontation had begun and Welles himself, in August, 1943, had been forced to resign.[65] Savouring somewhat of self-justification, it was couched in laudatory terms. The Ministers who attended it, his readers were informed, were 'profound students of international affairs' (except for one or two), and Welles used the very best butter in describing them. From the first day to the last, he asserted, he could feel the strength of the spirit animating them (again with one or two exceptions), and 'the force which moved them was not only a determination to achieve unity, but a realisation that Pan-Americanism had at last become a real, a vital and a living thing'.[66]

Inevitably, the recommendation that the republics should sever relations with the Axis and not renew them without prior consultation was the centre of the stage at Rio de Janeiro and also of world attention. But it was only one of forty resolutions, recommendations and declarations, some of them of great importance. Despite dissentient voices, the Conference resolved, if not to adhere to the Atlantic Charter, at least to take note of it and to express its satisfaction at the inclusion within it of principles declared to 'constitute a part of the juridical heritage of America'. Uruguay had announced her intention of proposing the extension of non-belligerent treatment to British vessels, and the United States had agreed with her.[67] But Argentina was only prepared to 'recommend that special facilities be granted to those countries which, in the opinion of each government, contribute to the defense of the interests of the hemisphere' during the emergency. It was agreed to establish an Emergency Advisory Committee for Political Defense, which would consider such matters as subversive activities, the abuses of citizenship, the control of dangerous aliens, and the like,[68] to transform the Inter-American Neutrality Committee into an Inter-American Juridical Committee, charged in part with the study of present and post-war juridical problems, and to establish an Inter-American Defense Board, composed of 'military and naval technicians' appointed by each government. And there were resolutions also on the co-ordination of national intelligence and investigation services and on the control of radio-telephone and radio-telegraph services.

But it was economic problems, quite as much as political, that interested the majority of the Latin American delegates. The corollory to the recommendation for a severance of diplomatic relations with the Axis was a recommendation to sever all commercial and financial relations and to eliminate all economic activities by the Axis and its nationals prejudicial to the welfare and security of the republics—a recommendation to which Argentina, in pursuit of neutrality, appended the reservation that she was prepared to control the activities of all firms or enterprises managed or controlled by aliens or from non-American belligerent countries, whether Axis or not. It was added that measures should be taken, severally or jointly, to counteract any adverse effects upon the economies of the republics which might result from the application of this recommendation. Welles, in his opening address to the Conference, had been careful to say that 'the arsenal of democracy' was mindful of its hemisphere responsibilities and to promise that the United States would provide for the essential civilian needs of the other American republics 'on the basis of

equal and proportionate consideration' with her own.[69] These
were heartening words for countries which were becoming
more and more dependent on the United States for the solution of their economic problems; and the economic conclu-
sions of the Conference were, for the most part, based on
United States proposals and what the Departments of State
and Commerce in Washington described as a Joint War Production Plan.[70] They had two main purposes. First, they were
intended to secure the 'economic mobilisation' of the hemisphere by such measures as the increased production of basic
and strategic materials, both for military and civilian use, the
improvement of communications by land, sea and air, and the
simplification of problems of exchange. Secondly, they aimed
at strengthening the internal economies of the republics by the
promotion of inter-American commerce, the establishment of
easy credit systems, the control of prices, the adoption of
simple systems of priorities and export controls, the development of natural resources, the promotion of industrial enterprises and similar measures. They called also for the meeting
of an Inter-American Technical Economic Conference
charged with the study of present and post-war economic
problems and a Conference on Systems of Economic and
Financial Control, which met at Washington in July.

Even Hull was constrained to congratulate Welles on some
of these measures,[71] which recognised the vital importance of
Latin America as a source of supply and the vital importance
of providing for its essential needs—no easy task. 'The United
States Government', observed Sir Noel Charles, some months
later, 'have every right to be pleased with the amount of
co-operation they obtained in mobilising the hemisphere in
their and our war against the Axis. Mr Sumner Welles had
little difficulty in forwarding the main interests of His Maj-
esty's Government at the Conference as they were more or less
identical with, or complementary to, those of the American
countries'. His considered conclusion, though it contained a
hint of criticism, was that the Conference represented 'a distinct advance in creating Pan American understanding, which
might have been still greater if more tactfully handled by the
framers of United States policy and/or the United States
Delegation'.[72] And while the Foreign Office, no doubt, would

have liked to see a unanimous breach of relations with the
Axis, and also the opening of South American ports to allied
warships, a minute of 4 April recorded the opinion that 'in
view of the war situation and the intransigent attitude of
Argentina, and, to a lesser extent, of Chile, Mr Sumner Welles
may be considered to have achieved no mean success . . .'[73]

ABBREVIATIONS

D.A.F.R.   *Documents on American Foreign Relations* (13 vols., various eds., Boston, World Peace Foundation, 1939–53).

D.G.F.P.   *Documents on German Foreign Policy, 1918–1945, Series D* (Washington and London, 1949–)

F.O.   Foreign Office Records, Public Record Office

F.R.   *Foreign Relations of the United States, Diplomatic Papers* (Washington, Government Printing Office, 1862–) [The series began as *Papers relating to the Foreign Relations of the United States*, etc.]

NOTES

NOTES TO CHAPTER I

[1] See Preston James, *Latin America* (London, 1943), pp. 4–6. The most densely populated of the mainland states was El Salvador. Of the island republics Haiti had a population of 280 to the square mile, Cuba of under 100, and the Dominican Republic of 72.

[2] It was out of service and under repair in 1939. The traveller by rail could, if the line was not blocked or washed out, complete the tedious journey from Buenos Aires to La Paz and then change to the Arica-La Paz railway, or, earlier, at Uyuni, join the La Paz-Antofagasta line. For Perú he crossed Lake Titicaca by steamer to the port of Puno.

[3] See W. H. Burden, *The Struggle for Airways in Latin America* (New York, 1943). Scadta (*Sociedad Colombo-Alemana de Transportes Aéreos*) of Colombia was the first Latin American air-line, established in 1920.

[4] There was no British line. The only trans-Atlantic services in 1939 were *Lufthansa* (till the outbreak of war), Air France (till the fall of France), the Dutch K.L.M. (till the fall of Holland), and the Italian Lati, inaugurated in December 1939.

[5] Taca (*Transportes Aéreos Centro-Americanos*), founded by a New Zealander in 1932 with its headquarters in Honduras, had been the enterprising pioneer in the transport of freight.

[6] The degree of urbanisation was greatest in Argentina, Uruguay, Chile and Cuba.

[7] J. F. Rippy, *British Investments in Latin America, 1822–1949* (Minneapolis, 1959), pp. 66 ff.; Irving Stone, 'British Long-Term Investment in Latin America, 1865–1913', *The Business History Review*, xlii (1968), p. 323; D. C. M. Platt, *Latin America and British Trade, 1806–1914* (London, 1972), pp. 286–9. *Foreign Capital in Latin America*, published by the United Nations Department of Economic and Social Affairs (New York, 1955) p. 5, gives a figure of only £750 million in 1914.

[8] Chile, Uruguay, Cuba, Perú and Guatemala were next in order of importance, Venezuela, by 1939, taking precedence of Guatemala.

[9] In Rippy's view, British capital invested in Latin America reached its peak near the end of 1928 when a gradual contraction began with the sale of several public utilities to corporations controlled by American capital. *op. cit.*, p. 75.

[10] Mexico and Cuba accounted for more than half the total of American investments. The total itself had fallen to some three and three quarter billions in 1939, the greater part being direct investments. More than a half of these were in so-called 'colonial' enterprises, the production for export of mineral, agricultural and forest products. Direct investments were largest in Cuba, Chile, Argentina and Mexico, portfolio in Brazil, Argentina, Chile and Colombia.

[11] See W. E. Feuerlein and Elizabeth Hannan, *Dollars in Latin America* (New York, 1941), pp. 19–21.

[12] Argentina, Venezuela, Cuba, Uruguay, Honduras, the Dominican Republic and Haiti were notable in fulfilling all or the greater part of their obligations. Brazil, Chile, Colombia and many other countries were still either wholly or mainly in default at the end of 1939.

[13] P. R. Olson and C. A. Hickman, *Pan American Economics* (New York, 1943), p. 407.

[14] The first organized emigration of Japanese labourers to Perú had taken place in 1899 and the first Japanese settlement in Brazil in 1908. But it was not till after the first World War that emigration, a controlled emigration, increased to any great extent.

[15] Robertson to Austen Chamberlain, 20 April, 1928; to F. W. Goodenough [n.d.], Public Record Office, F. O. 371/12737; *Evening Standard*, 11 Dec. 1928, F. O. 371/12737, Doc. A 8506/2687/2.

[16] For accounts of Brazilian German bilateral trade see P. W. Bidwell, *Economic Defense of Latin America* (Boston, 1914), pp. 41–4; F. D. McCann, Jr., *The Brazilian-American Alliance, 1937–1945* (Princeton, 1973), pp. 148–75, and S. E. Hilton, *Brazil and the Great Powers, 1930–1939. The Politics of Trade Rivalry* (Austin and London, 1937), *passim*. Barter agreements with Germany were signed by Argentina, Bolivia, Brazil, Chile, Costa Rica, Ecuador, Paraguay, Uruguay and Venezuela.

[17] *New York Times*, 9 April, 1939.

[18] *Cf.* Bryce Wood, *The Making of the Good Neighbor Policy* (New York and London, 1961), p. 286. The Act looked to the negotiation of reciprocal and non-discriminatory tariff reductions. Agreements had been signed with eleven Latin American states by the end of 1939. Of these Brazil was the most important. The Cuban Reciprocity Treaty of 1934 was an exception to the non-discriminatory principle. It increased the substantial measure of preference which United States exports enjoyed over the exports of other countries. The Act, of course, was not limited to Latin America.

[19] United States Tariff Commission, *The Foreign Trade of Latin America. Part I. Trade of Latin America with the World and with the United States* (Revised). Report No. 146. Second Series (Washington, D.C., 1942), pp. 22–3, 59; Olson and Hickman, *op. cit.*, pp. 406–7.

[20] Tariff Commission, *op. cit.*, pp. 17, 20.

[21] There were two longer coast-to-coast isthmian railways, traversing Costa Rica and Guatemala.

[22] This quasi-protectorate, under the terms of the so-called 'Platt Amendment' to the United States Army Appropriation Act of 1901, was imposed upon Cuba when the island received its independence in the aftermath of the Spanish-American War. After the withdrawal of United States forces in 1902 the right of intervention was exercised from September 1906 to January 1909, in 1912 and 1917, and, virtually, from 1921–23 in the person of General Enoch Crowder.

[23] For the part played by Sumner Welles see E. D. Cronon, *Josephus Daniels in Mexico* (Madison, 1960), pp. 67–72; Wood, *op. cit.*, pp. 62–117; and Irwin F. Gellman, *Roosevelt and Batista. Good Neighbor Diplomacy in Cuba, 1933–1945* (Albuquerque, New Mexico, 1973), pp. 12–83.

[24] Rees (Havana) to Eden, 8 May, 1936, F. O. 371/19779. Batista, by this time, was commander-in-chief. Hugh Thomas, *Cuba, or the Pursuit of Freedom* (London, 1971), and Gellman, *op. cit.*, provide excellent studies of events in the thirties.

[25] The Dominican Republic having defaulted on her debts, the Unites States took over the receivership of her customs in 1905, partly to avert European intervention, partly to protect her own interests. A similar receivership was established in Haiti in 1916. There, as in the Dominican Republic, the United States fiscal representative was withdrawn in 1941, but a measure of fiscal control was retained through American representation on the Board of the Haitian National Bank.

[26] Strictly speaking El Salvador is not a Caribbean state since she has only a Pacific coastline. But she qualifies as an honorary member.

[27] American marines had landed in Nicaragua in 1912 and remained there, with a brief interval, till 1923. They had intervened in Honduras in 1924. And though these

interventionist days were over, their memory remained. In all fairness it should be remembered that the United States had tried hard to preserve peace and order both in Central America and the islands.

[28] Between 1917 and 1919, during the régime of President Federico Tinoco Granados, who had come into power by a *coup d'état*. Curiously enough, the country was at war during these years with the only major power which had recognized the Tinoco régime — Germany.

[29] Adam (Panamá) to F.O., 26 Jan., 1939, F.O. 371/22781; Lyall (San José) to F.O., 5 Nov. 1940, F.O. 371/24219.

[30] Tel., Adam to Halifax, 12 Sept, 1939, F.O. 371/22781.

[31] Sugar and tobacco did compete. But American sugar production was quite insufficient for American demand, and Cuban cigar and leaf tobacco enjoyed a unique prestige.

[32] The number of Germans in Central America, some of them World War I veterans, and some refugees, was usually estimated at about 16,000 and of these over a half were in Guatemala.

[33] The population was of the order of three and a half millions in 1935, of which possibly a fifth was white, somewhat smaller proportions negro and Indian, and the remainder of mixed origin. It was predominantly rural and illiterate.

[34] *Cf.* Keeling (Caracas) to Simon, 5 Jan., 1934, F.O. 371/17618; MacGregor (Caracas) to Eden, 24 Dec., 1935, F.O. 371/19845. Only in the number of his children (over a hundred) did Gómez, who was unmarried, merit the title of *pater patriae*.

[35] MacGregor to Eden, 24 Dec., 1935, F.O. 371/19845.

[36] For a brief but dispassionate account of López Contreras see J. L. Salcedo Bastardo, *Historia Fundamental de Venezuela* (Caracas, 1970), pp. 581-3, and for his memoirs, E. López Contreras, *Gobierno y Administración, 1936–41* (Caracas, 1966).

[37] The total population was roughly eight and three quarter millions, of which about a fifth was white.

[38] *Cf.* Dickson (Bogotá) to Simon, 6 June, 1934, 7 Jan., 1935, F.O. 371/17513 and 371/18673.

[39] *Cf.* Paske Smith (Bogotá) to J. Balfour, 23 Jan., 1939; to Halifax, 7 Feb., 1939, F.O. 371/22744.

[40] A pipe line from the oil-fields to the Gulf had been completed in 1926 and another in 1939. The banana industry was in the hands of the United Fruit Company.

[41] See W. P. McGreevey, *An Economic History of Colombia, 1845–1930* (Cambridge, 1971), pp. 195–8, 207, 231.

[42] The population numbered rather more than 19,600,000 in 1940. Perhaps nearly a third consisted of pure-blooded Indians and sixty per cent of mestizos, the Indian blood predominating.

[43] Daniel Cosío Villegas, *Change in Latin America. The Mexican and Cuban Revolutions* (Lincoln, Nebraska, 1961), p. 24.

[44] Superseding, in effect, the Confederación Regional Obrera Mexicana, founded in 1918.

[45] Replacing the P.R.N., or National Revolutionary Party, and becoming in 1945 the P. R. I. or Institutional Revolutionary Party.

[46] Cronon, *op. cit.*, pp. 193–8; Wood, *op. cit.*, pp. 208–19.

[47] Wood, *op. cit.*, pp. 225–7.

[48] Cronon, *op. cit.*, pp. 208–19.

[49] *ibid.*, pp. 233–4. Sales to Japan were made difficult by the long haul from the east coast and the lack of facilities on the west. They ceased by the end of 1940.

[50] *Sociedad Ecuatoriana de Transportes Aéreos.*

[51] Graham (Quito) to Henderson, 3 March, 18 Aug., 1931, F. O. 371/15091.

[52] Lee (Quito) to Hoare, 26 Aug., 1935, F. O. 371/18681.

[53] It is fair to add that Sr. Federico Páez, installed by the army, survived for two years, and Dr. Aurelio Mosquera Narváez's presidency, beginning in December 1938, was cut short by his death in November 1939. For a portrait of Velasco see G. I. Blanksten, *Ecuador: Constitutions and Caudillos* (Berkeley and Los Angeles, 1951), pp. 46–54.

[54] According to the census of 1940 around seven million. The first census in Ecuador was not held till 1950.

[55] Forbes (Lima) to F. O., 24 March, 1939, F. O. 371/22758.

[56] Marlow (Lima) to Halifax, 11 March, 1938, F.O. 371/21488.

[57] Forbes to Eden, 16 Nov., 1936, F. O. 371/19801.

[58] Forbes to Troubeck, 13 Aug., 1935; Admiralty to Foreign Office, 5 Dec., 1935, F.O. 371/18724.

[59] Forbes to Eden, 27 June, 1936; to Halifax, 26 June, 1939, F.O. 371/19802 and 371/22784.

[60] *e.g.* the Gildermeisters, who, however, had been in Perú for two or three generations and were intermarried with Peruvians, controlled a high proportion of sugar production.

[61] Forbes to Eden, 1 Jan., 1937, F.O. 371/20644.

[62] Forbes to Craigie, 19 June, 1934, F.O. 371/17553.

[63] Apra had a long intellectual history. But the party itself was founded by Haya de la Torre and others in Mexico City in 1924. Born in 1895, Haya de la Torre first came into prominence as a university reformer. Incurring the displeasure of Leguía, he was exiled, travelled widely and spent some time both at Ruskin College, Oxford, and at the London School of Economics. He was narrowly defeated in the 1931 presidential elections, was imprisoned in 1932–3, was released by Benavides and later went into hiding (by no means difficult to locate). His views, including his hostility to capitalism and the United States, were greatly modified in the 1940's, and so were Apra's, which committed itself to Pan Americanism and the democratic cause generally.

[64] *New York Times*, 8 Dec. 1939

[65] Estimated to be 50 per cent Indian, still speaking their own languages, and 33 per cent mestizo or 'cholo'; 75 per cent were illiterate.

[66] See H. S. Klein, *Parties and Political Change in Bolivia, 1880–1952* (Cambridge, 1969), pp. 108 ff.

[67] *ibid.*, pp. 230 ff, 235, 244.

[68] .Wood, *op. cit.*, pp. 168–71

[69] Morris (La Paz) to Eden, 14 July, 1937, F.O. 371/20601.

[70] Rawlins (La Paz) to Halifax, 3, 22 May, 1939, F.O. 371/22716.

[71] Rawlins to Halifax, 14 Dec., 1938, F.O. 371/22752.

[72] Rawlins to Balfour, 23 March, 1939, F.O. 371/22756.

[73] Rawlins to Halifax, 26 April, 22 May, 1939, F.O. 361/22716; Cole Blasier, 'The United States, Germany, and the Bolivian Revolutionaries (1914–1946)', *Hispanic American Historical Review*, 52 (Feb., 1972). pp. 28–9.

[74] Rawlins to Halifax, 28 Aug., 1939, F.O. 371/22716.

[75] Klein, *op. cit.*, p. 321.

[76] Some four and a half millions in 1939.

[77] M. J. Francis, *The Limits of Hegemony. United States Relations with Argentina and Chile during World War II* (Notre Dame, 1977), p. 10.

[78] P.T. Ellsworth, *Chile. An Economy in Transition* (New York, 1945), p. 135.

[79] Alessandri remains a highly controversial figure. Ricardo Donoso, *Alessandri, Agitador y Demoledor. Cincuenta años de historia política de Chile* (2 vols., Mexico, 1952–4), is one of his bitterest critics.

[80] F. B. Pike, *Chile and the United States, 1880–1962* (Notre Dame, 1963), pp. 189, 195.

[81] Chilton (Santiago) to Henderson, 24 July, 1931, F.O. 371/15077; Thompson (Santiago) to Simon, 4 July, 1932, F.O. 371/15826.

[82] Chilton to Simon, 10 March, 1932; Tel., Thompson to F.O., 8 April, 1932; Thompson to Simon, 24 April, 1932, F.O. 371/15824.

[83] He had foolishly been put in command of the air force by Ibáñez's legally elected successor, Dr. Juan Montero.

[84] Tel., Thompson to F.O., 17 June, 1932; to Simon, 19 June, 1932, F.O. 371/15825.

[85] Chilton to Simon, 22, 24 Oct. 1932, F.O. 371/15828. In the opinion of Sir H. Chilton, the Dávila Administration, overthrown in September 1932 (Dávila's '100 days') was the worst ever experienced in Chile. Tel., Chilton to F.O., 16 Sept., 1932, F.O. 371/15827.

[86] Cf. J. R. Stevenson, The Chilean Popular Front (Philadelphia, 1942), p. 56.

[87] ibid., p. 59.

[88] Aguirre Cerda told a British diplomat that the management of his campaign was in the hands of the Ibáñistas and the Nacistas. Leigh-Smith to Halifax, 23 Oct., 1938, F.O. 371/21437. Cf. Stevenson, op. cit., p. 87. The Nacistas, organized in 1932, were led by Jorge González von Marées. They had strong fascist tendencies and were in some respects a carbon copy of the Nazi Party. Despite this, they had no more connection with Germany than the Falangists, who appeared in 1938, had with Spain. Cf. Bentinck (Santiago) to Halifax, 7 April 1938, F.O. 371/21437, and 6 May, 1938, F.O. 371/21651. The Nacistas later became the Vanguardia Popular Socialista and the Falange Nacional the Christian Democrats.

[89] Bentinck (Santiago) to Eden, 8 Sept., 1937, F.O. 371/20621, 4 Jan. 1938, F.O. 371/21437.

[90] See my Evolution of Modern Latin America (Oxford, 1946), pp. 68–9.

[91] Bidwell, op.cit., p. 13.

[92] The population in 1939 was very nearly thirteen million, of which a fifth was foreign-born.

[93] According to the Director of the Germanic Union the Reichsdeutsche in 1938 numbered 43,626; half of whom were in Buenos Aires itself. The Volksdeutsche, of whatever origin, numbered 193,129, making a total of 236,755 persons of Germanic or mixed German-Argentine blood. The largest concentrations were in Entre Ríos, Buenos Aires Province, Buenos Aires, Misiones and Santa Fe. But Germans had settled from one end of Argentina to the other. Cf. my Evolution of Modern Latin America, pp. 66–7.

[94] Cecil Jane, Liberty and Despotism in Latin America (Oxford, 1929), p. 173.

[95] Macleay (Buenos Aires) to Craigie, 28 June, 1930; to Henderson, 10 July, 1930, F.O. 371/14191; David Rock, Politics in Argentina, 1890–1930 (Cambridge, 1975), pp. 257–64; David Rock, ed., Argentina in the Twentieth Century (London, 1975), pp. 85–6; Peter Smith, Politics and Beef in Argentina. Patterns of Conflict and Change (New York and London, 1969), pp. 134, 137–8.

[96] Macleay to Henderson, 9 Sept., 1930, F.O. 371/14192.

[97] Macleay to Henderson, 9, 20 Sept., 1930, F.O. 371/14192. See Robert A. Potash, The Army and Politics in Argentina, 1928–1945. Yrigoyen to Perón (Stanford, 1969), pp. 43–50.

[98] Macleay to Henderson, 2 June, 1931, F.O. 371/15054; Leche (Buenos Aires) to Simon, 26 April, 1934, F.O. 371/17475. Potash, op.cit., pp. 49, 67–8.

[99] Dodd (Buenos Aires) to Halifax, 14 June, 12 Aug., 1938, F.O. 371/21415; Potash, op.cit., pp. 106–11.

[100] Board of Trade Memorandum, 7 Feb., 1933, F.O. 371/16531, Doc. A 1088/48/2. Cf. Smith, op.cit., pp. 35, 127.

[101] Waley (Treasury) to Troutbeck, 17 March, 1936, F.O. 371/19758. Cf. Rippy, op.cit., p. 159.

[102] R. B. Mitchell and Phyllis Deane, *Abstract of British Historical Statistics* (Cambridge, 1962), pp. 323–6.

[103] Sir Arthur Samuel, *News Chronicle*, 14 Feb. 1933, F.O. 395/501 Doc. P426/151/150. More discreetly and privately, Sir Malcolm Robertson, the Duke of Atholl (Chairman of Anglo-Argentine Tramways), and Sir Neville Henderson, made similar remarks or, at any rate, suggested that Argentina should be treated on the same footing as if she were a part of the Empire. Robertson to Henderson, 17 June, 1929, F.O. 371/13460; Atholl to Foreign Secretary, 18 Aug., 1932, F.O. 371/15797; Henderson to Vansittart, 29 Jan. 1936, F.O. 371/19578.

[104] *Cf.* Rock, *Politics in Argentina*, pp. 218–9.

[105] See Smith, *op.cit.*, pp. 142–7, and, for a succinct statement, George Pendle, *Argentina* (3rd ed., London, 1963), pp. 77–80.

[106] *Cf.* Lindsay (Washington) to Eden, 4, 23 June, 1936, F.O. 371/19759 and 19834, on American opposition to the Roca-Runciman Pact and also to the Anglo-Uruguyan Agreement of 1935, which reserved 80 per cent of the proceeds from Uruguayan exports to Britain for British payments.

[107] Adolf Berle, of the State Department, for example, was understood by the Foreign Office to have been under the delusion (wholly unfounded) that Britain instigated the independent attitude of the Argentine Delegation at the Lima Conference of 1938 (see above, p. 40) out of a desire to thwart United States policies in Latin America. Tel., F.O. to Lothian (Washington) and Forbes (Havana), 24 July, 1940, F.O. 371/24195, Doc. A. 3605/1/51. He certainly entertained also the singular notion that Britain had tried to break up the Buenos Aires conference in 1936. B. B. Berle and T. B. Jacobs, eds., *Navigating the Rapids, 1918–1971. From the Papers of Adolf Berle* (New York, 1973), p. 207.

[108] Smith, *op.cit.*, pp. 146–7.

[109] Tel., Macleay to Simon, 14 June, 1933, F.O. 371/16533.

[110] Smith, *op.cit.*, p. 164.

[111] The President of this body was General Juan Bautista Molina, at one time Military Attaché in Germany. It was alleged to be linked with Nazi and Fascist elements and was both anti-British and anti-American.

[112] Henderson to Eden, 26 May, 1936, F.O. 371/19760. The decree was signed by Dr. Manuel Fresco, celebrated for his contempt for democratic principles. But *La Nación* had only one fault to find with it, namely that it had been issued by the Provincial Governor and not by the Federal Government.

[113] Ovey (Buenos Aires) to Halifax, 3 March, 1938, F.O. 371/21650, Doc. C 2211/34/18; Minute by Balfour, 14 March, 1939, F.O. 371/22756, Doc. A 2455/105/51.

[114] Tel., Ovey to F.O. 5 April, 1938, F.O. 371/21651; Dodd to Halifax, 12 Aug., 1938, F.O. 371/21415.

[115] Ovey to Halifax, 29 April, 1938, F.O. 371/21651.

[116] Dodd to Halifax, 30 May, 1938, F.O. 371/21651.

[117] Ovey to Halifax, 6, 12 April, 1939; Tel., Dodd to Halifax, 16 May, 1939, F.O. 371/22756; Dodd to Halifax, 23, 29 May, 1939, F.O. 371/22714; Dodd to Halifax, 4 July, 1939, F.O. 471/22757; Alton Frye, *Nazi Germany and the American Hemisphere,1933–1941* (New Haven, 1967), pp. 114–16.

[118] Rather more than four million immigrants entered Brazil between 1884 and 1939. Nearly two-thirds were Italian and Portuguese. The Germans numbered 170,645, of whom a half came between 1918 and 1933. See the *Revista de Emigração e Colonização*, i, No. 4 (Rio de Janeiro, 1940).

These figures are exclusive of Austrians (85,790, mostly pre-1914 migrants), German-Swiss and German-Russians. They take no account of re-emigration to Argentina or Paraguay or of returns to Germany. Nor do they include data for the German settlements of the eighteen-forties and earlier.

[119] *e.g.* In Espríto Santo, Minas Gerais, Rio de Janeiro, Bahia and Recife.

[120] But also in Minas Gerais, Espírito Santo, Pará and Amazonas.

[121] For these foreign communities see my *Evolution of Modern Latin America*, pp. 59–66 and 72–3.

[122] Above, p. 6.

[123] *Cf.* Seeds (Rio) to Simon, 26 Dec, 1934, F.O. 371/18651, referring to the 'swelling wave of extreme national feeling directed against foreign public utilities and creditors of all sorts'.

[124] Hilton, *op.cit.*, p. 4.

[125] *ibid.*, pp. 15–19, 26–31, 178, 181.

[126] For a detailed analysis see T. E. Skidmore, *Politics in Brazil, 1930–1964* (New York, 1967), pp. 4–12, and, on the *tenentes*, R. M. Levine, *The Vargas Regime. The Critical Years, 1934–1938* (New York and London, 1970), pp. 2–6.

[127] 'Some are screaming for it, others are against it, so . . .', he told the British Amabassador, 'and he cocked his head at me with an *in medio tutissimus* smile'. Seeds to Simon, 23 Dec., 1931, F.O. 371/15807.

[128] Seeds to Henderson, 15 Dec., 1930, F.O. 371/15059.

[129] J. W. F. Dulles, *Vargas of Brazil. A Political Biography* (Austin and London, 1967), pp. 119–21.

[130] On these incipient mass movements see Peter Flynn, *Brazil. A Political Analysis* (London, 1978), pp. 71–84, and Levine, *op.cit.*, pp. 66–99.

[131] Gurney (Rio) to Eden, 21 June, 1937, F.O. 371/20603; Hilton, *op.cit.*, pp. 170–171.

[132] The so-called 'Cohen Plan', a document which seems to have been forged by the Integralists.

[133] The work of Francisco Campos of Minas Gerais, widely known for his totalitarian sympathies and Vargas's first Minister of Education.

[134] Lindsay (Washington) to Halifax, 1 March, 1938, F.O. 371/21422.

[135] The Foreign Organization of the Nazi Party.

[136] Gurney to Eden, 21 Feb., 8 March, 1938, F.O. 371/21422 and 21650.

[137] Tel., Gurney to F.O., 20 April, 1938, F.O. 371/21428. Gurney understood that the prohibition would not affect Britons, French or Americans. Gurney to Halifax, 28 April, 1938, F.O. 371/21428.

[138] Gurney to Halifax, 18 Feb., 1939, F.O. 371/22722; *New York Times*, 30 Aug., 1939.

[139] Hilton, *op.cit.*, p. 190.

[140] Halifax to H. M. Missions in Latin America, 5 March, 1938, Circular No. 023/1938; Thompson (Hendaye) to Balfour, 22 June, 1938, F.O. 371/21457. The Germans also had their anxieties. The representatives of the organisation held a conference in June, 1939, with German heads of missions in Latin America summoned to Berlin to discuss Latin America reactions to its activities. D[*ocuments on*] G[*erman*] F[*oreign*] P[*olicy*], *1918–1945*. *Series D* (Washington and London 1949-), vi, 700-07.

[141] Mallet (Washington) to Balfour, 23 Dec., 1938, F.O. 371/22756; to Halifax, 5 Aug., 1939; Tel., Lothian to F.O. 24 Oct., 1939, F.O. 371/22757; Notes on German Activities in South and Central America, 15 March, 1939, sent to the French and United States Governments, F.O. 371/22756, Doc, A 2455/105/51.

[142] *The Memoirs of Cordell Hull* (2 vols., London, 1948), i, 602.

[143] *Cf.* Hilton, *op.cit.*, p. 200.

[144] But Argentine-Brazilian rivalries were as apparent in the League as elsewhere. Argentina ceased to take an active part in 1920, having failed to wrest from Brazil the rôle of Latin American leadership in the League, and she did not resume full participation till 1933, after Brazil, not succeeding in obtaining a permanent seat on the Council, had herself withdrawn.

[145] It would seem from the instructions to the United States delegation that the United States had not intended to adhere to such a declaration, but Hull found himself compelled to do so, though not without a reservation. F[oreign] R[elations of the United States. Diplomatic Papers,]. 1933, iv, 67, and Gordon Connell-Smith, *The United States and Latin America* (London, 1974), pp. 163–5

[146] Hull, *Memoirs*, i, 497; I. F. Gellman, *Good Neighbor Diplomacy. United States Policies in Latin America, 1933–1945* (Baltimore, 1979), p. 67.

[147] Hull, *Memoirs*, i, 499; Minutes on Henderson to Eden, 20 Jan., 1937, F.O. 371/20631, Doc. A 1082/3/51.

[148] *Memoirs*, i, 605.

[149] Forbes (Lima) to Halifax, 28 Dec., 1938, F.O. 371/22752, Doc. A 145/51/51.

[150] Minutes on *ibid.*, 'It is not too much to say that the recent gathering in Lima was a check — and the first — to Nazi and Fascist progress in Latin America. It may be hoped that opposition, having once shown itself, may wax and grow'.

[151] Hull, *Memoirs*, i, 609.

[152] *ibid.* i, 604–9. Hull telephoned to the United States Ambassador in Argentina instructing him to get in touch with Ortiz and Ortiz in turn got in touch with Cantilo, who telegraphed new instructions to the Argentine delegation at Lima.

[153] *ibid.*, i, 605–6, 607; McCann, *op.cit.*, p. 121.

[154] Gurney to Balfour, 14 April, 1939, F.O. 371/22722.

[155] Gurney to Balfour, 3, 7 July, 1939, F.O. 371/22722.

NOTES TO CHAPTER II

[1] 2 Oct., 1939.

[2] 4 Nov., 1939.

[3] Tel. Bentinck (Chile) to F.O., 2 Oct., 1939, F.O. 371/22736.

[4] Gurney (Rio) to Balfour, 3 Oct., 1939, F.O. 371/22722. Aranha also said that British warships would be allowed to make repeated visits to Brazilian ports for refuelling provided the visits were discreet and the ports of call varied. Edy (Admiralty) to Beith (F.O.), 30 Sept., 1939, F.O. 371/22762.

[5] Forbes (Lima) to Halifax, 6 Sept., 1939, F.O. 371/22784, Doc A 6812/48/35.

[6] *El Día* (Montevideo), 5 Sept., 1939.

[7] *Panama Star and Herald*, 3 Sept., *El Tiempo* (Colombia), 4 Sept., 1939.

[8] Tel., Dodds (Buenos Aires), to F.O., 2 Sept., 1939, F.O. 371/22713.

[9] The United States proclaimed her neutrality on 5 September (the day after Argentina and Brazil), but repealed her embargo on the export of arms on 4 November, thus permitting sales on a 'cash and carry' basis. This, in effect, meant the sale of arms on an increasing scale to the Allies. The British & French established a Purchasing Commission in December. For Roosevelt's fight to secure this modification of the Neutrality Act see Robert Dallek, *Franklin D. Roosevelt and American Foreign Policy, 1932–1945* (New York, 1979), pp. 199–205.

[10] Tel., Millington-Drake (Montevideo) to F.O., 8 Sept., 1939, F.O. 371/22848.

[11] Gurney (Rio) to Halifax, 4 Sept., 1939, F.O. 371/22722; Anderson (Caracas) to Halifax, 15 Sept., 1939, F.O. 371/22852; *O Brasil e a Segunda Guerra Mundial* (2 vols., Ministério das Relações Exteriores, Rio de Janeiro, 1944), i, 72.

[12] *New York Times*, 14 Sept., 1939.

[13] Tel., Adam (Panamá) to F.O., 23 Sept., 1939, F.O. 371/22761.

[14] Tel., Ovey (Buenos Aires) to F.O., 2 Oct., 1939, F.O. 371/22762. The ban was imposed by Panamá and the United States as well as by Mexico, Brazil and Venezuela. Chile and Uruguay followed suit in 1940.

[15] While reserving her claims at Panamá and, later, at the Havana Conference in 1940, Argentina did not press them. President Ortiz was careful to say in October 1939 that the question in no way affected Argentina's cordial relations with Britain (Ovey to Halifax, 10 Oct., 1939, F.O. 371/22714), and *La Prensa*, on 23rd Oct., declared that the present was no time at which to seek a solution. As for Guatemala, President Ubico stated in December, 1939, that though he had 'a bone to pick' with Britain, it had nothing to do with the war. Tel., Leche to F.O., 27 Dec., 1939, F.O. 371/22765. For the 'bone' see my *Diplomatic History of British Honduras, 1638–1901* (London, 1961), and my article on 'The Anglo-Guatemalan Dispute', *International Affairs*, xxiv (July, 1948), pp. 387–404, and, for a convenient summary of the Falkland Islands question, J.C.J. Metford, 'Falklands or Malvinas. The Background to the Dispute', *ibid.*, xxxiv (July, 1968), pp. 463–81.

[16] Tel., Lothian to F.O., 11 Oct., 1939, and Minute by Perowne, 16 Oct., F.O. 371/22763; Minute by Perowne, 5 March, 1940, F.O. 371/24191, Doc. A 1880/1/51. See also W. L. Langer and S. E. Gleason, *The Challenge to Isolation, 1937–1940* (London, 1952), pp. 207–8, and Stetson Conn and Byron Fairchild, *The Framework of Hemisphere Defense* [The Western Hemisphere. United States Army in World War II] (Washington, D.C., 1960), pp. 22–3.

[17] Hull, *Memoirs*, i, 690. President Benavides of Perú thought it absurd and in Brazil its enforcement was felt to be impracticable. Tel., Forbes (Lima) to F.O., 6 Oct., 1939, F.O. 371/22762, Tel., Gurney (Rio) to F.O., 10 Oct., 1939, F.O. 371/22763. Neither Argentina nor Chile regarded it with favour.

[18] S. E. Morison, *The Battle of the Atlantic, September 1939 to May 1943* [History of United States Naval Operations in World War II] (London, 1948), p. 14.

[19] Adam (Panamá) to Halifax, 2 Oct., 1939, F.O. 371/22763, quoting the *Panama Star and Herald*, 27 Sept., 1939; Langer and Gleason, *op.cit.*, p. 212.

[20] Tel., Adam to F.O., 2 Oct., 1939, F.O. 371/22762.

[21] Tel., Lothian to F.O. 19 Oct., 1939, F.O. 371/22763.

[22] Sendall (Admiralty) to Gage (F.O.), 1 Nov., 1939, enclosing copy of letter sent by Churchill through the American Ambassador, and Minutes, F.O., 371/22763, Doc. A 7530/5992/51; *F.R.*, 1939, v, 85; Winston S. Churchill, *The Second World War. I. The Gathering Storm* (London, 1948), p. 405.

[23] Tels, Rees (Mexico) to F.O., 2 Oct., 1939, F.O. 371/22762; Leche (Guatemala) to F.O., 3 Nov., 1939, F.O. 371/22764; Patterson (Dominican Republic) to Halifax, 22 May 1940, Annual Report for 1939, F.O. 371/24212.

[24] Reid-Brown (El Salvador) to Halifax, 13 Sept., 1939, F.O. 371/22728; Hill to Halifax, 3 Jan., 1940, Annual Report for 1939, F.O. 371/24180.

[25] Tel., Leche to F.O., 16 Oct., 1939, F.O. 371/22763.

[26] Tel., Grant Watson (Havana) to F.O., 15 Sept., 1939, F.O. 371/22761.

[27] D[ocuments on] A[merican] F[oreign] R[elations] (13 vols., various editors, Boston, World Peace Foundation, 1939–53), iii, 134–5.

[28] Tel., Paske-Smith (Bogotá) to F.O., 5 Sept., 1939, F.O. 371/22757; Fox (Petroleum Dept.) to Balfour (F.O.), secret, 30 Dec. 1939, F.O. 371/24270.

[29] *Cf.* Langer and Gleason, *op.cit.*, pp. 215–6; Conn and Fairchild, *op.cit.*, pp. 10–11, 24.

[30] 23 Dec., 1939.

[31] Tel., Lothian to F.O., 14 Dec., 1939, F.O. 371/22048.

[32] Tel., Ovey to F.O., 14 Dec. 1939; Ovey to Halifax, 22 Dec., 1939, F.O. 371/24165.

[33] For the 'Battle of the River Plate' see Churchill, *op.cit.*, pp. 407–16 and the immense monograph of Sir Eugene Millington-Drake, *The Drama of Graf Spee and the Battle of the Plate* (London, 1964).

[34] *La Nación*. 25 Dec., 1939; *El Día*, 24 Dec., 1939.

[35] Tel., Bentinck (Santiago) to F.O., 31 Dec., 1939, F.O. 371/24189; *F.R.* 1939, v, 114.
[36] Personal for the President from Naval Person, 25 Dec., 1939, *F.R.*, 1939, v, 121–2; Churchill, *op.cit.*, p. 418.
[37] Statement on Behalf of the British Government, *F.R.*, 1940, i, 690–2; F.O. to Dodd (Panamá), 13 Jan., 1940, F.O. 371/24189. The German reply was delayed till 14 February.
[38] *La Nación* (Argentina), 16, 18 Jan., 1940; *Panama American*, 25 Jan., 1940.
[39] 27 April, 1940. *D.A.F.R.*, ii, 133–8
[40] Hull, *Memoirs*, i, 690.
[41] W. L. Langer and S. E. Gleason, *The Undeclared War, 1940–1941* (London, 1953), p. 171. Whether it would have been a violation of the 'letter' of the Panamá Declaration, which specifically excluded from the zone the territorial waters of the 'undisputed colonies' of European powers, is open to question. But it would certainly have been a violation of the spirit.
[42] Hull, *Memoirs*, i, 690. See also Conn and Fairchild, *op.cit.*, pp. 24–5.
[43] W. N. Medlicott, *The Economic Blockade* (2 vols., London, 1952), i, 54, 437.
[44] Report on War Trade Lists Policy in Latin America, 5 Dec., 1940, F.O. 371/25063.
[45] *La Prensa*, 6 Oct., *La Nación*, 4 Oct., 1939.
[46] *La Nación*, 1 Feb., 1940; *New York Times*, 6 March, 1940.
[47] Britain maintained that the arms had not been paid for by cash transfer. The Brazilians were infuriated, particularly the Chief of Staff. Eventually the ship was allowed to proceed, partly because of pressure from the United States, partly because a refusal might have seriously impaired Anglo-Brazilian relations and even, it was thought, have led to the fall of the friendly Foreign Minister, Dr. Aranha. *Cf.* Knox (Petrópolis) to Eden, 2 April, 1941 (Annual Report for 1940), F. O. 371/25807; *O Brasil e a Segunda Guerra Mundial*, i, 159–71; Dulles, *Vargas of Brazil*, p. 215.
[48] F.O. Minutes, 15 Feb., 1940, F.O. 371/24270, Doc. A 1423/308/47, and 8 Jan., 1941, F.O. 371/26310, Doc. A. 210/210/47.
[49] Fynes Clinton (La Paz) to Halifax, 25 April, 5 Sept., 1940, Memo., Economic Relations with Bolivia, F.O. 371/24169.
[50] *Cf.* the Anglo-Argentine Payments Agreement of 25 Oct., 1939, which was an extension of the principles laid down in the Anglo-Argentine Treaty of 1936. Similar agreements were concluded in 1940 and 1941 with Brazil, Uruguay, Bolivia, Chile, Paraguay and Perú.
[51] R. S. Sayers, *Financial Policy, 1939–45* (London, 1956), p. 443. Britain suggested in 1940 that the Argentine balances might be used for the purchase of Argentine sterling securities owned by persons in the sterling area. In particular she was anxious to be rid of the inefficient British-owned railways — a proposal not unacceptable to Dr. Federico Pinedo, when Minister of Finance.
[52] Circular Telegram No. 156, 7 Aug., 1940, F.O. 371/24200, Doc. A 3555/18/51; Minute by Perowne, 16 Aug., 1940, F.O. 371/24201, Doc. A 3927/18/51; Draft Instructions, 15 Oct., 1940, F.O. 371/24203, Doc. A 4681/18/51; Willingdon to Cadogan, 27 March, 1941, F.O. 371/25958; Secretary-General of Mission to Department of Overseas Trade, Washington, 7 March, 1941, F.O. 371/25958; Forbes (Lima) to Eden, 2 Jan., 1941, Political Review of the Year 1940, F.O. 371/26140.
[53] Medlicott, *op.cit.*, ii, 31
[54] *ibid, loc.cit.* Keynes added that the greatest act of 'imprudence' was the 'abandonment' of British export business. H. Duncan Hall, *North American Supply* (London 1955), p. 445. For malicious allegations that Britain used Lend-Lease materials in her export trade or obtained materials under Lend-Lease in order that she might export comparable materials, to the disadvantage of Americans, and for the rebuttal of these allegations see *D.A.F.R.* iv, 592–7.

55 Tel., Knox (Rio) to F.O., 9 Sept., 1940, F.O. 371/24201, Doc. A 3882/18/51; Knox to Eden, 2 April, 1941, Annual Report for 1940, F.O. 371/25807.

56 Hadow (Buenos Aires) to Eden, 7 Feb., 1940, F.O. 371/25709.

57 Tel., Forbes (Lima) to F.O., 31 May, 1940, F.O. 371/24220.

58 *El Día* (Uruguay), 14 Sept., 1940.

59 *La Nación* (Chile), 1 Oct., 1940.

60 28 Sept., 1940.

61 Stetson Conn, Rose C. Engelman, Byron Fairchild, *Guarding the United States and its Outposts* [United States Army in World War II] (Washington, 1964), p. 336; Forbes (Lima) to F.O., 6 May, 1941, F.O. 371/26133.

62 The Convention for its establishment was signed only by Bolivia, Brazil, Colombia, the Dominican Republic, Ecuador, Mexico, Nicaragua, Paraguay and the United States. For its fate see David Green, *The Containment of Latin America* (Chicago 1971), pp. 60–73.

63 For the genesis of this plan see Langer and Gleason, *Challenge to Isolation*, pp. 630–34.

64 Finally killed, it has been suggested, by Cordell Hull. *ibid.*, p. 635. See also Gellman, *Good Neighbor Diplomacy*, pp. 93–4, 161.

65 See the list in *D.A.F.R.*, ii, 553–5.

66 *The Time for Decision* (London, 1944), p. 169.

67 It was renamed the Office of the Co-ordinator of Inter-American Affairs in July 1941 and the Office of Inter-American Affairs in March 1945. Despite the initial hostility of Hull and Welles (who tended to regard Latin America as his private bailiwick), it rapidly grew in size and importance, exercised considerable economic influence and led to a proliferation of informational, educational, medical and cultural activities. It was primarily responsible for compiling the United States 'Black Lists'.

68 Hilton, *Brazil and the Great Powers*, p. 219.

69 Phillimore (La Paz), Annual Report for 1940, 12 Jan., 1941, F.O. 371/25768.

70 Welles, *op.cit.*, p. 170; Orde (Santiago) to Eden, 31 Dec., 1941, Annual Report for 1940, F.O. 371/30434.

71 Tariff Commission, *Foreign Trade of Latin America*, Part I, p. 60.

72 H. J. Trueblood, 'Hull Program Hits Snags in Argentina', *Foreign Policy Bulletin*, 12 Jan., 1940, provides a balanced statement.

73 Above, p. 30.

74 *La Nación*, 25 Feb. 1940. The Argentine navy was by no means large. But it did possess two battleships as well as three cruisers and a number of destroyers.

75 13 May, 1940. 'Non-belligerency' may be defined as the avowed support of one belligerent or group of belligerents, limited to non-military action.

76 It is detailed, however, in the great series of documents on American Foreign Relations, *F.R.*, 1940, i, 743–68.

77 Knox (Petrópolis) to Eden, Annual Report for 1940, 2 April, 1941, F.O. 371/25807.

78 *Cf. El Día* and *La Mañana* (Uruguay), 14 May, 1940; *El Mundo* (Argentina), 14 May, 1940.

79 On this remarkable episode see Langer and Gleason, *Challenge to Isolation*, pp. 608–9; S. E. Hilton, 'Argentine Neutrality, September 1939 – June 1940, a Re-Examination', *The Americas*, xxii (1966), pp. 227–57; J. S. Tulchin, 'The Argentine Proposal for Non-Belligerency, April 1940', *Journal of Inter-American Studies*, xi (1969), pp, 571–604; Francis, *Limits of Hegemony*, pp. 57–8.

80 *La Nación*, 15 May, 1940.

81 Above, p. 50.

82 Winston S. Churchill, *The Second World War. Vol II. Their Finest Hour* (London, 1949), pp. 22–3.

[83] Kennedy had been Ambassador since 1938. Fortunately, what Sir John Colville called his 'prophecies of woe' were somewhat counteracted by his second-in-command, Herschel Johnson. To Roosevelt's indignation his was the first Embassy to move out of London in September 1940. J. G. Winant, his successor, arrived early in 1941. John Colville, *Footprints in Time* (London, 1976), pp. 142–3, 146, 154. Roosevelt, in October 1939, had described Kennedy as 'just a pain in the neck to me'. Dallek, *op.cit.*, p. 207.

[84] Hull, *Memoirs*, i, 766; Langer and Gleason, *Challenge to Isolation*, pp. 481–2, and compare Churchill's statement in Parliament on 4 June, 1940.

[85] Potash, *Army and Politics in Argentina*, pp. 124–5.

[86] *D.G.F.P., Series D*, ix, 493–5, 543–7.

[87] *La Prensa*, 20, 22 June, 1940; *La Mañana* (Uruguay), 19 June, 1940.

[88] *D.G.F.P.*, Series D, ix, 660–1 (21 June). Some such note was handed to the Argentine Ambassador in Berlin on 26 June. *Ibid.*, p. 547n.

[89] See Potash, *op.cit.*, pp. 125–40.

[90] *Time for Decision*, p. 174.

[91] Above, pp. 35–7.

[92] Getúlio Vargas, *A Nova Política do Brasil* (11 vols., Rio de Janeiro, 1938–1947), vii, 198.

[93] *ibid.*, p. 198.

[94] *ibid.*, pp. 331–5; *F.R.*, 1940, v, 616–7; Dulles, *op.cit.*, pp. 210–13; McCann, *op.cit.*, pp. 184–7.

[95] *Tel.*, Knox (Rio) to F.O., 11 June, 1940, F.O. 371/24194; Langer and Gleason, *Challenge to Isolation*, p. 617.

[96] *D.G.F.P.*, Series D, ix, 599, 630.

[97] *ibid.*, p. 659 (21 June).

[98] *ibid.*, Series D, x, 41–2. See also Hilton, *Brazil and the Great Powers*, pp. 212–3, and his article, 'Brazilian Diplomacy and the Washington-Rio de Janeiro "Axis" during the World War II Era', *Hispanic American Historical Review*, 59 (May, 1979), especially pp. 206–10.

[99] Above, p. 57; Hilton, *Great Powers*, pp. 217–19.

[100] Tel., Bentinck to F.O., 28 May, 1940, F.O. 371/24193.

[101] Bentinck to Halifax, 22 May, 1940, F.O. 371/24194. Similar representations were made to other Latin American governments. *D.G.F.P.*, Series D, ix, 355–6.

[102] Above, p. 25.

[103] Stevenson, *The Chilean Popular Front*, p. 96.

[104] *ibid.*, pp. 102–4; *El Mercurio*, 16 July, *La Nación*, 15 July, 1940.

[105] Above, p. 28.

[106] Millington-Drake (Montevideo) to Halifax, 8 March, 1940, Review for 1939, F.O. 371/24269.

[107] Millington-Drake to Halifax, 25 May, 1940, F.O. 371/24194; Tel., Millington-Drake to F.O., 26 May, 1940, F.O. 371/24204; H. Fernández Artucio, *The Nazi Octopus in South America* (London, 1943), pp. 9–12, 91–102; *La Nación, La Mañana*, 18 June, 1940; *El Día, El País*, 20 June, 1940; *New York Times*, 11, 18, 19, 23 June, 1940.

[108] They were released, through German pressure, re-arrested, and ultimately imprisoned.

[109] Tel., Millington-Drake to F.O., 18 June, 1940, F.O. 371/24194; Tel. Knox (Rio) to F.O., 11 June, 1940, F.O. 371/24194; to Eden, 2 March, 1941, F.O. 371/25807; Tel., Lothian to F.O., 1 June, 1940, F.O. 371/24193.

[110] Hull, *Memoirs*, i, 821.

[111] Conn and Fairchild, *op.cit.*, pp. 34–5.

[112] *ibid.*, p. 34.

[113] Tel., Lothian to F.O., 26 May, 1940, F.O. 371/24192.

[114] Langer and Gleason, *Challenge to Isolation*, pp. 273–5; Conn and Fairchild, *op.cit.*, pp. 175, 184.

[115] Burden, *Struggle for Airways in Latin America*, pp. 72–3.

[116] Conn and Fairchild, *op.cit.*, pp. 175–7; Langer and Gleason, *op.cit.*, pp. 614–6. No approach was made to Bolivia, Paraguay and Panamá.

[117] *F.R.*, 1940, v, 22–3; Francis, *op.cit.*, pp. 65–66; Langer and Gleason, *Challenge to Isolation*, p. 616.

[118] Bentinck to Halifax, 13 June, 1940, F.O. 371/24194.

[119] *F.R.*, 1940, v, 14 ff. and, for Argentina and Chile in particular, pp. 31–4, 55; McCann *op.cit.*, p. 204; Francis, *op.cit.*, pp. 31, 66–7.

[120] Conn and Fairchild, *op.cit.*, pp. 38–9; Langer and Gleason, *op.cit.*, pp. 620–1.

[121] Langer and Gleason, *op.cit.*, pp. 623–5; Conn and Fairchild, *op.cit.*, pp. 35, 46–7.

[122] Tel., Ovey (Buenos Aires) to F.O., 24 May, 1940, F.O. 371/24204; Hull, *Memoirs*, i, 816–7; Conn and Fairchild, *op.cit.*, p. 47.

[123] *D.A.F.R.*, ii, 90. The Declaration was approved by the House on the 18th. It was sent to the Allied Governments 'for information'.

[124] Tel., Leche (Guatemala) to F.O., 25 May, 1940, F.O. 371/24192; Tel., Lothian to F.O., 12 July, and Reuter's Report, 15 July, 1940, F.O. 371/24195; Tel., Leche to F.O., 16 July, 1940, F.O. 371/24195; *F.R.*, 1940, i, 796–809; Hull, *Memoirs*, i, 821; Langer and Gleason, *Challenge to Isolation*, p. 636.

[125] *D.G.F.P.*, Series D, x, 102–3 (2 July).

[126] Bentinck to Halifax, 9 July, 1940, F.O. 371/24196. Forbes had already reported from Perú (5 June) the distribution of leaflets asserting that the war would be over in a month and that Germany would then buy Peruvian cotton. Tel., F.O. 371/24222.

[127] *D.G.F.P.*, Series D, x, 177–8 (10 July); Hilton, *op.cit.*, p. 213.

[128] *D.G.F.P.*, Series D, ix, 565–6, 698 (14, 22 June). In Argentina, too, arms deliveries had been discussed (10, 17 July), *ibid*, x, 530 n, as also in Chile.

[129] *La Nación*, 16 July, 1940; *New York Times*, 8, 13 July, 1940.

[130] Craigie (Tokyo) to F.O., 19 May, 1940, F.O. 371/24169; *New York Times*, 29 July, 1940.

[131] *La Nación* (Chile), 15 July, *El Mercurio*, 16 July, 1940; *New York Times*, 16, 17 July, 1940.

[132] Tel., Lyall (San José) to F.O. 13 July, 1940, F.O. 371/24195.

[133] Langer and Gleason, *Challenge to Isolation*, p. 573.

[134] Tel., Knox (Rio) to F.O., 18 July, 1940, F.O. 371/24195.

[135] *El Mundo* (Argentina), 19 July, 1940.

[136] Bentinck to Halifax, 9 July, 1940, F.O. 371/24196.

[137] Above, pp. 56–7.

[138] Above, pp. 50–1.

[139] J. L. Mecham, *The United States and Inter-American Security, 1889–1960* (Austin, 1961), p. 189, describes this as 'the first inter-American security instrument' aimed specifically at non-American powers, its broad principles affording a basis for numerous wartime military agreements.

[140] Langer and Gleason, *The Challenge to Isolation*, pp. 692–3.

[141] Tel., Ogilvie Forbes (Havana) to F.O. 23 July, 1940, F.O. 371/24195; *F.R.*, 1940, v, 240, 248–50.

[142] Tel., Adam (Panamá) to F.O., 29 Sept., 1939, F.O. 371/22762.

[143] Tel., Bentinck to F.O. 28 July, 1940, 371/24195.

[144] Tel., Ogilvie Forbes to F.O., 26 July, 1940, F.O. 371/24195.

[145] Hull, *Memoirs*, i, 826.

[146] *Cf.* Knox (Rio) to F.O., 18 July, 1940, F.O. 371/24195; *F.R.*, 1940, v, 233–4, 237–8.

[147] Tel., Bentinck to F.O. 31 July, 1940, F.O. 371/24196.

[148] The Emergency Committee came into existence on 24 October. The Convention was never properly ratified.

[149] Langer and Gleason, *Challenge to Isolation*, pp. 696–8.

[150] Ogilvie Forbes to F.O., 1 Aug., 1940, F.O. 371/24196.

[151] Conn, Engelman and Fairchild, *op.cit.*, pp. 328–9.

[152] Hull, *Memoirs*, i, 819; Conn and Fairchild, *op.cit.*, p. 50.

[153] Morison, *op.cit.*, p. 32.

[154] Conn and Fairchild, *op.cit.*, pp. 86–7. Robert turned over his authority to the French Committee of National Liberation in 1943.

[155] Hull, *Memoirs*, ii, 1128–36.

NOTES TO CHAPTER III

[1] *Cf.* Tels., Ogilvie Forbes (Havana) to F.O., 26 July, 1940, F.O. 371/24195 and 1 Aug., 1940, F.O. 371/24196.

[2] Langer and Gleason, *Challenge to Isolation*, pp. 516, 746.

[3] Churchill, *Their Finest Hour*, pp. 23, 353.

[4] Langer and Gleason, *The Undeclared War, 1940–1941*, p. 171. See also Hull, *Memoirs*, i, 841–2. The agreement for the use and operation of these bases was not formally signed till 27 March, 1941.

[5] *Their Finest Hour*, p. 358.

[6] *ibid.*, pp. 494–501.

[7] W. K. Hancock and M. W. Gowing, *British War Economy* (London, 1949), p. 233.

[8] Langer and Gleason, *The Undeclared War*, p. 419.

[9] The Anglo-American staff conversations which opened in Washington on 29 January and, continuing till 27 March, laid the basis of Anglo-American co-operation after the United States entered the war, were not, of course, public knowledge. Morison, *Battle of the Atlantic*, pp. 45–6.

[10] Langer and Gleason, *op.cit.*, pp. 426 ff. The State Department Geographer had already declared in June 1940 that Greenland lay within the western hemisphere.

[11] The Atlantic Fleet was created on 1st February 1941 and the United States Fleet then became the Pacific Fleet. Morison, *op.cit.*, pp. 14, 57.

[12] Langer and Gleason, *op.cit.*, pp. 522 ff.

[13] Later the Board of Economic Warfare, quickly countered by the State Department's Board of Economic Operations. Medlicott, *Economic Blockade*, ii, 43.

[14] Dallek, *Franklin D. Roosevelt and American Foreign Policy*, pp. 285–8.

[15] Langer and Gleason, *Challenge to Isolation*, p. 595.

[16] Above, pp. 68–9.

[17] Conn and Fairchild, *Framework of Hemisphere Defense*, pp. 179–82, *Cf. F.R.*, 1940, v, 20–1.

[18] *Cf.* the remarks of the Argentine Delegation at the Havana Conference, based on the testimony given by Admiral Stark to the Naval Committee of the House of Representatives. Hull, *Memoirs*, i, 824.

[19] *El Siglo*, 17 Oct., 1940.

[20] *New York Times*, 17 Oct., 1940.

[21] *ibid.*, 16, 18 Nov., 1940; *La Nación* (Argentina), 15, 16, 18 Nov., 1940.

[22] Despatch of John T. White, *New York Times*, 10 Nov., 1940.

[23] *ibid.*, 24 Aug., 15, 16 Nov., 1940.

[24] *Diario*, 12 Nov., 1940; *D.A.F.R.*, iii, 136.

[25] *El Mundo*, 15 Nov., 1940.

[26] *D.A.F.R.*, iii, 137.

[27] 19 Nov., 1940. *ibid.*, pp. 138–9.
[28] *ibid.*, p. 140.
[29] Above, p. 28. The agreements, according to *La Prensa*, 14 Dec., 1940, amounted to a political, military and economic alliance. But they were never implemented.
[30] *La Nación*, 28 Nov., 1940; *El País*, 10 Dec., 1940.
[31] Conn and Fairchild, *op.cit.*, pp. 253–5; McCann, *Brazilian-American Alliance*, pp. 223–8; and see above, p. 139.
[32] *Cf.* the President's Radio Address of 12 October.
[33] Knox to Eden, 2 April, 1941, Annual Report for 1940, F.O. 371/25807.
[34] *F.R.*, 1941, vi, 134–48; Conn and Fairchild, *op.cit.*, pp. 184–6, 213–24, 233; Mecham, *op.cit.*, pp. 199–200.
[35] With Haiti, Paraguay, Brazil, Nicaragua, Cuba and Bolivia. Eleven Lend-Lease Agreements with Latin American states had been negotiated by March, 1942, and eighteen by March 1943.
[36] Above, pp. 14, 17, 18, 20, 47.
[37] Above, pp. 34, 143; Burden, *Struggle for Airways*, pp. 59–77; Conn and Fairchild, *op.cit.*, pp. 204–9; McCann, *op.cit.*, pp. 219–20.
[38] Above, pp. 56–8.
[39] Above, p. 57.
[40] Tariff Commission, *Foreign Trade of Latin America*, Part I, p. 61; *F.R.*, 1941, vi, 151 ff., 357 ff. 452 ff., 528 ff., 556–8, 578 ff., vii, 403–8, 534–5; Medlicott, *Economic Blockade*, ii, 129–30. For United States dependence on Latin America for strategic supplies by 1943 see Laurence Duggan, *The Americas* (New York, 1949), p. 99.
[41] Above, p. 57.
[42] U.K. Purchases from Argentina, 7 July, 1941, F.O. 371/25715, Doc. A 4340/125/2.
[43] Ogilvie Forbes (Havana) to F.O., 24 May, 1941, F.O. 371/25926.
[44] *F.R.*, 1941, vi, 375 ff. vii, 337 ff., 590 ff.; Medlicott, *op.cit.*, p. 130; Sir Eric Roll, *The Combined Food Boards. A study in wartime international planning* (Stanford, 1956), pp. 39–40.
[45] Above, p. 55.
[46] *New York Times*, 7, 17, Feb., 1941; *Review of the River Plate*, 14 Feb., 1941. As a further example of regional ideas, an Inter-American Conference of the Caribbean held at Port-au-Prince in April discussed a project for an Inter-American Union of the Caribbean.
[47] Above, p. 57.
[48] *F.R.*, 1940, v, 414; 1941, vi, 185–206; *D.A.F.R.*, iii, 114–7, 621–2, 631; iv, 403–5. Some 80 ships totalling 456,000 tons were eventually brought into service. Duggan, *op.cit.*, p. 84.
[49] Knox (Petrópolis) to Eden, 2 April, 1941, F.O. 371/25807.
[50] *La Prensa*, 26 Aug., 1941.
[51] *Cf. F.R.*, 1941, vi, 161–3; *D.A.F.R.*, iv, 354, 384–9.
[52] Welles, *Time for Decision*, pp. 170–1; L.O. Ealy, *The Republic of Panama in World Affairs, 1903–1950* (Philadelphia, 1951), p. 116; Fundación John Boulton, *Política y Economía en Venezuela, 1810–1976* (Caracas, 1976), pp. 280–1.
[53] *El Nacional*, 5 Sept., 1940.
[54] *Cf. La Nación*, 20 Aug., 5 Sept, *La Prensa*, 5 Sept., 1940; *El Mercurio (Chile)*, 5 Oct., 1940.
[55] 22, 28, 31 Aug., 5, 8, Sept., 1940.
[56] *Cf.* A. P. Whitaker, ed., *Inter-American Affairs*, (5 vols., New York, 1942–6), i (1941), p. 45.
[57] 24 March, 1941.
[58] Langer and Gleason, *The Undeclared War*, p. 541.

[59] These three countries declared war on the United States between the 11th and 13th December, but the United States did not reciprocate till 5 June, 1942.

[60] *Time for Decision*, p. 154.

[61] Above, p. 8.

[62] Grant Watson (Havana) to Simon, 13 Dec., 1934, 29 March, 1935, F.O. 371/17518 and 18676; Rees to Eden, 8 May, 1936, F.O. 371/19779.

[63] *New York Times*, 11 Oct., 1940; Gellman, *Roosevelt and Batista*, p. 184.

[64] Grant Watson to Halifax, 30 March, 1938, F.O. 371/21451, on Batista's 'three-year plan'; Thomas, *Cuba or the Pursuit of Freedom*, pp. 707, 709.

[65] Thomas, *op.cit.*, pp. 710–14, 727; Ogilvie Forbes to F.O., 2 July, 27 Sept., 1941, F.O. 371/25925.

[66] *F.R.*, 1940, v, 99–100; Gellman, *op.cit.*, p. 193; Thomas, *op.cit.*, p. 723.

[67] *El Mundo* (Cuba), 30 Jan., 1941.

[68] *ibid.*, 12 March, 1941; *Diario de la Marina*, 15 April, 1941.

[69] *F.R.*, 1941, vii, 104.

[70] Gellman, *op.cit.*, p. 194; Conn and Fairchild, *op.cit.*, p. 254.

[71] *El Mundo*,18, 19 November, 1941.

[72] *Diario de la Marina*, 25 Nov., 2 Dec., 1941. Later in 1940 the Cuban Minister had delivered a gift of five thousand of the best Havana cigars to Churchill, and this graceful gesture was repeated every year till the war ended. Colville, *Footprints in Time*, pp. 105–6.

[73] *F.R.*, 1941, vii, 229.

[74] *ibid.*, p. 157; Ogilvie Forbes to F.O., 24 May, 1941, F.O. 371/25926; Gellman, *op.cit.*, p. 190.

[75] *F.R.*, 1941, vii, 122ff., 196ff., 237ff.; Gellman, *op.cit.*, pp. 191–2; Above, p. 86.

[76] Ogilvie Forbes to F.O., 19 Jan., 1942, F.O. 371/30455.

[77] *Cf.* Gellman, *op.cit.*, p. 232–3.

[78] According to R. W. Logan, *Haiti and the Dominican Republic* (London, 1968), p. 146, Vincent would have been happy to succeed himself for a third term, unconstitutionally, but abandoned this intention because of opposition from the State Department.

[79] *Haiti-Journal*, 16 May, 1941; Hillyer (Port-au Prince) to F.O., 29 May, 1941, F.O. 371/26045.

[80] *Haiti-Journal*, 2 July, 1941.

[81] *ibid.*, 1, 5 Jan., 1942.

[82] Above, p. 47, and see E. O. Guerrant, *Roosevelt's Good Neighbor Policy* (Albuquerque, New Mexico, 1950), p. 155.

[83] Above, p. 184, n. 25.

[84] *F.R.*, 1941, vii, 253, 319.

[85] *Haiti-Journal*, 11 Nov., 1941; *La Nación* (D.R.), 6 Nov., 1941.

[86] Above, p. 86.

[87] *La Nación*, 22 Dec., 1940.

[88] *F.R.*, 1941, vii, 87–8; Tel., Patterson (Ciudad Trujillo) to F.O., 18 Dec., 1941, F.O. 371/26045.

[89] *La Nación*, 28 Oct., 8 Nov., 4 Dec., 1941.

[90] *F.R.*, 1941, vii, 366–7; Hillyer to F.O., 20 Aug., 1941, F.O. 371/26058.

[91] 27 August, 1941.

[92] *F.R.*1941, vi, 95; Comprehensive Agreement of 6 April, 1942, *D.A.F.R.*, iv, 367–9; Minute by Hohler, 24 Jan., 1942, F.O. 371/30525, Doc A 765/223/20.

[93] *New York Herald Tribune*, 9 April, 1942.

[94] Dodd (Panamá) to F.O., 28 May, 1940, F.O. 371/24193.

[95] Lyall (San José) to F.O., 13 July, 1940, F.O. 371/24195. The President told Lyall that he believed the Nazis were organized from north to south to strike a blow at

Costa Rica as being near the Canal Zone, and that the signal would be a successful invasion of England.

[96] Lyall to F.O., 6 July, 1940, F.O. 371/24196.

[97] Lyall to F.O., 12 June, 5 Sept., 1940, F.O. 371/24194 and 24219.

[98] *F.R.*, 1941, vi, 86.

[99] Lyall to F.O., 1 May, 1941, F.O. 371/26098.

[100] Lyall to F.O., 3 July, 1941, F.O. 371/26100.

[101] Lyall to F.O., 24 Nov., 1941, F.O. 371/26100.

[102] *Diario de Costa Rica*, 3, 21 June, 1941. For the Lend-Lease agreement of January 1942 see *F.R.*, 1942, vi, 235–8.

[103] *F.R.*, 1940, v, 736; Lyall to F.O., 2 Oct., 1940, 7 Sept., 1941, F.O. 371/24219 and 26115.

[104] *New York Herald Tribune*, 19 Oct., 1940.

[105] *Estrella de Nicaragua*, 6 Nov., 1940; *New York Times*, 13 Nov., 1941.

[106] Kemball (Tegucigalpa) to Halifax, 23 May, 1940, F.O. 371/24180.

[107] Minutes on Kemball to F.O., 14 March, 1941, F.O. 371/25830, Doc. A 1785/359/8.

[108] *Cf.* Proposed National Policy *Re* Supply of Arms to Amer. Republics, 27 July, 1940, Conn and Fairchild, *op.cit.*, p. 213.

[109] *F.R.*, 1941, vii, 410; 1942, vi, 431, 479–82.

[110] *Cf. F.R.*, 1941, vi, 83, 97–8, 102; vii, 313–6, 368–9.

[111] Above, p. 70.

[112] *Cf.* Leche (Guatemala City) to F.O., 7 Oct., 1940, F.O. 371/24197; Washington Chancery to F.O., 30 Feb., 1940, F.O. 371/24204.

[113] Leche to F.O., 26 Dec., 1940, 3 Jan., 1941, F.O. 371/24104 and 25836; *Nuestro Diario*, 26 Dec., 1940, 3 Jan., 1941.

[114] *Nuestro Diario*, 14 June, 1941.

[115] 27 May, 1941. *F.R.*, 1941, vii, 313.

[116] See Conn and Fairchild, *op.cit.*, p. 255, and Conn, Engelman and Fairchild, *op.cit.*, p. 343.

[117] *F.R.*, 1941, vii, 313–6; Conn, Engelman and Fairchild, *op.cit.*, p. 343.

[118] *Nuestro Diario*, 3 March, 1941.

[119] Conn and Fairchild, *op.cit.*, pp. 18 and 180n.

[120] Above, p. 11.

[121] See Conn, Engelman and Fairchild, *op.cit.*, pp. 306–7, 309, 316; Langer and Gleason, *The Undeclared War*, p. 148; *F.R.*, 1940, v, 1073–6.

[122] *New York Herald Tribune*, 4 July, 1940.

[123] *Panama Star and Herald*, 23, Nov., 1940.

[124] Dodd to F.O., 5 March, 1941, F.O. 371/26092.

[125] *New York Times*, 29 Jan., 1941.

[126] Dodd to F.O., 5 March, 22 May, 1941, F.O. 371/26092 and 26095.

[127] *Cf.* Ealy, *The Republic of Panama in World Affairs*, pp. 18–19, 109.

[128] Dawson to State Department, 30 Dec., 1940, *F.R.*, 1940, v, 1087–9.

[129] *New York Herald Tribune*, 2 Sept., 1940; *New York Times*, 3 Jan., 1941; *Panama Star and Herald*, 3, 9 Jan., 1941; *F.R.*, 1940, v, 1087–9; 1941, vii, 414–5.

[130] *F.R.*, 1940, v, 1076–9, 1082–3, 1087–9; 1941, vii, 414–5.

[131] Dawson to Secretary of State, 14 Feb., 1941, *F.R.*, 1941, vii, 427.

[132] Secretary of State to Dawson, 17 Feb., 1941, *F.R.*, 1941, vii, 428–9.

[133] *ibid.*, 1941, vii, 435–6.

[134] Conn, Engelman and Fairchild, *op.cit.*, p. 345.

[135] *F.R.*, 1941, vii, 430–1, 438–9.

[136] *F.R.*, 1942, vi, 577–618; Conn, Engelman and Fairchild, *op.cit.*, p. 346.

[137] Morison, *op.cit.*, p.297; Hull, *Memoirs*, ii,1048.

[138] *Panama American*, 9 Oct., 1940.

[139] Hull, *Memoirs*, ii, 1048; *D.A.F.R.*, iv, 429–31.

[140] Arias again became President by a *coup d'état* in 1949 and was again overthrown in 1951.

[141] Signed by the United States, Britain, Soviet Russia, China, Australia, Belgium, Canada, Czechoslovakia, Greece, India, Luxemburg, the Netherlands, New Zealand, Norway, Poland, South Africa and Jugoslavia, making, with the nine Latin American signatories, twenty-six nations in all.

[142] Above, p. 13.

[143] *New York Times*, 29 April, 1941.

[144] Gainer (Caracas) to F.O., 12 Nov., 1940, F.O. 371/26315.

[145] *El Heraldo*, 28 May, 1940.

[146] For the Hydro-Carbons Law of 13 March 1943 and related legislation dealing with the question of taxes, royalties, concessions and refining, see Edwin Liewen, *Venezuela* (London, 1968), p. 58, and Bryce Wood, *Making of the Good Neighbor Policy*, pp. 274–80, and for relations between the oil companies and the government in general, Liewen, *Petroleum in Venezuela: a History* (Berkeley, 1954), and Rómulo Betancourt, *Venezuela: Política y Petróleo* (Mexico 1956).

[147] Tel., F.O. to Gainer, 18 Dec., 1940, F.O. 371/24271.

[148] Anderson (Caracas) to F.O., 18 Sept., 1939, F.O. 371/22652.

[149] Gainer to F.O., 6 June, 1941, F.O. 371/26315. Also Gainer to F.O., 31 Dec., 1939, F.O. 371/24270.

[150] *El Heraldo*, 3 April, 1941.

[151] *D.A.F.R.*, iv, 356–7. The functions of this Board were absorbed by the War Production Board in Jan. 1942.

[152] *New York Times*, 6 Dec., 1941.

[153] Conn and Fairchild, *op.cit.*, pp. 261–2.

[154] *ibid.*, p. 254; *New York Times*, 11 Jan., 1942.

[155] Conn and Fairchild, *op.cit.*, p. 203–4.

[156] Above, p. 69.

[157] Morison, *op.cit.*, p. 145.

[158] *El Heraldo*, 25 Feb., 1942.

[159] For sinkings in the Caribbean area in 1942 see Morison, *op.cit.*, pp. 198, 257–9, 347–8, 413–4; Conn, Engelman and Fairchild, *op.cit.*, pp. 430–1.

[160] David Bushnell, *Eduardo Santos and the Good Neighbor, 1938–1942* (Gainesville, 1967), pp. 15–16.

[161] Above, p. 83.

[162] Conn and Fairchild, *op.cit.*, p. 242.

[163] Bushnell, *op.cit.*, pp. 52–3; *F.R.*, 1940, v, 69.

[164] Bushnell, pp. 57–64.

[165] Conn and Fairchild, *op.cit.*, pp. 262–3.

[166] Bushnell, *op.cit.*, pp. 55–7, 74–80.

[167] *El Siglo*, 24, 22 Sept., 1940; 11 Jan., 1941; 17 Dec., 1940, 22 Jan., 1941; 30 Dec., 1940.

[168] Gómez was not primarily interested in foreign affairs and his real views on totalitarianism in Europe remain a matter of dispute. *Cf.* Bushnell, *op.cit.*, p. 25n. But in an extraordinary interview in January 1941 he certainly expressed his admiration for Hitler. *El Siglo*, 26 Jan., 1941.

[169] *El Tiempo*, 17 Sept., 1940.

[170] *ibid.*, 27 Sept., 1940; 3, 27 Jan., 1941; 31 Dec., 1940.

[171] *F.R.*, 1941, vi, 79–83; *El Tiempo*, 18 Dec., 1940; Bushnell, *op.cit.*, pp. 103–4 (citing *La Guerra Mundial y la Política Internacional de Colombia*, Bogotá, 1941, pp. 3–15) and p. 113.

[172] 8 Dec., 1941.

[173] Bushnell, *op.cit.*, pp. 104–5.

[174] See Nathan R. Whetten, *Rural Mexico* (Chicago, 1948), pp. 484–522. Officially the party was founded in 1937, but it seems to have been the outgrowth of an Anti-Communist Centre established by a German at Guanajuato in 1936.

[175] *Excelsior*, 17 March, 1940.

[176] Above, p. 15.

[177] *Excelsior*, 28 Nov., 1940. Lombardo Toledano had been both a university professor and Governor of the State of Puebla. He was Secretary of the C.T.M. from its foundation in 1936 till March 1941, thereafter devoting his energies to the Confederation of Latin American Workers, founded in 1938, of which he was President. By 1943 sixteen national trade unions were affiliated to it. Lombardo Toledano professed to be a Marxist but not a communist, though to his opponents the distinction sometimes seemed over-refined.

[178] *New York Times*, 5 Dec., 1940. Avila Camacho was a professed Catholic.

[179] The announcement on 12 November that Vice-President-Elect Henry Wallace would attend the inauguration seems to have been the final blow to the hopes of the *Almazanistas*. Consul-General Rees (Mexico City) to Eden, 22 May, 1941, F.O. 371/26067.

[180] *New York Times*, 6 Oct., 1940; *Nacional*, 2, 4 Dec., 1940; *Universal*, 2 Dec. 1940.

[181] Cronon, *Josephus Daniels in Mexico*, p. 258.

[182] *F.R.*, 1941, vii, 403–8.

[183] *F.R.*, 1939, v, 703–6; Cronon, *op.cit.*, p. 244; Langer and Gleason, *Challenge to Isolation*, p. 277.

[184] *Excelsior*, 7 April, 1940; Cronon, *op.cit.*, pp. 250–1; Rees to Eden, 22 May, 1941, 'Review of Political Events in Mexico during 1940', F.O. 371/26067.

[185] Cronon, *op.cit.*, p. 252; Wood, *Making of the Good Neighbor Policy*, p. 244.

[186] Cronon, *op.cit.*, p. 254, Wood, *op.cit.*, p. 247.

[187] *Nacional*, 20 May, 6 Aug., 1940.

[188] *Excelsior*, 3 June, 1940.

[189] *ibid.*, 10 June, 1940.

[190] He did not leave for Japan till 19 July on the ground that his children had measles.

[191] *Excelsior*, 14 June, *Nacional*, 13 June, *Universal*, 13, 15 June, 1940.

[192] Conn and Fairchild, *Framework of Hemisphere Defense*, p. 334.

[193] *El Nacional*, 18 Sept., 1940.

[194] *ibid.*, 4 Oct., 1940.

[195] Halifax to Cadogan, 26 May, 1941, F.O. 371/26063.

[196] Cronon, *op.cit.*, p. 258.

[197] *ibid.*, p. 259.

[198] Langer and Gleason, *Undeclared War*, p. 606; Conn and Fairchild, *op.cit.*, pp. 335–6.

[199] *El Popular*, 6 June, 1941; Bateman to Eden, 31 March, 1942, F.O. 371/30571.

[200] Conn and Fairchild, *op.cit.*, pp. 345 ff.

[201] *Excelsior*, 2 Aug., *Nacional*, 4 Aug., *Universal*, 18 Nov., 1941; Bateman to Eden, 31 March 1942, F.O. 371/30571.

[202] Above, p. 85.

[203] Bateman to Eden, 31 March, 1942, F.O. 371/30571; Hull, *Memoirs*, ii, 1141.

[204] For the agreements of 19 November see *D.A.F.R.*, iv, 358 ff, 420 ff. The American companies valued their properties and equipment at over $260,000,000. An independent estimate by the Department of the Interior arrived at a figure of $13,538,052, excluding the Sinclair interests, which had already settled for $8,500,000 plus a four-year contract for oil purchases at less than the market price. Wood, *op.cit.*,

p. 203; Cronon, *op.cit.*, pp. 260–1. The compensation awarded by the experts was $23,995,991 together with interest payments of rather more than $5 million. Mexico made a down payment of $9 million and discharged the total debt by September 1947. The Standard Oil Company of New Jersey received much the largest sum. Sumner Welles insisted that sub-soil rights had been taken into consideration. Halifax to F.O., 23 April, 1942, F.O. 371/30567. But this was not the opinion of the companies, nor was it Mexico's. See Lorenzo Meyer, *México y Estados Unidos en el Conflicto Petrolero (1917–1942)*, (México, 1968), p. 261.

[205] Halifax to Cadogan, 26 May, 1941, F.O. 371/26063; Bateman (Mexico City) to Eden, 31 March 1942, F.O. 371/30571; Leith Ross (M.E.W.) to Cadogan, 18 March, 1941, F.O. 371/26061; Memorandum by J. D. Murray in Halifax to Cadogan, 2 July, 1941, F.O. 371/26068.

[206] Minutes by D. C. Scott, 29 Jan., 1941, F.O. 371/26061, Doc. A 364/47/26; R. A. Gallop, 22 March, 1941, F.O. 371/26062, Doc. A 1928/47/26; Cadogan to Halifax, 12 June, 1941, F.O. 371/26063.

[207] Campbell (Washington) to F.O., 29 Aug., 1941 (Tels., Nos 4011 and 4012), F.O. 371/26064; Memorandum for War Cabinet (Secret), 6 Sept., 1941, F.O. 371/26064; Halifax to F.O., 9 Oct., 1941 (tel Nos. 4630 and 4639), F.O. 371/26064.

[208] Bateman to Eden, 31 March 1942, F.O., 371/30571; Tel., Bateman to F.O., 6 Feb., 1942, F.O. 371/30581.

[209] The total sum was rather more than $81 million, with interest from 1938. Paid off in 15 instalments, it reached the sum of $130 million.

[210] *F.R.* 1941, vi, 98–101; *El Popular*, 11 Dec., 1941.

[211] Conn and Fairchild, *op.cit.*, p. 341.

[212] Bateman to F.O., 6 Feb., 1942, F.O. 371/30581.

[213] Conn and Fairchild, *op.cit.*, p. 363; Howard F. Cline, *The United States and Mexico* (New York, 1963), p. 278.

NOTES TO CHAPTER IV

[1] *Cf. El Telégrafo* (Quito), 29 July, 27 Aug., *New York Times*, 2 Sept., 1940.

[2] Above, p. 17.

[3] *El Telégrafo*, 24 Jan., 1941.

[4] *ibid.*, 22, 30 Aug., 25, 29 Sept., 1940; Bullock (Quito) to F.O., 8 Oct., 1940, F.O. 371/25949.

[5] *El Telégrafo*, 2, 25 July, 1940.

[6] *ibid.*, 14 June, 7, 12 Sept., 1940, 10, 11 Feb., 1941; *F.R.*, 1941, vi, 225, vii, 265, 300–1; Langer and Gleason, *Undeclared War*, p. 616; Conn, Engelman and Fairchild, *Guarding the United States and its Outposts*, p. 340; Bryce Wood, *The United States and Latin American Wars, 1932–1942* (New York and London, 1966), p. 273.

[7] *F.R.*, 1940, v, 850–5; 1941, vii, 266–7, 300–1; Conn, Engelman and Fairchild, *op.cit.*, pp. 340–1.

[8] *F.R.*, 1941, vi, 88–91; 1942, vi, 362–8, 370–1; Mecham, *The United States and Inter-American Security*, p. 222 and note; Conn, Engelman and Fairchild, *op.cit.*, pp. 342–3.

[9] *Christian Science Monitor*, 26 July, 1940. See above, p. 19.

[10] *La Prensa* (Perú), 29 July, 1940.

[11] Forbes (Lima) to Eden, 2 Jan., 1941, 'Political Review of the Year 1940', F.O. 371/26140.

[12] *La Prensa*, 30 Aug., 1940.

[13] Forbes to Scott, 15 May, 1941, F.O. 371/26140, to Eden, 2 Jan., 1942, Political

Review of the Year 1941, F.O. 371/30627; *La Prensa*, 3 April, 1941; *New York Times*, 5 April, 1941.

[14] *F.R.*, 1941, vii, 534–5.

[15] Forbes to Eden, 2 Jan., 1942, F.O. 371/30627.

[16] She had also built a road to Tingo María across the Andes, to be extended to Pucallpa on the Ucayali and so facilitate communications with Iquitos on the Amazon.

[17] *F.R.*, 1940, v, 1140–42; Tel., Forbes to F.O., 6 May, 1941, F.O. 371/26133.

[18] Langer and Gleason, *Undeclared War*, p. 617; Conn, Engelman and Fairchild, *op.cit.*, p. 353. A reinforced United States coastal battery was sent there in March, 1942, and an American air-base was in operation from September, 1942, to July, 1943.

[19] Forbes to Eden, 12 Sept., 1941, F.O. 371/26136.

[20] *El Comercio*, 8 Dec., 1941; Forbes to Eden, 2 Jan., 1942, F.O. 371/30627; *F.R.*, 1941, vi, 109, 110–11, 124.

[21] *F.R.*, 1941, vi, 217, 223–7; Wood, *United States and Latin American Wars*, pp. 269–70.

[22] Forbes to Eden, 2 Jan., 1942, F.O. 371/30627; *F.R.*, 1941, vii, 508–24. Compensation was later offered to Perú for the bombers and twelve training planes were sent there in November.

[23] Forbes to Eden, 23 May, 1941, 2 Jan., 1942, F.O. 371/26134 and 30627; *El Telégrafo*, 30, 31 July, 3 Aug., 1941; Whitaker, *Inter-American Affairs*, i, 61–4. *Cf.* the remarks of the Ecuadorean Foreign Minister to the American Minister in December 1941. *F.R.*, 1941, vi, 123.

[24] Wood, *op.cit.*, p. 331.

[25] Alberto Ostria Gutiérrez, *Una Revolución Tras Los Andes* (Santiago, Chile, 1944), p. 124, stated that the Embassy employed 70 persons in 1941, though officially its staff numbered 17.

[26] See Rawlins (La Paz) to Halifax, 26 Oct., 1939, F.O. 371/22757.

[27] Above, p. 22.

[28] Ostria Gutiérrez, *op.cit.*, pp. 119–24; Blasier, 'The United States, Germany and the Bolivian Revolutionaries', pp. 36, 48–9.

[29] Above, p. 86.

[30] Above, p. 137.

[31] *Diario*, 16 April, 26 Nov., 1940, 15 April, 1941;. *La Nación* (Argentina) 4 May, 1941.

[32] Above, p. 57.

[33] *F.R.*, 1941, vi, 459.

[34] Above, p. 21; Wood, *Making of the Good Neighbor Policy*, pp. 189–91.

[35] *ibid.*, 191–2, 402; *F.R.*, 1941, vi, 466–77.

[36] Jenkins' words, 28 April, 1941, Wood, *op.cit.*, p. 195.

[37] Above, p. 71. Fynes-Clinton (La Paz) to Halifax, 1 July, 1940, F.O. 371/24169.

[38] Jenkins, 16, 28 April, 1941, Blasier, *op.cit.*, p. 34; Wood, *op.cit.*, p. 402.

[39] Copy of Memorandum A 5834/219/G marked Secret, F.O. 371/25762, Doc. A 5834/43/5. The British Minister doubted whether the Bolivian Government would ever summon up courage to open the bag, and the matter was referred to 'the appropriate quarter'.

[40] Ostria Gutiérrez, *op.cit.*, pp. 126–7; *F.R.* 1941, vi, 424.

[41] *F.R.*, 1941, vi, 403–10.

[42] *New York Times*, 13 June, 1941.

[43] *ibid.*, 13, 14 June, 1941.

[44] Blasier, *op.cit.*, p. 31; H. Montgomery Hyde, *The Quiet Canadian* (London, 1962), p. 143; Ostria Gutiérrez, *op.cit.*, pp. 138–40.

[45] The full text of the letter is in Ostria Gutiérrez, *op.cit.*, pp. 134–8, and, for citations, see Hyde, *op.cit.*, pp. 142–3; Augusto Céspedes (who was arrested), *El Presidente Colgado* (Buenos Aires, 1966), pp. 69–70; Blasier, *op.cit.*, p. 31.

[46] According to Céspedes, *op.cit.*, p. 71, Ostria Gutiérrez retracted his accusations against Belmonte in 1950, saying that Belmonte had explained his conduct satisfactorily.

[47] Ostria Gutiérrez, *op.cit.*, pp. 147–63; Blasier, *op.cit.*, pp. 32, 35–7; *Diario*, 26, 31 Aug., 4, 5 Sept., *La Prensa* (Argentina), 26, 28 Aug., 2 Sept., 1941.

[48] According to Hyde, *op.cit.*, pp. xi–xii, 24–7, 153–6, 171, B.S.C. had been instructed to establish close contact between the British Intelligence Service (S.I.S.) and the F.B.I., and was able to do so with the enthusiastic approval of Roosevelt, but without the knowledge, at first, of the State or any other Government Department. It was responsible for all British clandestine activities in the western hemisphere. Stephenson's services were so highly regarded that he received a knighthood and the United States Medal of Merit.

[49] Hyde, *op.cit.*, pp. 139–40, states that Stephenson had received a message from Hoover to the effect that Belmonte was in touch with Nazi elements in Bolivia and was understood to be planning a *coup* to establish a pro-Axis military dictatorship and saying that Roosevelt was anxious that confirmatory evidence should be obtained and put in his hands as soon as possible.

[50] For the account of how the letter was fabricated by Hyde and his wife and by Station M, a laboratory near Toronto, see Hyde's statements in Blasier, *op.cit.*, p. 39, and the *Daily Telegraph*, 22 Aug., 1979; for the 'cloak and dagger' stories, Hyde, *op.cit.*, pp. 141–2, and Spruille Braden, *Diplomats and Demagogues. The Memoirs of Spruille Braden* (New Rochelle, 1971), pp. 248–53, and, for the preparation of the ground, *ibid.*, p. 248, Blasier, *op.cit.*, p. 34, and Hyde, *loc.cit.*

[51] Hyde, *op.cit.*, p. 142, and Copy of Memorandum A 5834/219/G marked Secret, F.O. 371/25762, Doc. A 5834/43/5: 'It was decided that this information could most suitably reach the Bolivian Government through United States channels, and although Mr Dodds [the British Minister at La Paz] was informed of the existence of the letter, he was instructed to discuss it with no one, nor, subsequently, to admit to prior knowledge of its existence'. There was no suggestion here that the letter was a forgery.

[52] Ostria Gutiérrez, *op.cit.*, pp. 165–8.

[53] Blasier, *op.cit.*, p. 32; Braden, *op.cit.* p. 249.

[54] *D.A.F.R.*, iv, 18–19.

[55] Braden, *op.cit.*, p. 249, and see his telegram of 21 July in Blasier, *op.cit.*, p. 35.

[56] *ibid.*, *loc.cit.*

[57] *F.R.*, 1941, iv, 428, 435–7, 444; *D.A.F.R.*, vi, 353, 363; Wood, *Making of the Good Neighbor Policy*, pp. 195–6.

[58] *F.R.*, 1941, vi, 72, 433.

[59] The Company received a cheque for $1,729,374 on 22 April, 1942. Since it claimed to have invested some $17 millions, the result could hardly be hailed as a triumph, except for Bolivia. Wood, *op.cit.*, pp. 197–200; Klein, *Parties and Political Change in Bolivia*, p. 351.

[60] *F.R.*, 1942, v, 592–6.

[61] Above, p. 27; George Pendle, *Paraguay. A Riverside Nation* (3rd edn London, 1967), pp. 33–7, 80.

[62] They were actually held, but with Morínigo as the sole candidate.

[63] *La Nación* (Argentina), 25 Dec., 1940.

[64] Brickell (Asunción) to Eden, 30 Nov., 1941, F.O. 371/26122.

[65] F.O. 371/25969, Doc. A 2262/69/51.

[66] Whitaker, *Inter-American Affairs*, i, 93–5.

[67] *F.R.*, 1941, vii, 480–3, 489 ff. By the end of March, 1941, Paraguay had been awarded credits from the Export-Import Bank to the value of $1,485,000 and the Bank was committed to another $2,405,000. *D.A.F.R.*, iii, 551.

[68] *F.R.*, 1941, vi, 107–8.

[69] Brickell to Eden, 5 Aug., 1942, F.O. 371/30612.

[70] Above, pp. 35 ff, 62 ff.

[71] Confidential Report for the Willingdon Mission, 10 Dec., 1940, F.O. 371/25783, Doc. A 190/190/6; Knox (Rio) to Eden, 17 Sept., 1941, F.O. 371/25783; Annual Report for 1941, in Charles to Eden, 6 March, 1942, F.O. 371/30366.

[72] *O Jornal*, 6 Aug., 1940; Vargas, *Nova Política*, viii, 23–32, 77–81.

[73] A later champion was Juscelino Kubitschek, who moved the capital from the coast to the interior in 1960.

[74] I borrow Hilton's phrase, *Brazil and the Great Powers*, p. 28. The Volta Redonda plant went into production in 1946.

[75] Above, pp. 86, 128, 135; Vargas, *Nova Política*, ix, 41–4, 57–9.

[76] Canada also appointed a minister to Argentina and Chile jointly, separate legations being established in 1942.

[77] Above pp. 52–3, 85, and, for British purchases, F.O. to Knox, Tel., 15 Feb., 1941, F.O. 371/25784, Doc. A 702/230/6.

[78] Above, pp. 57, 64.

[79] Above, pp. 57, 85; *F.R.*, 1941, vi, 538–41; Charles to Eden, 6 March, 1942, enclosing Annual Report for 1941, F.O. 371/30366.

[80] The São Paulo and Brazil Railway Companies (both of them in low water) were expropriated in 1940 and a decree of April, 1941, looked to the nationalisation of foreign banks by July, 1946. By a later decree American Banks (that is, the National City Bank of New York) were exempt.

[81] *F.R.*, 1941, vi, 539, Hilton, 'Brazilian Diplomacy . . .', pp. 219–20.

[82] Hilton, *loc.cit.*, p. 221.

[83] Conn and Fairchild, *Framework of Hemisphere Defense*, pp. 33, 266, 273.

[84] Above, p. 82; McCann, *Brazilian-American Alliance*, p. 221.

[85] *F.R.*, 1940, v, 40–46; 1941, vi, 490; Conn and Fairchild, *op.cit.*, pp. 268, 277–8.

[86] *F.R.*, 1941, vi, 513; McCann, *op.cit.*, pp. 223–38; Conn and Fairchild, *op.cit.*, p. 296.

[87] *F.R.*, 1941, vi, 506 ff., 512; Conn and Fairchild, *op.cit.*, pp. 291–2; Langer and Gleason, *Undeclared War*, pp. 601–3.

[88] *F.R.*, 1941, vi, 493–4; Morison, *Battle of the Atlantic*, pp. 83, 378.

[89] *F.R.*, 1941, ii, 818–9, vi, 505, 511; Langer and Gleason, *op.cit.*, pp. 603–5.

[90] *F.R.*, 1941, vi, 497, 501, 502; Conn and Fairchild, *op.cit.*, pp. 288, 296.

[91] Above, pp. 52, 192 n. 47.

[92] *F.R.*, 1941, vi, 528–9, 534; Conn and Fairchild, *op.cit.*, pp. 279–80, 294.

[93] *New York Times*, 8 Sept., 1940.

[94] Dulles, *Vargas of Brazil*, p. 218.

[95] Knox to Eden, 17 Sept., 1941, F.O. 371/25783.

[96] Dulles, *op.cit.*, p. 219.

[97] *D.G.F.P.*, Series D, xii, 994. See also *ibid*, p. 974; McCann, *op.cit.*, p. 227; Frye, *Nazi Germany and the American Hemisphere*, pp. 166–7.

[98] *D.G.F.P.*, Series D, xiii, 895.

[99] Charles to Eden, 6 March, 1942, enclosing Annual Report for 1941, F.O. 371/30366.

[100] McCann, *op.cit.*, p. 219.

[101] Perowne (F.O.) to Cohen (M.E.W.), 19 July, 1941, F.O. 371/25776.

[102] Above, p. 83; Burden, *Struggle for Airways*, pp. 72, 75–6.

[103] *F.R.*, 1941, vi, 517, 526–8.

[104] Above, pp. 130–2.
[105] Hyde, *The Quiet Canadian*, pp. 145–7; W. Stevenson, *A Man Called Intrepid* (London, Sphere Books Ltd., 1979), pp. 285–7.
[106] Above, p. 84; McCann, *op.cit.*, p. 220.
[107] *F.R.*, 1941, vi, 73–4.
[108] Langer and Gleason, *Undeclared War*, p. 605.
[109] Charles to Eden, 6 March, 1942, enclosing Annual Report for 1941, F.O. 371/30366.
[110] Hilton, 'Brazilian Diplomacy . . .', p. 210.
[111] Above, pp. 66–7; Tels., Millington-Drake (Montevideo) to F.O., 14 April, 2, 4, June, 1940, F.O. 371/24266, 24193 and 24194; to Halifax, 8 June, 27 Aug., 1940, F.O. 371/24266 and 24267.
[112] Above, p. 28.
[113] It was suggested in 1944 that, though anti-American, Herrera was not really pro-Axis. Only the necessities of internal politics had made him appear to side with the Axis. Hadow (Washington) to Vereker (Montevideo), 15 March, 1944, F.O. 371/38755, Doc. AS 2220/1106/46. He was, that is to say, a cynical opportunist, though perhaps this is to place the most favourable interpretation upon his actions and opinions.
[114] This self-denying and stultifying resolution, meant as a protest against the *coup d'état* of March, 1933 (above, p. 27), naturally worked to the advantage of the Herreristas.
[115] *Cf. El País*, 4 Aug., 13 Sept., 5, 29 Oct.; *La Mañana*, 6 Aug., 4 Sept., 13 Oct.; *El Día*, 27 Oct., 8, 15 Nov., 1940.
[116] Tel., Millington-Drake to F.O., 5 Jan., 1941, F.O. 371/26292.
[117] Above, pp. 81–2; *D.A.F.R.*, iii, 136.
[118] *F.R.*, 1940, v, 1173.
[119] *F.R.*, 1941, vi, 19–38.
[120] Tel., Stevenson (Montevideo) to F.O., 8 Nov., 1941, F.O. 371/26303.
[121] *F.R.*, vii, 552.
[122] *F.R.*, 1941, vi, 112–4.
[123] Ovey (Buenos Aires) to Halifax, 10 Oct., 22 Dec., 1939, F.O. 371/22714 and 24165.
[124] Above, pp. 59–60.
[125] Tel., Ovey to F.O., 28 May, 1940, F.O. 371/24204.
[126] See his despatch of 8 June, 1940, *D.G.F.P.*, Series D, ix, 529–32; Frye, *Nazi Germany and the American Hemisphere*, pp. 124–5.
[127] Tel., Ovey to F.O. 23 May, 1940, F.O. 371/24204; Potash, *Army and Politics*, p. 120.
[128] Potash, *op.cit.*, p. 119.
[129] *Ibid.*, p. 120; Francis, *Limits of Hegemony*, p. 60; above, pp. 60–62.
[130] Ovey to Halifax, 1 March, 1940, F.O. 371/24165.
[131] Minute of 3 July on tel., Ovey to F.O., 1 July, 1940, F.O. 371/24195. On Argentine nationalism and its anti-British shafts see above, p. 32.
[132] Above, p. 69, and see Alberto Conil Paz and Gustavo Ferrari, *Argentina's Foreign Policy, 1930–1962* (translated by John F. Kennedy, Notre Dame, 1966), pp. 73–9, on the conversations with Captain W. O. Spears before the Havana Conference and Lt. Col. R. L. Christian after it.
[133] Ovey to Eden, 10 March, 1941, F.O. 371/25709.
[134] Above, p. 29.
[135] *Cf.* the opinion of the American Ambassador, Norman Armour, in February, 1942. Francis, *op.cit.*, p. 68.
[136] Above, p. 62.

[137] *El Mundo*, 4 Dec., *La Nación*, 7 Dec., 1940.
[138] Above, pp. 69, 80.
[139] Potash, *op.cit.*, p. 142; *El Mundo*, 24 July, *La Nación*, 30 Aug., 1940.
[140] *El Mundo*, 25 Oct., 1940.
[141] See, for an interesting discussion of the Pinedo Plan, Felix J. Weil (who had earlier been associated with 'Pinedito') *Argentine Riddle* (New York, 1944), pp. 164–8; also H. S. Ferns, *The Argentine Republic* (London, 1973), pp. 140–1.
[142] Above, p. 57.
[143] Above, p. 86.
[144] *La Nación*, 28 Jan., 1941.
[145] Above, p. 81.
[146] Potash, *op.cit.*, pp. 146–7.
[147] *ibid.*, p. 147; *La Prensa*, 12 Feb., 1941.
[148] Ovey to Eden, 24 April, 1941, F.O. 371/25709.
[149] Potash, *op.cit.*, pp. 149–52.
[150] Ovey to Eden, 24 April, 1941, F.O. 371/25709.
[151] Sumner Welles, *Seven Major Decisions* (London, 1951), p. 106; Ovey to Cadogan, 21 Nov., 1941, F.O. 371/30318; Memo. by G.A. Wallinger (Buenos Aires), 19 Dec., 1941, *ibid*, Doc. A 1109/173/2.
[152] Conil Paz and Ferrari, *op.cit.*, p. 62.
[153] *Cf.* the reports of the American and German Ambassadors in Potash, *op.cit.*, p. 152, note 30. And see also Norman Armour's later judgment: 'Stupidity and vanity are a bad enough combination in any individual, but when they are found in a Foreign Minister with pro-Axis leanings they become positively dangerous'. Gellman, *Good Neighbor Diplomacy*, p. 123.
[154] Wallinger Memorandum, 19 Dec., 1941, *loc.cit.*
[155] *New York Times*, 19 June, 1941.
[156] R. H. Hadow (Buenos Aires), Memorandum on the Argentine Political Situation, 18 Sept., 1941, F.O. 371/25711, Doc. A 8321/120/2.
[157] *ibid.*; Cámara de Diputados de la Nación, Comisión Investigadora de Actividades Anti-Argentinas, *Informes*, Nos. 1–5, Aug.–Nov., 1941.
[158] Hadow, Memorandum, *loc.cit.*; Whitaker, *Inter-American Affairs*, i, 219; D.G.F.P., Series D, xiii, 401–2, 469–70; Francis, *Limits of Hegemony*, pp. 74–5.
[159] *La Nación*, 25 June, 1941.
[160] Potash, *op.cit.*, pp. 153, 154–5.
[161] 26 Sept., 1941.
[162] Potash, *op.cit.*, pp. 156–9.
[163] *ibid.*, p. 160.
[164] *La Nación*, 17, 20 Dec., *La Prensa*, 17 Dec., 1941.
[165] F.R., 1941, vi, 323–34; Conil Paz and Ferrari, *op.cit.*, pp. 79–87; Francis, *op.cit.*, p. 69–71.
[166] Potash, *op.cit.*, p. 170.
[167] Langer and Gleason, *Undeclared War*, pp. 623–4; Francis, *op.cit.*, pp. 145–7.
[168] F.R., 1941, vi, 59–60, 63–4; *La Prensa*, 11 Dec., 1941.
[169] D.G.F.P., Series D, xiii, 1002–3; Potash, *op.cit.* pp. 163–4; Francis, *op.cit.*, p. 148.
[170] *New York Times*, 8 Jan., *La Nación*, 8 Jan., 1941; Conil Paz and Ferrari, *op.cit.*, pp. 64–5.
[171] Above, pp. 24–5; Stevenson, *Chilean Popular Front*, pp. 108–10; Francis, *Limits of Hegemony*, pp. 34–5.
[172] Orde (Santiago) to Eden, 9 May, 12 July, 1941, F.O. 371/25876.
[173] Claude G. Bowers, *Chile through Embassy Windows, 1939–1953* (New York, 1958), p. 63.

[174] Orde to Eden, 12 July, 1941, F.O. 371/25876.
[175] *La Nación* (Chile), 17 Nov., 1941.
[176] Orde to Eden, 16 Sept., 1941, F.O. 371/25876.
[177] 5 Nov., 1941.
[178] According to Claude Bowers, the American Ambassador, *op.cit.*, p. 64.
[179] Orde to Eden, 16 Sept., 1941, F.O. 371/25876; Allen (for Orde) to F.O., 30 Dec., 1941, F.O. 371/30439; and see *El Mercurio*, 24 Oct., 1941.
[180] Dr. Leonardo Guzmán. Orde to Eden, 24 Oct., 1941, F.O. 371/25876.
[181] Orde to Eden, 13 March, 1942, F.O. 371/30435.
[182] Above, p. 81.
[183] Above, p. 125.
[184] *F.R.*, 1940, v, 684. Above, pp. 57, 85.
[185] *F.R.* 1941, vi, 583–4.
[186] *Diario Ilustrado*, 5 June, 1941.
[187] *El Mercurio*, 5 July, 1941.
[188] *F.R.*, 1941, vi, 557–8.
[189] *ibid.* pp. 39–45.
[190] *ibid.*, pp. 572–77; and *cf.* Francis, *op.cit*, p. 39.
[191] *F.R.*, 1941, vi, 75, 559–60: Langer and Gleason, *op.cit.*, pp. 618–9.
[192] Above, p. 158.
[193] Orde to Eden, 24 Oct., 1941, F.O. 371/25876.
[194] Francis, *op.cit.*, p. 41.
[195] *F.R.*, 1941, vi, 74–6, 119–20, 560–1.
[196] 16, 23 Dec., 1941.
[197] *F.R.*, 1941, vi, 77, 561.
[198] Bowers to Secretary of State, 13 Dec., 1941, *ibid*, p. 77, and see also pp. 75–6, 78.
[199] Orde to Eden, 13 March, 1942, F.O. 371/30435.

NOTES TO CHAPTER V

[1] Francis, *Limits of Hegemony*, pp. 78–9.
[2] *F.R.*, 1941, vi, 55–6, 118–9.
[3] *ibid.*, pp. 125–6.
[4] *ibid.*, p. 123.
[5] *ibid.*, pp. 74, 121, 124, 126–9.
[6] *ibid.*, pp. 129–31.
[7] *ibid.*, pp. 122–3; *New York Times*, 18 Dec., 1941.
[8] *F.R.*, 1941, vi, 73–4.
[9] *ibid.*, pp. 127–8.
[10] *ibid.*, 1942, v, 7.
[11] *ibid.*, 1941, vi, 70; 1942, v, 6. Above, p. 158.
[12] *ibid.*, 1942, v, 6–9.
[13] Medlicott, *Economic Blockade*, ii, 140. See also *F.R.*, 1942, v, 13.
[14] *F.R.*, 1942, v, 10–11; Francis, *op.cit.*, p. 80.
[15] *F.R.*, 1941, vi, 131–2.
[16] See the Chief of Staff's statement in Conn and Fairchild, *Framework of Hemisphere Defense* p. 193, and the summary of matters discussed at the Standing Liaison Committee on 3 Jan., 1942, National Archives, Washington, R. G. 353, Box 2. I am indebted to Dr. Leslie Bethell for examining these records. Welles, *Seven Major Decisions*, p. 111, leaves a different impression.
[17] No. J. I.C. (41) 492 (Final), War Cabinet Offices to F.O., 27 Dec., 1941, F.O. 371/30767, Doc. A 65/65/51.

[18] Conn and Fairchild, *op.cit.*, pp. 193–5.

[19] Hull, *Memoirs*, ii, 1143; Welles, *Seven Major Decisions*, p. 111; *F.R.*, 1942, v, 23.

[20] Hull, *Memoirs*, ii, 1144; *F.R.*, 1942, v, 27.

[21] Above, pp. 158, 167, and see Helio Silva, *O Ciclo de Vargas*, (14 vols., Rio de Janeiro, 1964–76), xii, 187–9.

[22] *F.R.*, 1942, v, 15. She surrendered them at the request of the countries concerned in February.

[23] *ibid.*, p. 24, [7 Jan].

[24] *ibid.*, p. 25; Conil Paz and Ferrari, *Argentina's Foreign Policy*, p. 72; Welles, *Time for Decision*, p. 172, and *Seven Major Decisions*, p. 114. For Hull's explanation to Maxim Litvinov, of all people, of Argentina's policy, revealing, as it does, his ignorance of Latin American history and his belief in a hoary legend, see *Memoirs*, ii, 1146.

[25] *F.R.*, 1942, v, 43–4.

[26] Medlicott, *op.cit.*, ii, 142.

[27] Minutes by Bruce Lockhart and J. V. Perowne, 26 Dec., 1941, F.O. 371/30767, Doc. A 248/65/51.

[28] *F.R.*, 1942, v, 15.

[29] *ibid.*, p. 767. [13 Jan.].

[30] Silva, *op.cit.*, xii, 184; Charles (Rio) to Eden, 8 Aug., 1942, F.O. 371/30362.

[31] Welles to Secretary of State, For the President, 18 Jan., 1942, *F.R.*, 1942, v, 633–4; Dulles, *Vargas of Brazil*, pp. 222–3.

[32] *Nova Política*, ix, 195–8; Silva, *op.cit.*, xii, 189–94.

[33] *D.A.F.R.*, iv, 280–7.

[34] For contemporary accounts of the conference see C. G. Fenwick, 'The Third Meeting of Ministers of Foreign Affairs at Rio de Janeiro', *American Journal of International Law*, 36 (1942), pp. 169–203, and D. H. Popper, 'The Rio de Janeiro Conference of 1942', *Foreign Policy Reports*, 15 April, 1942.

[35] *International Conciliation*, May, 1942, No. 380, p. 291.

[36] *F.R.*, 1941, vi, 282. The statement occurs in a document concerned with blacklisting policy. On this a happier relationship was established in 1942 and the Ministry of Economic Warfare cordially agreed on 15 January that Welles should tell the Latin American delegates that British and American aims in the field of economic warfare were identical. Medlicott, *op.cit.*, ii, 144–5.

[37] Charles to Scott, 5 Feb., 1942, F.O. 371/30365; Hayter to Perowne, 24 Oct., 1941, on a conversation between Charles and Welles, F.O. 371/25783.

[38] Foreign Office Minutes, 26 Jan., 1942, F.O. 371/25761, Doc. A 10714/36/5; 23 Feb., 11 April, 1942, F.O. 371/304504, Doc. A 1817/234/51 and 371/3033, Doc. A 3369/3188/2; Charles to Scott, 5 Feb., 1942, F.O. 371/30365.

[39] Minute of 11 April, F.O. 371/3033, Doc. A 3369/3188/2.

[40] Minute of 18 March, 1942, on Doc. A 1817/234/51; Perowne to Charles, 21 April, 1942, F.O. 371/30365; Charles to Eden, 8 Aug., 1942, F.O. 371/30362.

[41] Tel. No. 185 Cypher, F.O. to Washington, 8 Jan., 1942, F.O. 371/26036.

[42] Medlicott, *op.cit.*, ii. 141–2.

[43] Conil Paz and Ferrari, *op.cit.*, p. 65.

[44] *F.R.*, 1942, v, 28, 634.

[45] Silva, *op.cit.*, xii, 193–7; *F.R.*, 1942, v, 634.

[46] *F.R.*, 1942, v, 634–6.

[47] *F.R.*, 1942, v, 30–2; Conil Paz and Ferrari, *op.cit.*, p. 66.

[48] *F.R.*, 1942, v, 32–3. Welles's account in *The Time for Decision*, p. 181, is not consistent with the record in *Foreign Relations*.

[49] Hull, *Memoirs*, ii, 1147.

[50] *F.R.*, 1942, v, 33–4.

[51] *ibid.*, p. 37; Dulles, *op.cit.*, p. 224.

⁵² *F.R.*, 1942, v, 34; Welles. *Seven Major Decisions*, p. 116; McCann, *Brazilian-American Alliance*, p. 254.
⁵³ *F.R.* 1942, v, 35.
⁵⁴ *D.A.F.R.*, iv, 287–8.
⁵⁵ Hull, *Memoirs* ii, 1148–9; Welles, *Seven Major Decisions*, pp. 119–21. The two accounts are widely discrepant.
⁵⁶ *F.R.*, 1942, v, 36–9. See, on the whole episode, Julius W. Pratt, *Cordell Hull, 1933–44* (2 vols., New York, 1964), ii, 705–9, Francis, *op.cit.*, pp. 89–91, Gellman, *Good Neighbor Diplomacy*, pp. 124–6, R. B. Woods, *The Roosevelt Foreign Policy Establishment and the "Good Neighbor". The United States and Argentina, 1941–1945* (Lawrence, Kansas, 1979), pp. 38–42.
⁵⁷ Silva, *Ciclo de Vargas*, xii, 202–8.
⁵⁸ McCann, *op.cit.*, pp. 255–7.
⁵⁹ Above, p. 126.
⁶⁰ *F.R.*, 1942, v, 516–8.
⁶¹ Francis, *op.cit.*, p. 94; *F.R.*, 1942, 39–40, 41–2.
⁶² Gellman, *Good Neighbor Diplomacy*, p. 125.
⁶³ *Memoirs*, ii, 1150. Chile finally severed relations on 20 Jan., 1943, Argentina (after Italy had been granted co-belligerency status) with Germany and Japan on 26 Jan., 1944.
⁶⁴ *Time for Decision*, pp. 182–31, *Seven Major Decisions*, pp. 120–1, 124; *F.R.*, 1942, v, 36–9. The American edition of *Seven Major Decisions* was published in 1950, the English, which I have used, in 1951, See also Duggan, *The Americas*, p. 88. Duggan shared Welles's view.
⁶⁵ Hull's relationship with Welles had long been strained. After Rio de Janeiro it was over-strained. A threat by Ambassador William Bullitt to make public a deplorable episode in Welles's private life, hitherto hushed up, precipitated his resignation.
⁶⁶ *Time for Decision*, pp. 177–8, 318–20.
⁶⁷ *F.R.*, 1942, v, 11–12.
⁶⁸ It first met at Montevideo in April, 1942. Argentina and Chile were both represented.
⁶⁹ *D.A.F.R.*, iv, 285. Welles was quoting from a resolution of the Board of Economic Warfare on 26 Dec., 1941.
⁷⁰ *New York Times*, 21, 23 Jan., 1942.
⁷¹· Hull, *Memoirs*, ii, 1150.
⁷² Charles to Eden, 8 Aug., 1942, F.O. 371/30362.
⁷³ Minute, 4 April, 1942, on F.O. 371/30767, Doc. A 3246/65/51. By this time Uruguay, Venezuela and Mexico and, less categorically, Brazil had granted non-belligerent facilities to British warships.

NEWSPAPERS

Christian Science Monitor
Daily Telegraph
Evening Standard
New York Herald Tribune
New York Times
News Chronicle
Diario de Costa Rica
Diario de la Marina (Cuba)
El Comercio (Perú)
El Día (Uruguay)
El Diario (Bolivia)
El Diario (Uruguay)
El Diario Ilustrado (Chile)
El Heraldo (Venezuela)
El Mercurio (Chile)
El Mundo (Argentina)
El Mundo (Cuba)
El Nacional (Mexico)
El País (Uruguay)
El Popular (Mexico)

El Siglo (Colombia)
El Telégrafo (Ecuador)
El Tiempo (Colombia)
El Universal (Mexico)
Estrella de Nicaragua
Excelsior (Mexico)
Haiti-Journal
La Mañana (Uruguay)
La Nación (Argentina)
La Nación (Chile)
La Nación (Dominican Republic)
La Prensa (Argentina)
La Prensa (Perú)
Nuestro Diario (Guatemala)
O Estado de São Paulo (Brazil)
O Jornal (Brazil)
Panama American
Panama Star and Herald
Review of the River Plate
   (Argentina)

INDEX OF AUTHORS AND SHORT TITLES

The numbers after each entry refer to the chapter and note where a first citation is made and full bibliographical details will be found.

GENERAL INDEX